THE
COMPLETE
STITCH
ENCYCLOPEDIA

THE
COMPLETE
STITCH
ENCYCLOPEDIA
JAN EATON

BARRON'S

A QUARTO BOOK

First U.S. edition 1986 by Barron's Educational
Series, Inc.
Barron's Educational Series, Inc. has exclusive
publication rights in the English language in
the U.S.A., its territories, and possessions.

Copyright © Quarto Publishing Ltd

Reprinted 1987, 1991,1993, 1994, 1995

All inquiries should be addressed to:
Barron's Educational Series, Inc.
250 Wireless Boulevard
Hauppauge, New York 11788

International Standard Book No. 0-8120-5731-7
International Standard Book No. 0-8120-9257-0

This book was designed and produced by
Quarto Publishing Ltd
The Old Brewery, 6 Blundell Street
London N7 9BH

Senior editor Jane Laing

Art editor Alex Arthur

Editorial Caroline Mordaunt, Alison Berry,
Jac Buchan

Designer Fraser Newman

Photographer Rose Jones

Consultant Maggie McCormack
Indexer Hilary Bird

Art director Nigel Osborne
Editorial director Jim Miles

Typeset by Leaper and Gard Ltd, Bristol
Paste-up by Patrizio Semproni
Manufactured in Hong Kong by Regent
Publishing Services Ltd
Printed by Leefung-Asco Printers Ltd, China

The author would like to take this opportunity
to thank Gavin Fry and Ronald Wilson for their
kind help and assistance.

Contents

Introduction

From Algerian eye stitch to Gobelin stitch and from tête de boeuf filling stitch to zig-zag stitch, every stitch in *The Complete Stitch Encyclopedia* is described in detail. In this comprehensive reference book and self-instruction manual combined, all the stitches are accompanied by clear, full-color photographs, with step-by-step progressions for the more complicated stitches.

For every stitch, the method of working is clearly explained and advice is offered on the most suitable type of threads to use. Alternative names are provided and the interesting and involved history of some of the more unusual or older stitches is also given.

To make the book straightforward to use, the stitches are divided according to kind, so that if you know the type of stitch you require but do not have a specific stitch in mind, you need only turn to the relevant section from which you can easily choose the most appropriate stitch.

The introductory section contains easy-to-work stitches, such as chain stitch and cross stitch. If you are new to embroidery, practice these stitches first, as they form the basis for many of the complex, composite stitches found later in the book.

The next ten sections contain free embroidery stitches grouped according to their usage — for example, line stitches, filling stitches, isolated stitches, motif stitches, edging stitches and insertion stitches. Many of the line and isolated stitches can also be used as fillings and details of these can be found in the text, where appropriate.

Canvas stitches can be found in the final four sections of the book and are grouped according to their construction — for example, straight stiches and crossed stiches.

Also to help you decide on the stitch you wish to use, the stitches are arranged in order of difficulty within each section and each one is accompanied by a degree-of-difficulty symbol to indicate the amount of skill needed to work the stitch successfully.

When looking for a stitch with a particular name, consult the index at the back of the book. This has been organized so that in addition to their own individual entries all the stitches that make up a family group can be found under the initial letter of the main stitch. For example, threaded herringbone stitch is also listed under "H" as herringbone stitch — threaded. The technical terms mentioned in the text are fully explained in the glossary, which begins on page 172.

Degree of difficulty ratings

Within each section, the stitches are arranged into three groups, according to the degree of difficulty involved in working them. The number of star symbols accompanying each entry indicates the group into which the stitch falls: a stitch with one star is easy to work, one with two requires a little more skill and a stitch with three stars is difficult to effect. These at-a-glance symbol ratings should further help you to decide which stitch to use.

☆   **Easy**

☆ ☆   **Medium**

☆ ☆ ☆ **Difficult**

Matching text and photographs

Each double page of photographs illustrates the stitches described on the preceding double page of text and for greatest benefit, text and photographs should be used in conjunction. Once you have decided on the stitch you wish to use, read through the method of working the stitch and follow the steps on the photograph of the corresponding stitched example. Every stitch is numbered so that you can quickly match the description of a stitch to its photograph.

94/1 *Portuguese knotted stem stitch*   ☆ ☆ ☆

---

20   FABRIC STITCHES

32 Whipped chain stitch ☆
Whipped chain stitch is a simple line stitch used on plain- and even-weave fabrics and gives a neat, slightly raised, line. The whipping thread can be of a contrasting colour, weight or texture.
A foundation row of chain stitch *(see page 12)* is worked first, and then whipped at regular intervals with a second thread

the threading will tighten them. A second thread, of a contrasting weight, colour or texture, is then laced through the back stitch foundation. The needle should enter the fabric only at the beginning and end of each row. Use a blunt-ended tapestry needle for the lacing to avoid splitting the foundation stitches. The lacing thread should be tightened

36 Rosette of thorns stitch ☆
Rosette of thorns stitch is an ornamental line stitch used on plain- and even-weave fabrics. It makes a pattern of crown shapes linked together to form a line and is a variation of buttonhole stitch *(see page 13)*. It looks equally effective worked in straight rows or round

LINE STITCHES 21

39 Twisted chain stitch and detached twisted chain stitch
Twisted chain stitch is a useful line stitch as it follows curves well and has a neat, slightly textured look. It is always worked downwards, and is used on plain- and even-weave fabrics. A simple variation of chain

as an edging stitch on a hemmed piece of fabric, the top row of stitching should follow the turned over edge of the hem; the second row is worked on the very edge of the hem.

worked first, and then a second thread is whipped over the line without picking up any ground fabric. Use a blunt-ended tapestry needle for the whipping to avoid splitting the stitches on the foundation row. The effect of whipping

---

22   FABRIC STITCHES

32 Whipped chain stitch ☆
35/1 Plaited fly stitch ☆
36 Rosette of thorns stitch ☆
33 Pekinese stitch
35/2 Plaited fly stitch ☆
37 Single feather stitch ☆
34 Open Cretan stitch
35/3 Plaited fly stitch ☆
38 Knotted cable stitch ☆

LINE STITCHES 23

39 Twisted chain stitch and detached twisted chain stitch
42/1 Pearl stitch ☆
43 Whipped stem stitch ☆
40 Double buttonhole stitch ☆
42/2 Pearl stitch ☆
44 Ship's ladder stitch ☆
41 Half chevron stitch ☆
42/3 Pearl stitch ☆
45 Thorn stitch ☆

BASIC STITCHES

1 Couching ☆
also known as **convent stitch** *and* **kloster stitch**

and puffy couching
also known as **bunched couching**
Couching takes its name from the French word "coucher," meaning to lay down. The technique involves tying a thread or group of threads on the surface of a common- or even-weave fabric, and then tying them down by means of a second, often finer, thread. Couching was extensively used on medieval embroideries to keep scarce and expensive threads, especially those made from precious metals, on the surface of the work to avoid any waste. It was also used to attach threads to the fabric when they were too thick, rigid or textured to be stitched directly into the fabric without damaging either fabric or thread. Couching can be used to work linear designs, to cover the edge of an appliquéd shape, or to fill an area solidly. This technique is used for laid-work *(see page 84)*: the surface threads are laid side by side on the fabric and then anchored by a second thread, which is couched down in a pattern. In other types of couching the thread is laid across the fabric, and then tied down with the same thread before the next line of thread is laid; Bokhara couching *(see page 77)* and Roumanian couching *(see page 81)* are good examples.

Ordinary couching is the simplest form of this technique, and it should always be worked with the fabric stretched in an embroidery hoop or frame. It is worked from right to left, usually along a guideline marked on the fabric, unless it is being worked as a filling. The thick thread (or group of threads) is brought to the surface of the fabric, laid loosely along the line to be couched and, if you are right-handed, held in place and guided by the left hand. The couching thread is brought through,

and small, straight stitches are taken over the thick thread and back through the fabric. The line of thick thread should lie evenly on the surface after it has been couched. When the line is completed, all the threads are taken to the back of the work and secured. When working curves, arrange the couching stitches closer together so that the curved line lies flat. An extra stitch or two may need to be worked when negotiating an angle to make sure that the corner of the couched thread lies flat. When this stitch is used solidly, row on row, for filling a shape, the couching stitches can be arranged so they form parallel rows across the laid threads. They can also be placed alternatively on each row, or arranged to make a small geometric pattern.

Puffy couching is worked in a similar way but over a group of threads rather than a single one. The threads are laid on the surface and the couching stitches are made small enough to compress them into bunches. The couching thread should be pulled tightly after each stitch, and the laid threads should be kept fairly loose on the surface of the fabric so that they puff out between each stitch.

2 Herringbone stitch ☆
also known as **Mossoul stitch, Persian stitch, Russian stitch, Russian cross stitch, plaited stitch, catch stitch** *and* **witch stitch**
Herringbone stitch is a line stitch which is used on common- and even-weave fabrics. It makes a pretty, crossed zig-zag line and the stitches must be perfectly regular. It is worked from left to right and is very easy and quick to work. Guidelines may need to be marked on the fabric if the threads cannot be counted to keep the row straight. When the stitch is used as a filling, the rows can be placed so that the tips of the

stitches on the second and subsequent rows touch those on the row immediately preceding them. This will give a light trellis effect. For a heavier look, arrange the rows underneath each other so that the zig-zags interlock. Herringbone stitch is also used as the foundation row for a number of more complicated stitches. Any type of thread can be used for this stitch, the choice depending on the size of stitch required and the weight of the ground fabric.

3 Chevron stitch ☆
Chevron stitch is a line and filling stitch used on common- and even-weave fabrics. It is also used as a smocking stitch to make both the diamond and surface honeycomb patterns. Chevron stitch is worked from left to right between two parallel lines, in a similar way to herringbone stitch *(see above)*, and makes a pretty zig-zag line. This stitch does not follow curves well unless they are very gradual. It is composed of diagonal stitches set at an angle to a shorter horizontal stitch worked where these stitches meet. To keep the width of the stitches even, guidelines need to be marked on the fabric, unless the threads can be counted.

When used as a filling stitch, the rows are placed close together to give a lattice effect, which benefits from being worked neatly and regularly. An isolated stitch such as daisy stitch *(see page 92)* or dot stitch *(see page 92)* can be worked in the center of the diamond-shaped spaces to make the filling more decorative. Chevron stitch can be threaded with a contrasting color in the same way as threaded herringbone stitch *(see page 45)*.

4 *Holbein stitch* ☆
also known as double running stitch, line stitch, stroke stitch, square stitch, two-sided line stitch, two-sided stroke stitch, Roumanian stitch and Chiara stitch

Holbein stitch is a simple line stitch used on even-weave fabrics. It is a very old stitch and is an important component of two distinct types of counted thread embroidery: Assisi work and blackwork. Assisi work evolved in the town of that name in central Italy, probably during the fourteenth century, and is characterized by an unworked design and an embroidered background. The designs, often heraldic, were outlined by a row of Holbein stitch worked in black thread, with the background areas solidly filled in with long-armed cross stitch *(see page 141)*, and later with cross stitch *(see page 14)*. The backgrounds were of one color only, traditionally red or blue, and these colors were also occasionally used for the Holbein stitch.

Blackwork, also known as Spanish blackwork or Spanish work, was worked in a black thread on a white or natural fabric, using Holbein stitch extensively as an outline. The designs were very formal, with strongly outlined shapes and regular geometric fillings, and were sometimes enlivened by the use of metal thread or spangles. The designs were probably of Moorish origin and blackwork spread from Spain to England and the rest of Europe some time during the fifteenth century when it was used as a decoration for clothing, particularly on shirts, collars and ruffs, and household linens. The use of blackwork as a costume decoration can be seen in many sixteenth-century English portraits, particularly those by Hans Holbein (1497-1543) after whom this stitch was named.

Holbein stitch is extremely easy to work and is a useful stitch, both for outlines and for intricate linear details. A row of evenly spaced running stitch *(see page 12)* is worked first and the spaces are filled in on the return journey. It is exactly the same on both sides of the fabric, and can also be stepped to give a zig-zag line.

5 *Split stitch* ☆
also known as Kensington outline stitch

Split stitch is a line stitch used on common- and even-weave fabrics. It is used for outlines, as it follows intricate designs well, and it is also worked solidly as a shaded filling, especially for figurative embroideries, because of its brush-stroke quality. The type of thread suitable for use with split stitch is confined to a soft, untwisted thread which can be split by the needle. The method of working this stitch is similar to stem stitch *(see below)* but in this case the thread is split by the needle as it emerges from the fabric. The result is rather like chain stitch *(see page 12)* in appearance.

Split stitch was used during the Middle Ages for embroidering figures, particularly hands and faces. Examples of "opus anglicanum" still exist which show the extensive use of this stitch.

6 *Coral stitch* ☆
also known as coral knot, beaded stitch, German knot stitch, knotted stitch, scroll stitch and snail trail

Coral stitch is a knotted line stitch used on common- and even-weave fabrics. It is one of the oldest embroidery stitches, and many examples of it can be found on seventeenth- and eighteenth-century English crewel embroidery work. It is worked from right to left.

Hold the thread loosely on the surface of the fabric with your left thumb (if you are right-handed) and pull the needle through the fabric and over the thread to form a knot. The stitch can be varied by altering the angle of the needle as it takes up the fabric, and by changing the spacing of the knots along the row. Any type of embroidery thread can be used; the effect made depends on the weight and composition of the thread. Coral stitch is used for outlines, as it follows curves well, and for linear details. It can also be worked solidly to cover an area with a pretty, knotted filling. The knots can be arranged so that they form lines across the filling, or they can be set alternately on every row.

7 *Stem stitch* ☆
also known as crewel stitch, stalk stitch and South Kensington stitch

Stem stitch is a line stitch used on common- and even-weave fabrics. One of the most frequently-used outline stitches, it is quite easy to work and follows curves and intricate linear details well. It can also be used for filling and shading areas *(see stem stitch filling, page 69)*.

The stitch is simply worked, with a forward and backward motion along the line; the stitches should be evenly worked and equally sized. The working thread must always be kept at the right of the needle; if it is at the left, the effect is slightly different, and the stitch is then known as outline stitch *(see page 12)*. A slightly wider stem stitch line can be made by inserting the needle into the fabric at a slight angle to the line instead of directly along it. Any type of embroidery thread can be used, providing that it is compatible with the size of the stitch and the weight of the ground fabric.

1 *Couching* ☆

4 *Holbein stitch* ☆

7 *Stem stitch* ☆

2 *Herringbone stitch* ☆

5 *Split stitch* ☆

8 *Chain stitch* ☆

3 *Chevron stitch* ☆

6 *Coral stitch* ☆

9 *Outline stitch*   ☆   11 *Feather stitch*   ☆   13 *Cretan stitch*   ☆

10 *Running stitch*   ☆   12 *Blanket stitch*   ☆   14 *Buttonhole stitch*   ☆

8 *Chain stitch* ☆
also known as **tambour stitch** *and* **point de chainette**

Chain stitch is one of the oldest embroidery stitches. Its use is widespread, and examples of the stitch can be found on many antique and contemporary textiles throughout the world. Chain stitch probably originated in Persia and India, where it is usually worked by hand with a fine hook known as an "ari," which speeds up the work considerably. From the front of the embroidery, it is virtually impossible to distinguish chain stitch worked with a hook from that worked with a needle, although it is possible to tell from the back of the work: a continuous embroidery thread without any joins indicates that the chain stitch has been worked with a hook. Chain stitch is also worked in Western countries with a similar tool, known as a "tambour" hook. The Eastern and Western methods differ slightly: in India, the rows of chain stitch are worked on the right side of the fabric, which is hand held; using the tambour method, the stitch is worked from the reverse of the fabric, which is always mounted in a frame with the wrong side uppermost. Chain stitch was also one of the two stitches produced by the early sewing machines.

Chain stitch, worked either by needle or hook, forms a line stitch on common- and even-weave fabrics. It can also be worked solidly to produce a dense filling, which lends itself well to shading. It is a simple stitch to work, but care should be taken to keep the stitches even and of the same size. Chain stitch makes a good outline stitch and is very useful for defining curves and intricate shapes when worked quite small. Any thread is suitable, but the size of the stitch will depend on the weight of the embroidery thread used. When used as a filling, chain stitch can either be worked in close rows to fill the shape, or the rows can be worked from the center outward in a spiral, using one or more colors or textures.

Chain stitch can be worked with a needle on mono canvas in the same way as on fabric. It is often used for backgrounds and gives a dense, almost knitted texture. Care should be taken when matching the weight of the thread to the gauge of the canvas to ensure that the canvas threads are completely covered. Chain stitch on fabric or canvas can have a row of backstitch *(see page 14)* worked down the center either in the same color, or with a contrasting thread. This line of backstitch is useful for covering the background threads when chain stitch is worked on canvas.

9 *Outline stitch* ☆
Outline stitch is a line stitch used on common- and even-weave fabrics. An extremely versatile stitch, it is used for outlining shapes in single or multiple rows and, as it follows intricate curves well, for complicated linear details. It makes a neat, twisted line and can be worked in any type of embroidery thread, depending on the required weight of the line. It is worked in almost the same way as stem stitch *(see page 9)*, but the working thread always lies to the left of the needle, rather than to the right. A line of outline stitches twists in a reverse direction to a line of stem stitches.

10 *Running stitch* ☆
Running stitch is a line stitch used on common- and even-weave fabrics. It is the simplest and most basic of all stitches and is made by passing the needle and thread in and out of the fabric at regular intervals. This stitch has many uses: as an outline stitch, for working linear details, as it follows intricate shapes well; as a foundation row, for more complex stitches, such as Croatian stitch *(see page 73)*; as a strengthening stitch in cutwork; and for hand quilting. The stiches should all be of equal length and any type of embroidery thread can be used, providing that it is compatible with the weight of the ground fabric.

11 *Feather stitch* ☆
also known as **single coral stitch** *and* **briar stitch**

Feather stitch is a decorative line and smocking stitch used on common- and even-weave fabrics. This stitch has been extensively used on traditional English smocks, both as a smocking stitch and as surface embroidery; it is also used as a decorative joining stitch on crazy patchwork. It makes a pretty, feathery line, which is equally effective when worked in straight lines or following curves. Worked downward, it is a quick stitch, easy to perfect. The thread is brought through at the top of the line to be covered and a slanting loop stitch is made alternately to the left and to the right of the line. Any type of embroidery thread can be used with feather stitch but the effect required and the weight of the ground fabric must be taken into account.

12 Blanket stitch ☆
also known as **open buttonhole stitch**

Blanket stitch is a looped line stitch worked on common- and even-weave fabrics in exactly the same way as buttonhole stitch *(see below)*. The only difference between the two stitches is the spacing between the uprights: in blanket stitch, a space is left between each upright. Blanket stitch is frequently used as an edging stitch to cover a turned-over raw edge and makes a good appliqué stitch. The name probably originates from the use of the stitch, sometimes worked by hand but more often by machine, as a method of finishing the edges of blankets. As a line stitch on the surface of the fabric, blanket stitch can be made more decorative by altering the lengths of the uprights; a simple variation is to make the stitches alternately long and short, either singly or in groups of two or three. The lengths can also be varied to form pyramid shapes or the loops at the bottom of the stitch can be whipped with a contrasting color *(see whipped back stitch, page 16)*. Blanket stitch also forms the foundation for composite stitches, such as barb stitch *(see page 16)*.

13 Cretan stitch ☆
also known as **Persian stitch, long-armed feather stitch** *and* **quill stitch** *(when it is worked in a straight vertical line)*

Cretan stitch is a line stitch or filling for narrow shapes, used on common- and even-weave fabrics. The name is derived from the island of Crete, where the stitch has been used for centuries to decorate clothing. It is also found on Persian embroideries, and the stitch is called Persian stitch in France.

When used as a filling, the stitch is worked from alternate sides of the shape to completely cover it. A plait forms down the center of the shape to make a very decorative filling. This stitch can be worked with the stitches close together, or they can be spaced apart to let the ground fabric show through. Whether it is used as a filling or as a line stitch, different effects can be achieved by varying the amount of fabric picked up and by altering the slant of the needle. When used as a line stitch, it is usually worked with an open finish, and it makes a pretty, spiked line, which follows curves well. Any type of embroidery thread can be used with Cretan stitch, but when it is being used to fill a shape solidly, a stranded silk or cotton floss will give better cover.

14 Buttonhole stitch ☆
also known as **button stitch** *and* **close stitch**

Buttonhole stitch is a simple, looped line stitch used on common- and even-weave fabrics and has a variety of applications, both practical and decorative. It is frequently used for finishing raw edges and for buttonholes, although a knotted variation, tailor's buttonhole stitch *(see page 33)*, is more hard-wearing and therefore more suitable for this purpose. Variations of this stitch are used for many types of decorative embroidery, including cutwork, couching and filling. Work buttonhole stitch from left to right, pulling the needle through the fabric and over the working thread; this action forms a row of vertical straight stitches joined together by a looped edge at the bottom. The stitch is equally successful worked in straight lines or following curves, and the size of the vertical stitches can be graduated to give a wavy line or a sawtooth edge at the top of the row. The stitches are placed close together so that no ground fabric shows between them; if they are widely spaced, the stitch is known as blanket stitch *(see above)*.

15 *Cross stitch* ☆
*also known as **sampler stitch, Berlin stitch** and **point de marque***

Cross stitch is probably the oldest and best known of all decorative embroidery stitches. It has many variations and has been known world-wide for centuries. Cross stitch is still used on traditional embroideries in many areas, including the Greek Islands, Scandinavia, Central and Eastern Europe and India. It is extremely quick and easy to work and is used mainly on even-weave fabrics, and on canvas where the threads can be counted to keep the crosses even. The stitch can also be used on common-weave fabrics, but guidelines will need to be marked on the fabric unless a commercially produced transfer is being used. Among its many uses, cross stitch is excellent for outlines, solid fillings, formalized motifs, borders and lettering. Cross stitch on canvas makes an excellent and hard-wearing stitch, suitable for upholstery.

Although the actual construction of crossed diagonal stitches remains the same, there are different methods of working ordinary cross stitch, depending on the choice of ground fabric or canvas. One rule applies to all methods: the top diagonal stitches must always fall in the same direction, unless a deliberate light and shade effect is required, in which case their direction can be varied to catch the light.

1 Cross stitch worked individually
Work a complete cross stitch before proceeding to the next stitch to form neat, slightly raised crosses. Cross stitch on canvas should always be worked in this way, and Penelope canvas should be used for the best result. Care should be taken when matching the weight of the thread to the gauge of the canvas to ensure that the canvas is completely covered.

2 Cross stitch worked in rows
This method works well on common- and even-weave fabrics. First, work a line of diagonals in one direction. Then, cover them with the top diagonals on the second journey in the opposite direction.

3 Alternate cross stitch   This method is only suitable for even-weave fabrics. It will ensure an even tension and finish, particularly important when covering a large area. The bottom diagonal rows are worked alternately on two journeys, and then the top diagonals are worked over them in two more journeys.

16 *Darning* ☆
*also known as **basting stitch***

Darning stitch is a simple line and filling stitch used on common- and even-weave fabrics. It is a variation of running stitch *(see page 12)* but, instead of the stitches and spaces being of equal length, the surface stitches are made longer and only a tiny amount of fabric is picked up by the needle. Many different patterns can be made by varying the arrangement of rows of stitches; one of the simplest, a brick pattern, is shown. Any type of embroidery thread can be used; choose the thread according to the weight of the ground fabric and the size of the stitch required.

In many parts of the world, notably the Greek Islands and Eastern Europe, darning stitch is used to create complex, geometric patterns by using multiple rows of the stitch.

17 *Backstitch* ☆
*also known as **stitching** and **point de sable***

Backstitch is one of the most adaptable stitches in this book. It can be used as a line stitch on common- and even-weave fabrics; as a firm foundation row for composite stitches, such as Pekinese stitch *(see page 20)* and herringbone ladder filling stitch *(see page 73)*; and occasionally on canvas in conjunction with another stitch, where a well-defined outline or center line is needed. When used alone it should be worked in small, even stitches to look rather like machine stitching. This stitch follows intricate curves well if the stitches are kept tiny to let the curve flow. The front of the work is similar in appearance to Holbein stitch *(see page 9)* but, where Holbein stitch is quite flat, backstitch is slightly raised.

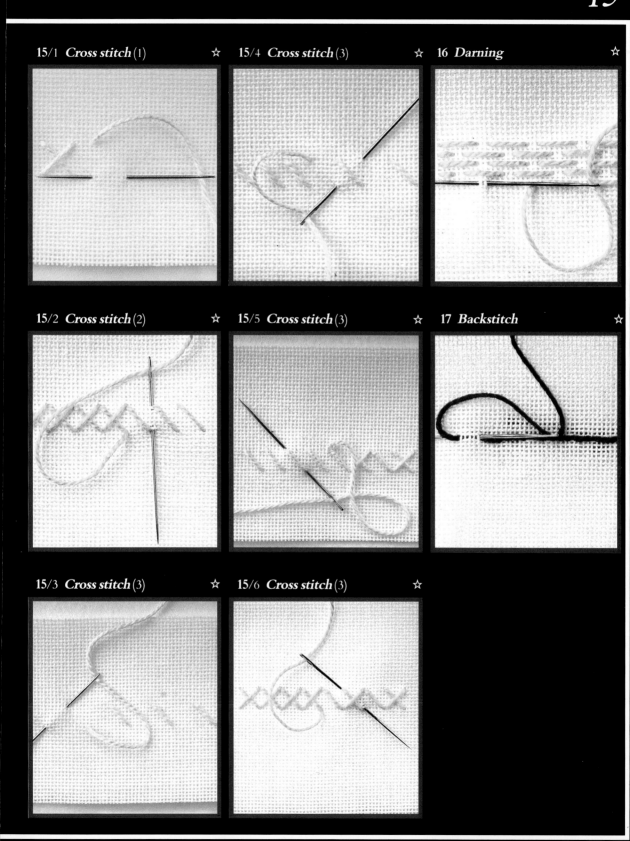

15/1 *Cross stitch* (1) ☆

15/4 *Cross stitch* (3) ☆

16 *Darning* ☆

15/2 *Cross stitch* (2) ☆

15/5 *Cross stitch* (3) ☆

17 *Backstitch* ☆

15/3 *Cross stitch* (3) ☆

15/6 *Cross stitch* (3) ☆

18 *Threaded backstitch* ☆

Threaded backstitch is quick to work and gives a decorative outline on common- and even-weave fabrics; the line is heavier and wider than a plain backstitch line. A foundation row of ordinary backstitch is worked, although the stitches should be slightly longer than usual. Using a blunt-ended tapestry needle, a second thread is then passed alternately up and down behind these stitches, without entering the fabric. A third thread is then used to fill in the spaces left on the first journey to create a richer, heavier line. Threaded backstitch can be worked in one, two or three colors and will give an embossed effect if a much thicker yarn is used for the threading than for the foundation row. If the backstitches are made fairly large, textured threads can be used for the threading to give an interesting effect on delicate fabric.

19 *Whipped backstitch* ☆

Whipped backstitch is used as a line stitch on common- and even-weave fabrics. It gives a heavier line than ordinary backstitch, and has a narrower, more raised appearance than threaded backstitch *(see page 16)*. First, work a foundation row of backstitches slightly longer than usual, and then whip a second thread over the line, without picking up any ground fabric; use a blunt-ended tapestry needle for the whipping to avoid splitting the foundation thread. The effect of whipped backstitch varies depending on the choice of whipping thread: if a heavy, shiny thread in the same color as the foundation stitching is used, the line will look like a fine cord. Such a thread is used when a raised line is required on a fabric that is too delicate for a thick thread to be embroidered through the weave: a very fine thread can be used for the foundation row and then whipped with the thick one.

20 *Barb stitch* ☆

Barb stitch is an ornamental line stitch used on common-weave fabrics. A foundation of two rows of blanket stitch *(see page 13)* worked close together is first laid down with the loops facing each other. These loops are then whipped together with a second thread without picking up the ground fabric. A blunt-ended tapestry needle should be used for the second thread, which can be of a contrasting color, texture or thickness to the first thread, or a metallic yarn can be used for a richer effect. Barb stitch can be worked in a single line, or rows of the stitch can be repeated to make a wide border. The second row can be placed edge to edge with the first one, or the stitches of each row can interlock.

21 *Basque stitch* ☆
also known as **twisted daisy border stitch**

Basque stitch, as its name suggests, has its origins in the Basque provinces of northern Spain. Often used in conjunction with the Basque knot *(see page 36)*, this stitch has been found on old embroideries of that area of Spain, and also in Portugal and southern France. Traditionally, the stitch was worked with red thread on green fabric, or white thread on a blue-green background. Basque stitch is a looped line stitch with a twist, which is always worked on common-weave fabrics. It lends itself particularly well to curved lines and scroll shapes, and is most effective embroidered in white or another light-colored thread on a dark fabric. At first sight, this stitch looks quite complicated, but it will prove quick and easy to work after some practice.

22 *Berwick stitch* ☆

Berwick stitch is a line stitch worked on common-weave fabrics. It forms a knotted base line with straight stitches protruding like spines from the top. Two rows of stitches can be worked with the knotted edges close together and the spines making a fishbone shape at each side. Each knot should be tightened slightly before proceeding to the next stitch. It is a quick and easy stitch to work, and is useful for outlining circular shapes, looking equally effective with the knotted edge on the inside or outside of the curve. Work French knots *(see page 96)* or Chinese knots *(see page 96)* at the top of the spines for a more ornate line, or vary the lengths of the spines to make a zigzag edge.

23 *Closed feather stitch* ☆

Closed feather stitch is a wide line stitch used on common- and even-weave fabrics and is a variation of feather stitch *(see page 12)*. It makes a decorative lacy line, which is worked downward between two parallel lines, and it makes a pretty border when worked in multiple rows. To keep the rows even, guidelines may need to be marked on the fabric if the threads cannot be counted. Closed feather stitch can be used as a couching stitch to anchor groups of threads and narrow ribbon or flat cord. This stitch does not follow curves well, unless they are extremely gradual, and it is usually worked in a straight line. It is worked in the same way as feather stitch but the needle is inserted vertically, rather than at an angle, and the loops are worked rather more closely together.

24 *Whipped fly stitch* ☆
also known as **whipped attached fly stitch**

Whipped fly stitch is a line and filling stitch used on common- and even-weave fabrics. It produces an attractive branched line with a ridged center, which can be used on the straight or as an outline stitch. A variation of ordinary fly stitch *(see page 93)*, it is usually worked in two colors. A row of vertical fly stitch is worked with the tying-down stitches almost but not quite touching the center of the shapes. A second thread is then used to whip the tying-down stitches, without picking up the ground fabric *(see whipped backstitch, page 16)*. Use a blunt-ended tapestry needle for the whipping thread to avoid splitting the stitches on the fly stitch row. The whipping thread can be of a contrasting weight, color or texture and a metallic thread can look very attractive, providing that it is supple enough to follow the line well. Rows of whipped fly stitch can be worked solidly to fill a shape, giving a lacy, ridged effect.

25 Open chain stitch ☆
also known as ladder stitch, square chain stitch, Roman chain stitch, small writing *(when the stitches are narrow) and* big writing *(when the stitches are wide)*
Open chain stitch is a line stitch worked downward on common- and even-weave fabrics. A variation of chain stitch *(see page 12)* it is quick and easy to work. Carefully follow the sequence shown and anchor the last chain in each row by a tiny straight stitch through each of the bottom corners. Open chain stitch can be worked to give either an open or closed effect by simply adjusting the spacing between the stitches. It can be worked between parallel lines to make a heavy outline, and can couch down cords, narrow ribbons or other threads. This stitch is also suitable for filling narrow shapes of graduated widths, or it can be worked solidly row upon row to fill a larger area. It is essential that the line should be of an even width and guidelines may need to be marked on the fabric when the stitch is worked in a straight line if the fabric threads cannot be counted.

When this stitch is spaced so that the ground fabric shows through, the space in the center of each chain stitch can be decorated with an isolated stitch, such as a Chinese knot *(see page 96)*. Running stitch *(see page 12)* or chain stitch can be worked down the center of each row in a contrasting color or a different weight of embroidery thread. Open chain stitch worked close together to make a solid line with no ground fabric showing through is characteristic of both Indian and East European embroidery, particularly that of Hungary and Yugoslavia.

26 Knotted Cretan stitch ☆
Knotted Cretan stitch is a decorative line stitch and filling used on common- and even-weave fabrics. It is a simple variation of open Cretan stitch *(see page 20)* and is similar in appearance to zig-zag coral stitch *(see page 25)*. It makes a pretty, zig-zag line, with a knotted effect, and is suitable for use with any type of embroidery thread, the choice

depending on the weight of line required. It is worked in the same way as open Cretan stitch but a knot is made after each slanting stitch is completed. Each knot should be tightened firmly, before proceeding to the next stitch.

Knotted Cretan stitch makes a good outline, especially when it is worked on a small scale, and it follows gradual curves well. It can also be used as a light filling over a shape, with the zig-zags arranged to make an attractive lattice pattern.

27 Pagoda chevron stitch ☆
Pagoda chevron stitch is a line and filling stitch used on common- and even-weave fabrics. It is a pretty and simply worked variation of chevron stitch *(see page 8)*, and is worked from left to right between two parallel lines. Any type of thread can be used with this stitch, the choice depending on the effect required. It is worked in a similar way to chevron stitch but in this case the diagonal stitches pass over the straight horizontal stitches, rather than underneath. Follow the sequence of stitches shown. To keep the stitches even, guidelines may need to be marked on the fabric if the threads cannot be counted.

Pagoda chevron stitch can also be worked in closely placed rows to make a lattice filling.

28 Reversed fly stitch ☆
Reversed fly stitch is a line or filling stitch used on common- and even-weave fabrics. It is a variation of ordinary fly stitch *(see page 93)* and, as the name suggests, consists of a row of vertical fly stitches with superimposed upside-down fly stitches. The tail stitches are normally kept quite short but can be made much longer to give a completely different effect. The stitch is usually worked in one journey, but two contrasting colors or weights of thread can be used if two journeys are made. It makes a pretty filling stitch worked solidly in vertical rows over the shape, or each pair of fly stitches can be scattered to make a powdering.

29 Whipped running stitch ☆
also known as cordonnet stitch
Whipped running stitch is a line stitch used on common- and even-weave fabrics. It makes a heavier line than ordinary running stitch *(see page 12)*, but has a narrower, more raised appearance than interlaced running stitch *(see page 25)*. This stitch is used for outlines and linear details, as it will follow intricate curves well.

First work a foundation of small, evenly spaced running stitches over the line to be covered. Then whip a second thread over this foundation, without picking up any ground fabric *(see whipped backstitch, page 6)*. A much heavier thread can be used for the whipping, and it can also be of a contrasting color and texture. Alternatively a metallic thread can be used for the whipping, provided that it is quite supple.

30 Closed fly stitch ☆
Closed fly stitch is a line or filling stitch used on common- and even-weave fabrics. A variation of ordinary fly stitch *(see page 93)*, it makes a heavy line and is worked downward. It can be used to fill long, narrow shapes by graduating the widths of the stitches, or it can be worked solidly, row on row, for filling a larger shape. It is worked in exactly the same way as fly stitch when that stitch is worked in a vertical row, but the tying-down stitch is tiny and the V-shaped loops are packed very closely together. When this stitch is worked in a straight line, if the threads cannot be counted, guidelines may need to be marked on the fabric to keep the row even.

31 Crossed buttonhole stitch ☆
Crossed buttonhole stitch is another simple but attractive variation of buttonhole stitch *(see page 13)*, and is used on common- and even-weave fabrics. It can be used as an edging or line stitch, or as a filling, and consists of pairs of buttonhole stitches worked at an angle so that they cross each other. When the spaces between the stitches are narrowed and the stitch is worked row upon row as a filling, a pretty, trellis-like grid effect is achieved.

18 Threaded backstitch ☆

21/1 Basque stitch ☆

23/1 Closed feather stitch ☆

19 Whipped backstitch ☆

21/2 Basque stitch ☆

23/2 Closed feather stitch ☆

20 Barb stitch ☆

22 Berwick stitch ☆

24 Whipped fly stitch ☆

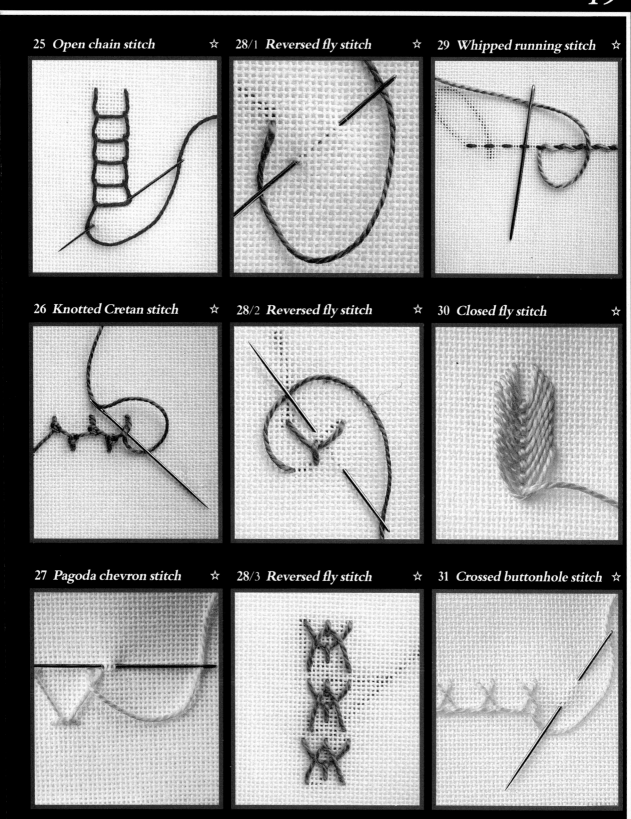

25 *Open chain stitch* ☆

28/1 *Reversed fly stitch* ☆

29 *Whipped running stitch* ☆

26 *Knotted Cretan stitch* ☆

28/2 *Reversed fly stitch* ☆

30 *Closed fly stitch* ☆

27 *Pagoda chevron stitch* ☆

28/3 *Reversed fly stitch* ☆

31 *Crossed buttonhole stitch* ☆

32 Whipped chain stitch ☆

Whipped chain stitch is a simple line stitch used on common- and even-weave fabrics and gives a neat, slightly raised, line. The whipping thread can be of a contrasting color, weight or texture.

A foundation row of chain stitch (see page 12) is worked first, and then whipped at regular intervals with a second thread (do not pick up any ground fabric). The whipping stitches fall across the junctions of the chain stitches. Use a blunt-ended tapestry needle for the whipping to avoid splitting the stitches on the foundation row. Other variations of this stitch can also be worked:

1 The chain stitch row can be whipped back in the opposite direction to give a heavy, raised line.
2 The whipping stitch can be worked over the top and bottom of the chain loops, rather than over the whole stitch, to give a lighter effect.
3 An interesting solid filling can be made by working spaced parallel rows of chain stitch with the links directly underneath each other. These rows are then whipped loosely together through the opposite links, the whipping stitches spanning the spaces between the rows. This filling technique can also be worked with cable stitch (see page 33), and looks very decorative when the whipping thread is shiny or metallic.

33 Pekinese stitch ☆

also known as **Chinese stitch, blind stitch** and **forbidden stitch**

Pekinese stitch is a composite line stitch used on common- and even-weave fabrics. One of the principal stitches used on old Chinese embroideries, it was worked on a tiny scale, and was reputed to affect the eyesight of the worker, hence its alternative name, blind stitch. It was worked in silk and used to fill shapes solidly with carefully blended shapes. Pekinese stitch makes an attractive braided line which follows any linear design well, and can be used as a filling stitch in the Chinese manner.

The stitch is worked on a foundation of backstitch (see page. 14); the stitches should be left fairly loose, as the threading will tighten

them. A second thread, of a contrasting weight, color or texture, is then laced through the backstitch foundation. The needle should enter the fabric only at the beginning and end of each row. Use a blunt-ended tapestry needle for the lacing to avoid splitting the foundation stitches. The lacing thread should be tightened slightly after each loop has been formed to make a neat, textured line.

34 Open Cretan stitch ☆

Open Cretan stitch is a line stitch and filling used on common- and even-weave fabrics. A variation of ordinary Cretan stitch (see page 13), the needle is inserted vertically into the fabric, rather than at a slant, and the stitches are spaced apart, it makes a light, zig-zag line and follows gradual curves well. Any type of embroidery thread can be used; the choice depends on the size of the stitch and the weight of the fabric.

When used as a filling, the rows are arranged to make a lattice pattern, which can be decorated by the addition of isolated stitches worked in the spaces, and in a contrasting thread: French knots (see page 96), Chinese knots (see page 96), or daisy stitches (see page 92) all look effective. Isolated stitches can also be worked as a decoration when open Cretan stitch is worked in a single straight line to build up quite complex borders.

35 Plaited fly stitch ☆

Plaited fly stitch is a line or filling stitch used on common- and even-weave fabrics. It is an easily worked variation of ordinary fly stitch (see page 93) and makes an attractive plaited line or light filling. The stitch consists of a row of fly stitches with long tails, worked horizontally, from left to right. Each new stitch overlaps the previous stitch. A wide, double line can be made by working two rows of the stitch, with the "V" shapes touching, creating spines along each side. By graduating the length of the tying-down stitches, a wavy edge can be made. Plaited fly stitch can be worked solidly, row on row, to fill a shape. The tying-down stitches can be made smaller.

36 Rosette of thorns stitch ☆

Rosette of thorns stitch is an ornamental line stitch used on common- and even-weave fabrics. It makes a pattern of crown shapes linked together to form a line and is a variation of buttonhole stitch (see page 13). It looks equally effective worked in straight rows or round gradual curves, with the branching stitches fanning out along the outside of the curve. Any type of embroidery thread can be used, but a fine, rounded thread such as fine crochet cotton shows off the delicacy of the stitch. The line is worked from left to right and consists of groups of five buttonhole stitches worked with the bases close together and the upright stitches fanning out. A long buttonhole stitch links the groups of stitches. The crown shapes can be decorated by the addition of an isolated knot stitch, such as a Chinese knot (see page 96), or a Danish knot (see page 97), at the tip of each upright stitch.

37 Single feather stitch ☆

also known as **slanted buttonhole stitch**

Single feather stitch is a line and smocking stitch used on common- and even-weave fabrics. A variation of feather stitch (see page 12), it makes a much plainer line, which is equally effective worked straight or following a curve. It is worked downward and the looped stitches are made only to the right of the line. It has a similar appearance to blanket stitch (see page 13), but the arms of the stitch are set at an angle.

38 Knotted cable stitch ☆

also known as **knotted cable chain stitch**

Knotted cable stitch is a composite line stitch used on common- and even-weave fabrics; it is made up of chain stitch (see page 12) and coral stitch (see page 9). More ornate than ordinary cable stitch, it makes a broader line with a knotted appearance. Although this stitch looks more complicated to work than cable stitch, it is in fact easier, as the knots hold the chains in place during stitching.

39 Twisted chain stitch and detached twisted chain stitch ☆

Twisted chain stitch is a useful line stitch as it follows curves well and has a neat, slightly textured look. It is always worked downward, and is used on common- and even-weave fabrics. A simple variation of chain stitch *(see page 12)*, a twist is made at the top of each chain. It may help to hold the chain loop down on the fabric with the left thumb while pulling the working thread through the fabric (if you are right-handed). Twisted chain stitch gives a more satisfactory line than ordinary chain stitch and is ideal for outlining shapes and for linear details. Any type of embroidery thread can be used: a rounded thread, such as pearl cotton, will make the line slightly more raised than a flatter thread, such as stranded silk or cotton floss. The stitch is most effective when the stitches are fairly small and close together.

Twisted chain stitch can also be worked as an isolated stitch in the same way as daisy stitch *(see page 92)*, when it is known as detached twisted chain stitch. Each loop is anchored to the fabric by a tiny straight stitch worked at the bottom. It can be used either as an accent stitch or in multiples as a pretty, textured powdering over a wide area of fabric.

---

40 Double buttonhole stitch ☆

Double buttonhole stitch is an attractive edging or outline stitch used on common- and even-weave fabrics. It is quick and easy to work and consists of two parallel rows of blanket stitch *(see page 13)* worked facing each other. The second parallel row is placed so that the vertical stitches fit into the spaces of the first row. The spacing and size of the stitches can be varied, depending on the weight of thread used and the effect required. This stitch is equally effective worked in straight lines or following curves. When the two rows are worked close together with long verticals, a second thicker and contrasting thread or narrow ribbon can be slotted through the center to make a more decorative line. When worked as an edging stitch on a

hemmed piece of fabric, the top row of stitching should follow the turned-under edge of the hem; the second row is worked on the very edge of the hem.

---

41 Half chevron stitch ☆

Half chevron stitch is a line stitch used on common- and even-weave fabrics. It is a variation of chevron stitch *(see page 8)* and is worked from left to right. Half chevron stitch can be used with any type of embroidery thread and makes a useful border or outline stitch. The lower edge of the stitch is exactly the same as chevron stitch. This stitch follows curves well, and makes a good circular outline; the chevron edge can be worked on either the outside or inside of the circle. It can also be worked row on row to make a light, lacy filling stitch.

---

42 Pearl stitch ☆

Pearl stitch is a line stitch used on common- and even-weave fabrics. It makes a raised, beaded line, which is suitable for outlines and intricate linear details, and looks most effective when worked with a heavy thread, such as pearl cotton. It can also be worked with a more open finish, but the resulting line can look rather ragged. The line is worked from right to left of the area and, after the tiny horizontal stitch is made, the needle is inserted through the loop and then downward through the fabric. The working thread should be tightened firmly before the needle is pulled through to begin the next stitch.

---

43 Whipped stem stitch ☆

Whipped stem stitch is a raised line stitch used on common- and even-weave fabrics. It makes a heavier line than ordinary stem stitch *(see page 9)* and it is more raised than its sister stitches, whipped running stitch *(see page 17)* and whipped backstitch *(see page 16)*.

Whipped stem stitch is used where a bold line is needed as it follows curves and linear details well. It can be made more decorative by using a contrasting color for the whipping. A foundation row of stem stitch is worked first, and then a

second thread is whipped over the line without picking up any ground fabric. Use a blunt-ended tapestry needle for the whipping to avoid splitting the stitches on the foundation row. The effect of whipped stem stitch varies, depending on the choice of whipping thread: by using a heavy, lustrous thread in the same color as the foundation row, the line will look like a fine cord, whereas a stranded thread on a contrasting color will give a flatter effect.

---

44 Ship's ladder stitch ☆

Ship's ladder stitch is a line stitch used on common- and even-weave fabrics. It makes a delicate, angular line, which is best used on the straight as it does not follow a curve well. It is very simple to work and is always worked from the bottom to the top. The stitch consists of a central line of vertical straight stitches divided by diagonal straight stitches set across the line. Any type of embroidery thread can be used, the choice depending on the weight of the ground fabric and the required width of the line. The central line of vertical stitches can be whipped, using the same or a contrasting weight of thread to give a heavier effect *(see whipped backstitch, page 16)*.

---

45 Thorn stitch ☆

Thorn stitch is a line stitch used on common- and even-weave fabrics. It makes a pretty, branched line, and is often used to depict stems and ferns on a naturalistic embroidery. Actually a form of couching *(see page 8)*, a long, laid thread forms the center of the line. Diagonal straight stitches are then worked in pairs, crossing over the central thread and anchoring it to the fabric. The diagonal stitches create the ''thorns'' at each side of the line, and the lengths of these stitches can be varied as required. To prevent the fabric from puckering, thorn stitch is best worked on fabric that is stretched in an embroidery hoop or frame. The laid thread can be of a contrasting weight and color to that used for the diagonal stitches.

32 Whipped chain stitch ☆

35/1 Plaited fly stitch ☆

36 Rosette of thorns stitch ☆

33 Pekinese stitch ☆

35/2 Plaited fly stitch ☆

37 Single feather stitch ☆

34 Open Cretan stitch ☆

35/3 Plaited fly stitch ☆

38 Knotted cable stitch ☆

39 Twisted chain stitch and detached twisted chain stitch ☆

42/1 Pearl stitch ☆

43 Whipped stem stitch ☆

40 Double buttonhole stitch ☆

42/2 Pearl stitch ☆

44 Ship's ladder stitch ☆

41 Half chevron stitch ☆

42/3 Pearl stitch ☆

45 Thorn stitch ☆

46 *Pueblo stitch*   ☆

Pueblo stitch is a line stitch used on common- and even-weave fabrics. It is a variation of backstitch *(see page 14)* and must be worked with a two-ply, lightly twisted wool thread to achieve the correct appearance. Two strands of crewel yarn can be used instead, perhaps in two contrasting colors, in which case the twists are made as each stitch is worked. The stitch makes an unusual twisted line and was probably invented by the Pueblo Indians who have used it to produce some very fine examples of embroidery.

Pueblo stitch consists of large backstitches, and the effect of the line depends on the loosely twisted thread which is split as each section is made. It can be used for outlines and also looks extremely effective when worked solidly to make a filling.

47 *Satin stitch*   ☆

also known as ***damask stitch***

Satin stitch is a line and filling stitch used on common- and even-weave fabrics. It is one of the oldest embroidery stitches and, like cross stitch *(see page 14)*, examples of satin stitch can be found worked on traditional embroideries in practically every country, but notably in China and Japan. Satin stitch consists of straight stitches worked side by side and, although it appears to be an easy stitch to work, some practice is required to work satin stitch evenly. It should be worked on fabric stretched in an embroidery hoop or frame to prevent the material from puckering, and the stitches should lie evenly and close together to cover the ground fabric completely.

When used as a line stitch, it is worked between two lines with the stitches either slanting or at a right angle to the lines to give a perfectly smooth surface. When worked as a filling, the stitches are taken right across the shape and can be worked vertically or diagonally, with changes of direction giving the effect of light and shade. This effect is enhanced by the use of a lustrous thread, such as stranded floss or silk, but any other embroidery thread can be used, the choice depending on the effect required and the weight of the ground fabric. Since long satin stiches can become loose and untidy, only small shapes should be attempted, or, if a large shape is required, it should be split into smaller, more workable shapes first. For a very large shape, use long and short stich *(see page 72)* or encroaching satin stitch *(see page 68)*. Areas of satin stitch can be made slightly raised by first working a padding of rows of stem stitch *(see page 9)*, chain stitch *(see page 12)*, or running stitch *(see page 12)* over the shape. Satin stitch can also be used on mono canvas for outlines and small shapes, with the stitches running vertically, horizontally or diagonally.

48 *Double fly stitch*   ☆

Double fly stitch is a line stitch used on common- and even-weave fabrics. It is a simply worked variation of ordinary fly stitch *(see page 93)* and it makes a pretty line, which can be worked in two colors. The stitch consists of a row of spaced fly stitches worked vertically, with each fly stitch over-stitched by a second fly stitch. The tail of the second fly fills the space underneath the first, and so on. The line can be worked in one or two journeys, depending on how many colors are being used. If one color only is being used, work the stitch as a continuous line. For two colors, work the underneath stitches on one journey, and the top stitches on the second journey.

49 *Scroll stitch*   ☆

also known as ***single knotted line stitch***; *see also* ***coral stitch***

Scroll stitch is a line stitch used on common- and even-weave fabrics. It makes a simple knotted line which flows around curves and follows intricate details well, and is often used to depict areas of water. Any type of embroidery thread can be used with scroll stitch, provided that it is compatible with the weight of the ground fabric. A stranded thread gives a much flatter effect than a rounded thread such as pearl cotton. It is very quick and easy to work and runs from left to right along the line. It consists of a series of simple knots which are linked together. The knots should not be pulled tightly and they can be worked close together or spaced quite widely apart, depending on the effect required.

50 *Closed buttonhole stitch*   ☆

Closed buttonhole stitch is a very simple variation of buttonhole stitch *(see page 13)*. It makes an attractive alternative edging for hems instead of blanket stitch *(see page 13)*, or it can be worked row upon row to make a border or filling. It is worked from left to right in the same way as buttonhole stitch, but the spacing between the stitches is more open. Each pair of verticals is worked into the same place in the fabric so that they form a triangular shape; a variation of this is to work three verticals in the same space. When working this stitch as a border or filling, different effects can be achieved by placing the rows with the loops facing one another, or with the vertical stitches touching each other, or interlocking.

51 *Rope stitch*   ☆

Rope stitch is a line stitch used on common- and even-weave fabrics. It makes a solidly stitched line, which is raised along the lower edge. This stitch is extremely effective for working curves and spirals, especially when a lustrous thread, such as stranded cotton or silk floss, is used. It is easy to work, but the stitches should lie close together and evenly to give the correct effect. The stitch is worked from right to left by working slanting stitches which should slant sharply backward. A small knot is formed by pulling the needle through over the working thread; these knots should not show on the surface but merely act as a padding to raise the lower edge of each stitch.

52 Broad chain stitch ☆
also known as reverse chain stitch
Broad chain stitch is a line stitch used on common- and even-weave fabrics. It makes a bold, broad line, suitable for where a heavily defined outline is needed. A firm thread should be chosen so that the individual stitches keep their shape well. Begin the row by working a short straight stitch; this will anchor the top chain. Bring the needle out of the fabric further along the line and then work the top chain through the straight stitch; work the second and subsequent chains as shown. When the needle passes under the chain loops, no ground fabric should be picked up: the chain stitches should be left quite loose on the surface of the fabric to make the line flat and broad.

53 Spine chain stitch ☆
Spine chain stitch is a decorative variation of chain stitch *(see page 12)*. A line stitch, it is used on common- and even-weave fabrics. It is most attractive when worked on a small scale and can be used for outlining, as it follows all types of curves well. Any kind of embroidery thread can be used for this stitch, depending on the weight of the ground fabric and the effect required. It is worked in exactly the same manner as chain stitch but with the addition of a diagonal straight stitch at the base of each chain. These diagonal stitches or "spines" can be worked alternately to the right and left of the chains, or they can be grouped in multiples on each side. The spines can conform to one length or vary along the row. They can be embellished by the addition of an isolated stitch, such as

a French knot *(see page 96)* or a daisy stitch *(see page 92)*, at the tip.

A variation of this stitch can be made by whipping the central chain stitch row in a contrasting color or different texture of thread, or by working an isolated knot stitch in the center of each chain.

54 Heavy chain stitch ☆
also known as heavy braid chain stitch
Heavy chain stitch is a solid line stitch used on common- and even-weave fabrics. It makes a heavy, cord-like line which is useful where a well-defined outline is needed. It is similar in construction to broad chain stitch *(see page 25)* and is also worked downward. The row starts with a vertical straight stitch worked in exactly the same way as broad chain stitch; the second and subsequent chains are then worked as shown. The difference between this stitch and broad chain stitch is that the needle is passed back under the previous two chain loops, rather than just the previous one, to form the next stitch. When the needle passes under the chain loops, no ground fabric should be picked up. This stitch can be worked row on row to fill an area, but the effect can berather solid and uninteresting, and choice of thread is important. Any type of embroidery thread can be used when heavy chain stitch is worked in a single row, although a round, twisted thread will make the line stand out best from the background. A stranded floss will create a flatter, wider line.

55 Interlaced running stitch ☆
Interlaced running stitch is a line stitch used on common- and even-weave fabrics. It makes an attractive threaded line, which follows curves and intricate shapes well and is used for outlines and decorative details. This stitch is an easily worked variation of ordinary running stitch *(see page 12)*, which is threaded in

two journeys. A heavy thread is normally used for the interlacing and a rounded thread, such as pearl cotton, gives a slightly raised line. The stitch can be monochrome, or contrasting colors can be used for the interlacing. Use a blunt-ended tapestry needle to avoid splitting the running stitches. Interlaced running stitch can also be worked solidly to fill a shape, either in vertical or horizontal rows, or arranged in a spiral, working outward from the center of the shape.

56 Paris stitch ☆
Paris stitch is a line stitch used only on even-weave fabrics. It makes a neat line with branched stitches along the upper edge, and should be worked in straight rows. It is a variation of backstitch *(see page 14)*, which is used to make a horizontal line. After each backstitch is worked, a vertical stitch is made. This vertical stitch can be worked diagonally to give a different effect. When used on a loosely woven fabric, each stitch can be pulled slightly to create a pattern of holes along the row. Paris stitch can also be worked row upon row to fill a shape.

57 Zig-zag coral stitch ☆
Zig-zag coral stitch is a wide, decorative line stitch used on common- and even-weave fabrics. It forms a knotted zig-zag line, which follows gradual curves well, and it makes an attractive outline when the stitches are kept small and even. It is a variation of coral stitch *(see page 9)* and is usually worked downward between two parallel lines. Guidelines may need to be marked on the fabric to keep the lines of stitching straight and even. Each left-hand stitch is worked in exactly the same way as a coral stitch, but the right-hand stitches are worked slightly differently. Any type of thread can be used with zig-zag coral stitch, but a medium-weight, slightly twisted thread will give the most pleasing result.

46 *Pueblo stitch* ☆

48/2 *Double fly stitch* ☆

49 *Scroll stitch* ☆

47 *Satin stitch* ☆

48/3 *Double fly stitch* ☆

50 *Closed buttonhole stitch* ☆

48/1 *Double fly stitch* ☆

48/4 *Double fly stitch* ☆

51 *Rope stitch* ☆

54/1 *Heavy chain stitch* ☆

55 *Interlaced running stitch* ☆

52 *Broad chain stitch* ☆

54/2 *Heavy chain stitch* ☆

56 *Paris stitch* ☆

53 *Spine chain stitch* ☆

54/3 *Heavy chain stitch* ☆

57 *Zig-zag coral stitch* ☆

58 *Double feather stitch*   ☆

also known as double coral stitch

Double feather stitch is a wide line stitch used on common- and even-weave fabrics. It is a great favorite as it makes a branched, feathery line, which is more decorative than that made by feather stitch *(see page 12)*. A variation of feather stitch, it is worked in a zig-zag pattern. It is used for borders, or multiple rows can be worked to fill a shape. It is worked downward in a similar way to feather stitch, but two or more stitches are made alternately to the right and the left of the line. It can also be worked irregularly, with the numbers of stitches at each side varying, depending on the shape of line required.

59 *Petal stitch*   ☆

also known as pendant chain stitch

Petal stitch is a composite line stitch used on common- and even-weave fabrics. It makes an attractive line with daisy stitches *(see page 92)* arranged so that they hang down to form pendants. This stitch is especially suited to working circular and spiral lines, but it can also be used on the straight, either singly or in multiple rows, to make a textured filling. It is worked from right to left and consists of a row of stem stitch *(see page 9)* with daisy stitches worked below each stem stitch, as shown. Any type of embroidery thread can be used, although the weight of the ground fabric must be taken into consideration, but this stitch looks very effective worked in stranded cotton or silk floss.

60 *Bonnet stitch*   ☆

Bonnet stitch came by its name after an example of the stitch, which does not seem to have been previously known, was found embroidered on a bonnet in a 1923 issue of *Embroidery Magazine*. It is a looped line stitch with a twist, suitable for common-weave fabrics. Worked from right to left, this stitch is a twisted variation of blanket stitch *(see page 13)*. Bonnet stitch can also be worked in rows that touch, to produce a light, lacy filling. The stitch can be varied by altering the lengths of the twisted uprights and the spaces between

them. Most types of thread are suitable for use with this stitch, depending on the effect required and the weight of the fabric to be used. A fine pearl cotton, for example, will give a delicate, spidery look, while a thick wool yarn will create a more solid texture.

61 *Fern stitch*   ☆

Fern stitch is a line stitch used on common- and even-weave fabric. It is extremely simple to work and any type of embroidery thread can be used, but the weight of the background fabric must be taken into account. Fern stitch makes a pretty, branched line and is often used for decorating leaf and flower shapes and for working fern-like sprays in a floral embroidery. It consists of groups of three straight stitches of equal length, worked at angles to each other and sharing the same base hole; the groups are arranged to form a line. Evenly sized and spaced stitches are essential, so care should be taken when working this stitch.

62 *Overcast stitch and detached overcast stitch*   ☆ ☆

Overcast stitch is a raised line stitch used on common- and even-weave fabrics. It is used for outlines, as it follows an intricate pattern well, and it is particularly useful for working letters and monograms, and for figurative designs. This stitch should always be worked with the fabric stretched in an embroidery hoop or frame, as the ground fabric can become puckered and distorted. A padding row of running stitch *(see page 12)* or Holbein stitch *(see page 9)* is worked along the desired line first. This line is then closely covered by small straight stitches, worked at right angles to the padding. The stitches must be worked tightly together and pick up a very small amount of ground fabric each time. A flat thread, such as stranded cotton or silk floss, gives better coverage, while a round thread, such as pearl cotton, should be used for the padding row.

    Detached overcast stitch is worked in a similar way but with two differences. The padding consists of

two loosely worked rows of stem stitch *(see page 9)*: the two rows pick up the fabric alternately. The overcast stitch over the padding is worked in the same way as above, but the ground fabric is not picked up. The stitches must be worked evenly and very close together to make a well-formed line. This stitch is especially useful for working branched lines and for lines that cross one another.

63 *Basket stitch no.1*   ☆ ☆

This and basket stitch no.2 *(see page 80)* bear the same name but are, in fact, entirely different. Basket stitch no.1 is a line stitch used on common-weave fabrics, which gives a braided effect, useful for both edgings and fillings. It can be worked to give an open or closed finish, and looks best when the outside edges are kept parallel; guidelines drawn on the fabric are helpful here. Basket stitch no.1 is worked with a forward and backward motion, and is similar in construction to long-armed cross stitch *(see page 14)*. These plaited or braided stitches are very effective when worked with a fairly shiny thread, such as stranded floss, to enhance the light and shade effect made by the different slants of the stitched threads.

64 *Zig-zag cable stitch*   ☆ ☆

also known as double cable stitch

Zig-zag cable stitch is a simple but effective variation of ordinary cable stitch *(see page 33)*. It is a line stitch and filling used on common- and even-weave fabrics. The stitches are formed in exactly the same manner as cable stitch, but each one is worked at a right angle to the previous one to make a zig-zag line. When used as a line stitch, zig-zag cable stitch is usually worked in straight lines, as it does not follow curves well. It makes an attractive light filling when several spaced parallel rows are worked together: the apex of each pair of stitches should be placed between those on the row below. This stitch works well with any type of embroidery thread.

65 Feathered chain stitch ☆
also known as chained feather stitch

Feathered chain stitch is a pretty, wide line stitch used on common- and even-weave fabrics. It makes a delicate zig-zag line, and is suitable for use with any type of embroidery thread, although a fine thread will enhance the delicacy of the stitch. It is essential that the stitches are of an even size and equally spaced along the line: if an even-weave fabric is used, the threads can be counted to keep the stitches evenly spaced; if a common-weave fabric is used, guidelines will need to be marked on the fabric, or the zig-zag line will be lost. The stitch is always worked downward and consists of chain stitches *(see page 12)* worked alternately to the left and right at a slant. These stitches are then connected by straight diagonal stitches. Short rows of feathered chain stitch can be scattered at random over an area to make a light powdering, or rows can be worked solidly to give an interesting texture to a shape.

66 Breton stitch ☆ ☆

Breton stitch is a relatively little-known stitch, characteristic of the embroidery of Brittany, and is reminiscent of the shape of the curved spindles found on the furniture of that area. It is a line stitch used on common- and even-weave fabrics and is traditionally worked with a dark blue thread on a white fabric, or with white thread on blue linen. Breton stitch is based on closed herringbone stitch *(see page 60)* but differs from that stitch in the way that the crossing stitches are twisted around each other. It is worked with the stitches quite close together between parallel lines; the width between these lines depends on the weight of the embroidery thread. When rows of Breton stitch are worked together to make a filling, an attractive grill-work pattern is created over the fabric, which allows the color of the background to show through. This stitch should be worked on tightly stretched fabric in an embroidery hoop or frame, using a thread with a definite twist for best results. It is equally effective as a line

or filling stitch, or to outline curved shapes.

67 Satin stitch couching ☆ ☆
also known as trailing stitch

Satin stitch couching makes a solid, raised line and is used on common- and even-weave fabrics. A variation of ordinary couching *(see page 8)*, the laid threads are used as a padding and are completely covered by couching stitches. It is used exclusively as a line stitch; it follows both tight and gradual curves well, and can be used for very intricate linear patterns. To give a varying diameter of line, vary the weight of the laid threads. Any type of embroidery thread is suitable for the couching stitches, although a stranded floss or silk will give the most effective cover. Bring the laid threads to the surface and guide them with your left hand (if you are right-handed) along the line to be stitched. Then bring through the couching thread, and work small, close satin stitches *(see page 24)* over the laid thread. The satin stitches can be worked either at a right angle to the laid thread, or they can be slanted, depending on the effect required.

68 German buttonhole stitch ☆ ☆

German buttonhole stitch is a lacy, looped line stitch, which gives a knotted effect; it is used on common- and even-weave fabrics. This stitch makes a very decorative line which looks very complicated to work but is, in fact, quite easy. A rounded, twisted thread, such as pearl cotton, will make the line stand out from the fabric, while stranded floss or silk will give a flatter appearance. It is usually worked downward on the fabric, unlike most other variations of buttonhole stitch, which are worked from left to right. A pair of buttonhole stitches *(see page 13)* are worked with a slant. The working thread is then looped under both stitches in an upward direction, without entering the fabric. To complete the stitch, the thread must be pulled in a downward direction. Like most decorative line stitches, German buttonhole stitch can be used as an outline or worked solidly

to make a border or filling. It looks very unusual when worked in a spiral.

69 Laced Antwerp edging stitch and fringed Antwerp edging stitch ☆ ☆

Laced Antwerp edging stitch is a line stitch used on common-weave fabric, not an edging stitch. It consists of two rows of Antwerp edging stitch running parallel to each other on the surface of the fabric, with the loops facing one another. A second thread is then laced through the loops with a blunt-ended tapestry needle, without picking up the ground fabric.

Fringed Antwerp edging stitch is another decorative border stitch but it can also be used as a fancy fringe edging. Work one row of Antwerp edging stitch, then, to form the fringe, attach lengths of thread to each loop using a lark's head knot *(see Glossary)*. This fringing technique can also be used with Armenian edging stitch *(see page 108)* and braid edging stitch *(see page 109)*.

70 Rosette chain stitch ☆ ☆
also known as bead edging stitch

Rosette chain stitch is a decorative line stitch used on common- and even-weave fabrics. It makes a pretty, braided line, and is a useful finishing device, worked close to the turned-under edge of a piece of fabric. A variation of twisted chain stitch *(see page 21)*, it is always worked from right to left and is fairly simple to stitch. The loop must be held loosely in place on the fabric with the left thumb (if you are right-handed) while the twisted chain stitch is completed. Pass the needle under the right-hand top thread of the stitch, without picking up the ground fabric; the next twisted chain stitch can then be worked.

A heavy thread, such as pearl cotton, is the most suitable for this stitch, as stranded threads give a flat effect. Rosette chain stitch is a useful outline stitch, equally effective when worked in a straight line or when following a curve. It is also used to make floral motifs by working it in a small circle, with the chain stitches pointing outward.

58 *Double feather stitch* ☆

60/1 *Bonnet stitch* ☆

61 *Fern stitch* ☆

59/1 *Petal stitch* ☆

60/2 *Bonnet stitch* ☆

62 *Overcast stitch and detached overcast stitch* ☆ ☆

59/2 *Petal stitch* ☆

60/3 *Bonnet stitch* ☆

63 *Basket stitch no. 1* ☆ ☆

64 Zig-zag cable stitch ☆ ☆

67 Satin stitch couching ☆ ☆

70/1 Rosette chain stitch ☆ ☆

65 Feathered chain stitch ☆ ☆

68 German buttonhole stitch ☆ ☆

70/2 Rosette chain stitch ☆ ☆

66 Breton stitch ☆ ☆

69 Laced Antwerp edging stitch ☆ ☆

71 *Whipped satin stitch* ☆ ☆

Whipped satin stitch is a variation of ordinary satin stitch *(see page 24)* used on common- and even-weave fabrics. It gives a raised, corded finish to lines and narrow shapes worked in satin stitch, by whipping the same or a contrasting thread across the surface. The satin stitches should be slanted, and the whipping stitches should be set at a right angle to them and spaced slightly apart. The whipping stitches enter the ground fabric close to the outside of the shape or line, and should be perfectly regular.

72 *Mirrored buttonhole stitch* ☆ ☆
also known as up and down buttonhole stitch

Mirrored buttonhole stitch is a variation of buttonhole stitch *(see page 13)*, and is used as a line stitch on common- and even-weave fabrics. It forms pairs of vertical stitches crossed by a small bar, each pair linked by a loop. It is fairly simple to work; the pairs of stitches should be made in two separate movements. After the first stitch has been worked, hold the loop down with the left thumb to prevent it from slipping while completing the second stitch. Mirrored buttonhole stitch makes a bold outline, which is particularly attractive when worked

around curves and circles. It can be worked solidly for filling shapes, with the rows placed next to each other or overlapping.

73 *Knotted pearl stitch* ☆ ☆

Knotted pearl stitch is a line stitch used on common- and even-weave fabrics. A variation of pearl stitch *(see page 21)*, it makes a more open line with a knotted surface. It is also suitable for outlines and linear details, but is not as effective as ordinary pearl stitch for following very intricate designs. A round thread, such as pearl cotton, accentuates the knotted appearance of the stitch more than a flat, stranded cotton floss. It is worked from right to left, and the working thread should be tightened after each knot before proceeding to the next stitch. The lower stitches can be made longer to create a less densely knotted effect, or the lengths can be varied to give an undulating line.

74 *Wheatear stitch* ☆ ☆

Wheatear stitch is a decorative line stitch used on common- and even-weave fabrics. It makes a branched line with a heavy central strip and looks rather like an ear of corn, especially when used in short lengths. This stitch follows a gentle curve but is normally used on the

straight. Wheatear stitch was often used as a surface decoration on traditional English smocks. The stitch is worked downward and consists of two diagonal stitches set at a right angle and then joined by a broad chain stitch *(see page 25)*, as shown. The length of the diagonal stitches can be varied to give an attractive, irregular line, and any type of embroidery thread can be used.

75 *Looped edging stitch no. 2* ☆ ☆

Looped edging stitch no. 2 is a line stitch used on common- and even-weave fabrics and not an edging stitch as its name implies. It makes a looped line, with regular downward straight stitches, and follows a curve well, provided that the looped line is worked on the inside of the curve, with the straight stitches fanning out from it. This stitch can also be worked solidly row on row, to make an attractive filling. It is simple to work, and each row is worked from right to left along parallel lines. Guidelines may need to be marked on the fabric if the stitch is being worked in straight lines and the fabric threads cannot be counted. A short, horizontal stitch is made at the beginning of each row to act as a foundation for the first loop. A series of straight stitches and loops are then made along the row.

76 Tailor's buttonhole stitch ☆ ☆

Tailor's buttonhole stitch is similar to ordinary buttonhole stitch *(see page 13)* but it has a stronger edge, which is more hard-wearing and particularly suitable for the heavyweight fabrics. It is used both to finish raw edges and as a line stitch on common- and even-weave fabrics. It is worked from left to right in the same way as buttonhole stitch, but with an extra loop of thread, which is wound around the needle before it is pulled through the stitch. This extra loop makes a firm knotted edge to the stitch. Tailor's buttonhole stitch should be worked with the stitches very close together, so that no fabric shows between them. This will ensure that the knots lie neatly next to each other along the edge. The lengths of the uprights can be graduated to give a zig-zag or undulating top edge to the stitch for a more decorative line.

77 Cable stitch ☆ ☆
*also known as **cable chain stitch***

Cable stitch is a variation of chain stitch *(see page 12)* used as a line or filling stitch on common- and even-weave fabrics. It is worked in a similar way to ordinary chain stitch but in this case the thread is twisted around the needle after each chain loop, and before it enters the fabric. This makes an intervening link between the chains. The stitch follows curved lines well and makes a good filling stitch when worked solidly. A contrasting stitch, such as coral stitch *(see page 9)* or stem stitch *(see page 9)*, can be worked on alternate rows to make an unusual filling. Another method of filling a shape with cable stitch is to work evenly spaced parallel rows of it over the whole area to be filled. Then lace adjoining rows together through the chains with a contrasting thread and a blunt-ended tapestry needle.

78 Loop stitch ☆ ☆
*also known as **centipede stitch** and **knotted loop stitch**; see also **daisy stitch***

Loop stitch is a line stitch used on common- and even-weave fabrics, and it has a raised, plaited center. It is normally used on the straight, but it will follow a curve, provided that it is gradual. Loop stitch can also be used to fill narrow shapes by varying the length of the outside stitches and outlining the shape with backstitch *(see page 14)* or stem stitch *(see page 9)* for greater definition. It is worked horizontally from right to left along parallel lines, and guidelines may need to be drawn on the fabric to keep the stitches even, if the fabric threads cannot be counted. Straight stitches are worked between the two lines, and loop under each preceding stitch to make the plaited center. Any type of thread can be used, but a round, twisted thread, such as pearl cotton, enhances the raised plait.

79 Double-sided cross stitch ☆ ☆
*also known as **marking stitch** and **brave bred stitch***

Double-sided cross stitch is used on common- and even-weave fabrics. As its name suggests, it makes an identical stitch on both sides of the fabric; it is a reversible variation of ordinary cross stitch *(see page 14)*. It is an ideal stitch for fine, semi-transparent fabrics, such as organdy or fine silk, and for work which is viewed from both sides. Each row is worked in four journeys: at the end of the first journey and the beginning of the fourth, work extra half-diagonals. If it is necessary to work over a cross stitch to get to a point of continuation (to keep the stitch identical on both sides) it should be done as neatly as possible. Care should be taken to conceal the beginning and end of each length of embroidery thread under an existing stitch.

71 Whipped satin stitch ☆ ☆

73/1 Knotted pearl stitch ☆ ☆

74 Wheatear stitch ☆ ☆

72/1 Mirrored buttonhole stitch ☆ ☆

73/2 Knotted pearl stitch ☆ ☆

75/1 Looped edging stitch no. 2 ☆ ☆

72/2 Mirrored buttonhole stitch ☆ ☆

73/3 Knotted pearl stitch ☆ ☆

75/2 Looped edging stitch no. 2 ☆ ☆

76 Tailor's buttonhole stitch ☆ ☆

78 Loop stitch ☆ ☆

79/3 Double-sided cross stitch ☆ ☆

77/1 Cable stitch ☆ ☆

79/1 Double-sided cross stitch ☆ ☆

79/4 Double-sided cross stitch ☆ ☆

77/2 Cable stitch ☆ ☆

79/2 Double-sided cross stitch ☆ ☆

79/5 Double-sided cross stitch ☆ ☆

80 *Braid stitch*   ☆ ☆

also known as **Gordian knot stitch**

Braid stitch is a line stitch used on common- and even-weave fabrics. It makes a textured border with a braided, slightly raised look, which can be worked easily around curves. It should be worked between close parallel lines, using a firm, twisted thread, such as pearl cotton or fine crochet cotton; stranded floss is too flat to work well with this stitch. The stitches should be kept small, otherwise the loops slip and become loose, and the braided effect is lost. When working braid stitch on an even-weave linen along the grain of the fabric, one or two of the fabric threads can be drawn out behind the stitches to give the stitch a lacy look. This stitch is not suitable for use on articles which will be laundered unless the stitches are less than 1/4 inch high, as the loops are inclined to pull out of shape if they are any longer.

81 *Basque knot*   ☆ ☆

also known as **knotted loop stitch**

Basque knots can be used singly, scattered at random over an area of common-weave fabric to provide a textured finish, or they can be joined together to form a line stitch which gives a well-defined knotted line. By packing the row of lines close together and using a heavy thread, this stitch can be used as a solid filling. Basque knot is similar to double knot stitch *(see page 36)*, but differs from it because it is always worked from right to left rather than left to right, and also because the base stitch is slightly larger. This knot was often used an old embroideries to ornament rows of Basque stitch *(see page 16)*.

82 *Sorbello stitch*   ☆ ☆

Sorbello stitch is a looped stitch used on common- and even-weave fabrics. The stitch originates in the Italian village of Sorbello where it is used extensively, often in a heavy white cotton thread on an unbleached linen background. The Italians use it not only for working straight and curved lines, but also as an individual stitch to fill complex geometric designs in the same way as cross stitch *(see page 14)*.

The stitch should be worked quite loosely and each stitch covers a small square area. First, a horizontal straight stitch is made at the top of the square; the thread is then brought through at the bottom left-hand corner, looped under and over the horizontal stitch and taken through the fabric at the bottom right-hand corner. The stitches are worked close together from left to right to make a line, or they can be used individually, in the Italian manner. A round thread, such as matte embroidery cotton or heavyweight pearl cotton, shows off the textured quality of this stitch well, but it also looks effective when worked in a finer thread.

83 *Double knot stitch*   ☆ ☆

also known as **tied coral stitch, old English knot stitch, Smyrna stitch** *and* **Palestrina stitch**

Double knit stitch is a line stitch used on common- and even-weave fabrics. Characteristic of Italian embroidery, this stitch makes an attractive knotted line with a beaded effect. It is used for outlines, linear details, curves and, by working it solidly, as a textured filling. It can also be worked as an isolated stitch and be used as a powdering. Work the stitch from left to right: make a straight stitch and loop the thread under and over it to form a knot at the end. The knots can be arranged more closely together and the straight stitch made very small to give a heavy line. Use a round, twisted thread, such as pearl cotton, for this stitch to show the knots to their best advantage.

84 Zig-zag chain stitch ☆☆
also known as Vandyke chain stitch
Zig-zag chain stitch is a line stitch and filling used on common- and even-weave fabrics, and is suitable for use with any type of embroidery thread. It is a very old variation of chain stitch *(see page 12)* and small-scale examples of it have been found on ancient Chinese embroideries. As its name suggests, it makes a decorative zig-zag line — an unusual outline for a shape. It is worked in the same way as ordinary chain stitch but each chain loop is set at a right angle to the previous one to create the zig-zag line. To ensure that the chains lie flat on the surface of the fabric, the needle should pierce the end of the previous loop as it enters the fabric. This stitch also makes an effective filling when worked solidly over an area and lends itself to being striped or shaded gradually in bands.

85 Marking cross stitch ☆☆
Marking cross stitch is a variation of ordinary cross stitch *(see page 14)* and is used on common- and even-weave fabrics. It is reversible and forms an ordinary cross stitch on one side of the fabric, and a neat square of four straight stitches on the reverse. As its name suggests, it is particularly useful for working lettering and monograms on clothing and household linen, or for any item where both sides are viewed. It is also extremely decorative when worked on a semi-transparent fabric, such as organdy or voile, since the squares on the back of the fabric show through, creating a shadow effect. Each cross is covered twice to form the square of stitches on the reverse. It is sometimes necessary to make further re-crosses, especially when working lettering, in order to complete the squares on the back, and this should be done very neatly. Care should be taken to conceal the beginning and end of each length of embroidery thread under an existing stitch.

86 Checkered chain stitch ☆☆
also known as magic chain and magic stitch
Checkered chain stitch is a variation of ordinary chain stitch *(see page 12)*. It is a decorative line or filling stitch used on common- and even-weave fabrics, worked with two contrasting threads. Both threads are threaded through the same needle, and a row of chain stitch is worked using the threas alternately. When making a stitch with one of the threads, the thread not in use is kept above the point of the needle before both threads are pulled through. (If a loop of the wrong color thread remains on the surface, a slight pull on the thread will cause it to disappear.) The position of the threads is then reversed, and the next stitch worked. The threads need not be altered after each stitch — two or more stitches can be worked in one color before reversing the position of the threads.

87 Knotted chain stitch ☆☆
also known as link stitch
Knotted chain stitch is a fancy line stitch used on common- and even-weave fabrics. It makes a raised, knotted line and follows intricate curves well. To show this stitch to its best advantage, work it in a rounded, fairly heavy thread, such as matte embroidery cotton or pearl cotton, in the heaviest weight available. Adjust the loop of each stitch to the required size, hold it in place on the fabric with the left thumb and at the same time pull the working thread through the loop to complete the knot. Although this stitch is easy to work by following the sequence shown, it takes practice to work the loops completely evenly.

80 Braid stitch ☆ ☆

82/1 Sorbello stitch ☆ ☆

83/1 Double knot stitch ☆ ☆

81/1 Basque knot ☆ ☆

82/2 Sorbello stitch ☆ ☆

83/2 Double knot stitch ☆ ☆

81/2 Basque knot ☆ ☆

82/3 Sorbello stitch ☆ ☆

83/3 Double knot stitch ☆ ☆

84 *Zig-zag chain stitch* ☆ ☆

85/3 *Marking cross stitch* ☆ ☆

86 *Checkered chain stitch* ☆ ☆

85/1 *Marking cross stitch* ☆ ☆

85/4 *Marking cross stitch* ☆ ☆

87/1 *Knotted chain stitch* ☆ ☆

85/2 *Marking cross stitch* ☆ ☆

85/5 *Marking cross stitch* ☆ ☆

87/2 *Knotted chain stitch* ☆ ☆

88 *Crested chain stitch* ☆ ☆
also known as Spanish coral stitch

Crested chain stitch is a composite line stitch used on common- and even-weave fabrics. It gives a decorative, braided line when worked close together, and has a light, lacy appearance if the stitches are spread out. It is particularly effective when used to outline a gradual curve with the coral stitch edge on the outside of the curve. This stitch combines chain stitch *(see page 12)* and coral stitch *(see page 9)*, and it is much easier to work crested chain stitch successfully if both of these stitches are already familiar. It is worked downward and spans two parallel lines, which may first need to be marked on the fabric to keep the stitches evenly spaced. First work a small chain stitch at the top right-hand side of the fabric, then work the coral and chain stitches alternately. A round, twisted thread, such as pearl cotton, illustrates the beauty of this stitch better than a flat stranded thread.

89 *Knotted diamond stitch* ☆ ☆ ☆

Knotted diamond stitch is a complex line stitch used on common- and even-weave fabrics. It makes a bold, strongly textured lline, which can be worked as a border or an outline. Any type of thread can be used for this stitch, but a firm, rounded thread, such as the heaviest available weight of pearl cotton, makes the knots more pronounced than a flat, stranded thread. It is worked from left to right and consists of complicated knots linked together in a line. Each knot is worked on a foundation of a diagonal straight stitch slanting from bottom left to top right. The thread is brought through the fabric at the bottom right-hand corner and a series of loops is worked to make the knot over the foundation, without picking up the ground fabric. The thread should be tightened at each stage. When the knot is completed, the next foundation stitch is made, and so on to the end of the row.

90 *Knotted buttonhole stitch* ☆ ☆

Knotted buttonhole stitch is a very useful and decorative variation of ordinary buttonhole stitch *(see page 13)*. A line stitch used on common- and even-weave fabrics, each vertical stitch has a knot at the tip. Knotted buttonhole stitch is effective when used as an outline, as it follows curves well. Two rows can be worked close together, back to back for a feathery line, and with the heights of the vertical stitches graduated. This stitch makes an attractive outline for a circle, with the vertical stitches either inside the shape, or fanning out around the edge. It is a little tricky to keep the knots an even size at first, and some practice will be needed. The knots are made by winding the thread once around the thumb of the left hand (if you are right-handed) before passing the needle through the resulting loop, making a buttonhole stitch. The loop on the needle forms the knot at the top of the vertical stitch. Knotted buttonhole stitch looks best when worked with a rounded, heavy thread, such as pearl or matte embroidery cotton; a stranded thread will flatten the stitch.

91 Plaited braid stitch ☆ ☆ ☆

Plaited braid stitch is a heavy line stitch used on common-weave fabrics, which requires practice if it is to work successfully. It has been in use since the early sixteenth century, and was popular during that period and during the early seventeenth century when it was usually worked in metal threads to adorn clothes and furnishings. The effect this stitch creates is of a slightly raised, heavy braid, very rich and complex in appearance. It is essential to use a heavy, stiff thread when working plaited braid stitch, otherwise the loops will tangle and lose their shape. Always work the stitch from the top of the fabric downward, passing the needle alternately under the threads and through the fabric. The back of the work should show small horizontal stitches, all of the same length, lying in a straight line. Study the sequence of loops and stitches carefully when trying this stitch for the first time; gradually, experience will tell you how loose to leave the loops to form an even line of stitching. Metallic threads work well with this stitch, as does a shiny, twisted thread, provided that it is heavy enough.

92 Three-sided stitch ☆ ☆ ☆
also known as point Turc, lace stitch, Turkish stitch and Bermuda faggoting

Three-sided stitch is a line stitch used on a finely woven, common-weave fabric. It makes a pretty line with a triangular pattern of stitches and holes and can be used as a border, to follow curves, or as a decorative seam when applying lace. It should be worked with a fine thread and a very heavy needle. The stitches should be pulled quite tightly to accentuate the holes made by the needle every time it enters the fabric, as they form an integral part of the pattern. The triangles are outlined by working two backstitches *(see page 14)* on each side, which must all be of equal size to give the correct effect.

93 Crossed Cretan stitch ☆ ☆ ☆

Crossed Cretan stitch is a decorative line stitch used on common- and even-weave fabrics. It makes a zig-zag line and is best worked in straight lines on a fairly small scale to make borders and bands. It can also be combined with a plainer line stitch, such as chain stitch *(see page 12)*. The line has a delicate, almost spidery appearance and needs a thread which will accentuate this delicacy. It consists of diagonal stitches, which make the zig-zag, and two crossed slanting stitches worked where the diagonal stitches meet. The slanting stitches should be left fairly loose on the fabric. It is quite complicated to work, and the sequence of stitches shown should be followed carefully.

94 Portuguese knotted stem stitch ☆ ☆ ☆

Portuguese knotted stem stitch is a line stitch used on common- and even-weave fabrics. It makes a knotted, rope-like line, which is accentuated when a heavy thread, such as pearl cotton, is used. The stitch is ideal for outlining shapes and working quite intricate linear designs as it follows curves well. A variation of ordinary stem stitch *(see page 9)*, it is worked in the same way, with two whipping stitches added to form the knots. The whipping stitches are worked over two consecutive stem stitches and do not pick up any ground fabric.

88/1 Crested chain stitch ☆☆

89/1 Knotted diamond stitch ☆☆☆

89/4 Knotted diamond stitch ☆☆☆

88/2 Crested chain stitch ☆☆

89/2 Knotted diamond stitch ☆☆☆

89/5 Knotted diamond stitch ☆☆☆

88/3 Crested chain stitch ☆☆

89/3 Knotted diamond stitch ☆☆☆

90 Knotted buttonhole stitch ☆☆☆

91/1 **Plaited braid stitch** ☆ ☆ ☆

92 **Three-sided stitch** ☆ ☆ ☆

94/2 **Portuguese knotted stem stitch** ☆ ☆ ☆

91/2 **Plaited braid stitch** ☆ ☆ ☆

93 **Crossed Cretan stitch** ☆ ☆ ☆

94/3 **Portuguese knotted stem stitch** ☆ ☆ ☆

91/3 **Plaited braid stitch** ☆ ☆ ☆

94/1 **Portuguese knotted stem stitch** ☆ ☆ ☆

94/4 **Portuguese knotted stem stitch** ☆ ☆ ☆

Border stitches

95 Threaded chain stitch ☆
Threaded chain stitch is a composite line stitch used on common- and even-weave fabrics. It consists of a foundation row of spaced daisy stitches (see page 92), all facing the same direction. These stitches are then threaded with a similar or contrasting color thread along the row from left to right. For a more decorative line, a second threading can be made, perhaps in a third color, with the second thread filling the spaces left on the first journey. Any type of embroidery thread is suitable for this stitch, and a metallic thread can be used for the threading. A blunt-ended tapestry needle should be used for the threading to avoid splitting the stitches on the foundation row. Extra decorative touches can be added after the threading, by working isolated French knots (see page 96) or cross stitches (see page 14) between the daisy stitches.

96 Sham hemstitch ☆
also known as zig-zag sham hemstitch
Sham hemstitch is a line stitch used on common- and even-weave fabrics. It was originally used to imitate a hemstitch border (see page 112) on fabric which was too fine for the threads to be removed, but it is now used as a decorative zig-zag line stitch and worked in two colors. This stitch is worked in straight lines, as it does not follow curves well. To keep the row straight, guidelines may need to be marked on the fabric if the threads cannot be counted. It is worked in two journeys. A zig-zag row of diagonal straight stitches is worked first, and a second thread of contrasting color or weight is then laced over these foundation stitches. The needle enters the fabric only at the beginning and end of each row and a blunt-ended tapestry needle should be used for the lacing to avoid splitting the foundation stitches.

97 Fancy herringbone stitch ☆
Fancy herringbone stitch is a wide, ornamental line stitch for common- and even-weave fabrics. It makes a rich border, particularly if a metallic thread is used for the interlacing, and it can look stunning if worked in spaced multiple rows, using a carefully chosen color scheme. It is deceptively simple to work, in spite of its rather complex appearance. Each row is worked in three journeys. First, a foundation row of ordinary herringbone stitch (see page 8) is worked, using guidelines marked on the fabric, unless the fabric threads can be counted, to keep the row of an even width. A row of St George cross stitch (see page 68) is then worked over the top and bottom crosses of the herringbone rows, taking care that the horizontal bar of the St George cross stitch is always worked over the vertical one. These two journeys can be worked in the same color thread, or two contrasting threads. On the third journey, the horizontal bars are interlaced without the ground fabric being picked up. Use a blunt-ended tapestry needle for the interlacing to avoid splitting the stitches on the two preceding rows.

98 Interlaced band ☆
Interlaced band is a composite line stitch used on common- and even-weave fabrics. Guidelines may need to be drawn to keep the edges of the stitch straight, unless the fabric threads can be counted. This stitch can be worked in any type of thread, and looks very effective when a fairly stiff metallic thread is used for the interlacing. It makes a pretty border when two colors are used, or it can be worked in multiple rows to make a stunning filling stitch.

Each row has a foundation of vertical straight stitches placed fairly close together. A second thread is then laced through the center of these stitches, twisting each pair in turn. This thread enters the fabric only at the beginning and end of the row, and a blunt-ended tapestry needle should be used to avoid splitting the foundation stitches. A heavier effect can be achieved by twisting four threads in two groups. If the foundation stitches are made quite long and spaced closely together, two or even three threads can be used to make a more complicated twist. The fabric will then need to be stretched in an embroidery hoop or frame to prevent it from pulling out of shape.

99 Chinese stitch ☆
also known as Chinese cross stitch; see also Pekinese stitch
Chinese stitch is a border or filling stitch used on even-weave fabrics. It is extremely simple to work and looks most effective when a loosely woven linen provides the background fabric: the loose threads of the linen are drawn together by the stitching if it is pulled quite tightly after each stitch. It can also be used as a decorative surface stitch, or the blocks can be scattered at random over a shape as a powdering. It is simply constructed in blocks and each block covers six vertical and four horizontal fabric threads. A central horizontal stitch is worked first over six vertical threads and then crossed by two vertical stitches, each worked over four horizontal threads. The next block is set with a half drop, as shown. When used as a filling stitch, the blocks can be worked solidly or can be arranged to make a chessboard pattern with rectangles of the fabric left unworked.

100 Roman stitch ☆
also known as branch stitch
Roman stitch is a wide line stitch used on common- and even-weave fabrics. It makes a pretty branched line and can be used to make a border or it can be worked solidly to fill a shape. It is worked from left to right between two widely spaced parallel lines, and if the threads cannot be counted, guidelines may need to be marked on the fabric, to keep the width of the line even. It is very simple to work; a long straight stitch is taken from the lower edge of the line to the top edge and then tied down by a short crossing stitch. The long stitches can be pulled slightly by the crossing stitches to give them a gentle curve, or they can be worked straight. The stitches should be placed close together to make a solid line and any type of embroidery thread can be used for this attractive border stitch.

101 *Raised chevron stitch* ☆

Raised chevron stitch is a heavy composite line stitch used in straight rows on common- and even-weave fabrics. It is a variation of chevron stitch *(see page 8)* and makes a bold, raised line useful for borders and bands. It is quite simple to work but the foundation row must be worked neatly and with even spaces between the stitches for good results. A foundation row is worked first, consisting of diagonal stitches arranged in "V" shapes. Guidelines may need to be marked on the fabric to keep the "V" shapes even, unless the threads of the fabric can be counted. The chevron stitch is then threaded over the foundation row, without the needle entering the fabric except at the beginning and end of the row. It is advisable to use a blunt-ended tapestry needle for the second thread to avoid splitting the stitches on the foundation row.

Raised chevron stitch should be worked with the fabric stretched in an embroidery hoop or frame to prevent the fabric from distorting when the chevron threading is worked. The chevron threading can be worked in a contrasting color, texture or weight of thread for a more decorative effect.

102 *Triangle stitch* ☆

Triangle stitch is a border stitch or filling used on common- and even-weave fabrics and has a triangular pattern. This stitch will work more successfully on a fabric where the threads can be counted, as regularity is crucial to give the correct geometric effect. A common-weave fabric can, however, be used, but guidelines will need to be marked on the surface.

Triangle stitch is worked in vertical rows, and two journeys are needed to complete one row. Each journey consists of a line of alternate horizontal and diagonal stitches. On the second journey, the direction of the diagonal stitches is reversed. Triangle stitch makes an attractive border, and each triangle can be decorated by working a daisy stitch *(see page 92)* or a French knot *(see page 96)* at the center. This stitch is also used in multiple rows as a light filling. Any type of embroidery thread can be used, the choice depending on the size of the stitch being worked, and the weight of the ground fabric.

103 *Sailor stitch* ☆

also known as sailor edge stitch

Sailor stitch is a line stitch used on common- and even-weave fabrics. It makes a delicate looped border when worked on a small scale in a fine, rounded thread such as fine crochet cotton. It is quite an easy stitch to work, but practice is needed to keep the loops even. It is worked downward and consists of a series of loops which are anchored by chain stitches *(see page 12)* as shown.

Hold each loop firmly on the fabric with your left thumb (if you are right-handed) until the anchoring stitch has been made and tightened slightly. A different effect can be made by working very large loops and anchoring them to the fabric at the center of each loop by a daisy stitch *(see page 92)*. Sailor stitch can also be worked in multiple rows to fill a shape. Two rows can be worked along the same line, so that the chain stitches on the second row fit between those on the first. This looks very attractive if two shades of the same color are used, or if two different weights of thread are worked and the finer thread used for the second row.

104 *Interlaced buttonhole stitch* ☆

Interlaced buttonhole stitch is a wide, composite line stitch used on common- and even-weave fabrics. Simple to work, it can be made more ornate by using a rich metallic or textured thread for the interlacing. Two parallel rows of the buttonhole stitch *(see page 13)*, with the stitches spaced, are worked with the looped edges facing each other and a gap lying between them. A second thread is then interlaced through these foundation rows without entering the ground fabric; a blunt-ended tapestry needle should be used to avoid splitting the threads of the foundation stitches. Stretch the fabric in an embroidery hoop or frame while working the stitch, otherwise the interlacing will pucker and distort the fabric. The tension of the second thread is also important: if it is too loose, the interlacing will lose its shape, but if it is too tight, the foundation rows will be pulled toward each other and will no longer be parallel.

105 *Maidenhair stitch* ☆

Maidenhair stitch is a line stitch used on common- and even-weave fabrics. It makes a delicate, branched line and has a fern-like quality, hence the name; it is a variation of single feather stitch *(see page 12)*. This stitch looks most attractive when worked in single, straight rows, using a round thread such as pearl cotton or fine crochet cotton. Worked downward, groups of stitches are placed alternately on each side of the central line. Three single feather stitches are made to the right of the line with the lengths graduated so that they line up horizontally. A similar group is then made on the left of the line, and so on down the line. Maidenhair stitch looks equally effective whether it is worked on a large or a small scale.

106 *Threaded herringbone stitch* ☆

also known as barred witch stitch

Threaded herringbone stitch is a composite line stitch used on common- and even-weave fabrics. It makes an attractive line, which is usually worked in two contrasting colors of thread. This stitch is used as a simple, straight border, or in multiple rows as a rich, lacy filling, which can be threaded with a metallic thread to create an unusual effect. A row of ordinary herringbone stitch *(see page 8)* is worked first, and then a second thread is laced up and down through the foundation stitches. The second thread passes through the fabric at only the beginning and end of each row, and a blunt-ended tapestry needle should be used to avoid splitting the foundation stitches. When worked as a filling, the foundation rows should touch at the tips of the crosses. The color of the lacing thread can be graduated to give a subtle color change over the area.

95 **Threaded chain stitch** ☆

97/1 *Fancy herringbone stitch* ☆

98 **Interlaced band** ☆

96/1 **Sham hemstitch** ☆

97/2 *Fancy herringbone stitch* ☆

99 **Chinese stitch** ☆

96/2 **Sham hemstitch** ☆

97/3 *Fancy herringbone stitch* ☆

100 **Roman stitch** ☆

101 *Raised chevron stitch* ☆

103/1 *Sailor stitch* ☆

105 *Maidenhair stitch* ☆

102/1 *Triangle stitch* ☆

103/2 *Sailor stitch* ☆

106 *Threaded herringbone stitch* ☆

102/2 *Triangle stitch* ☆

104 *Interlaced buttonhole stitch* ☆

107 Laced buttonhole stitch ☆

Laced buttonhole stitch is a wide, composite line stitch worked on common- and even-weave fabrics. It is similar in construction to interlaced buttonhole stitch *(see page 45)* but the effect is simpler. Work two parallel rows of buttonhole stitch *(see page 13)* with spaced stitches; the looped edges should face each other and a gap should be left between the rows. Then, lace a second thread between the foundation rows, taking care not to enter the ground fabric. A contrasting color or texture or a metallic finish for the second thread will make this stitch look more decorative. Use a blunt-ended tapestry needle for the lacing to avoid splitting the threads on the foundation rows.

A variation on this stitch is to work the buttonhole stitch foundation with the verticals, rather than the loops, facing each other. A second thread can then be faced across the gap and through alternate vertical stitches in the same way as a single row of cloud filling stitch *(see page 69)*. The looped edges of the buttonhole stitch can then be whipped with a contrasting color in the same manner as whipped backstitch *(see page 16)*. This stitch should be worked with the fabric stretched in an embroidery hoop or frame, otherwise the lacing will pucker and distort the background. The lacing thread should remain fairly loose or the foundation rows will be pulled toward each other and no longer be parallel.

108 Two-sided plaited Spanish stitch ☆

Two-sided plaited Spanish stitch is a border stitch used only on even-weave fabrics. It makes a simple pattern of "V" shapes, pointing from left to right; the stitch is identical on both sides of the fabric. Each row requires two journeys, one immediately above the other, to complete it — both halves of the row are composed of slanting straight stitches. On the first journey, the stitches slant from the bottom left to the top right, and each stitch spans five vertical and three horizontal fabric threads. On the second

journey, the stitches slant in the opposite direction, and this line is placed above the first one. If both sides of the work will be visible, break the thread off at the end of the first journey, securing it neatly, and use a second length of thread for the second journey. Any type of embroidery thread can be used, provided that it is compatible with the weight of the ground fabric, but a fine thread accentuates the delicacy of this attractive border stitch.

109 Lock stitch and lock stitch band ☆

Lock stitch is a composite line stitch used on common- and even-weave fabrics. It makes a delicate, laced line with a looped lower edge and is always used on the straight, never around curves. Any type of thread is suitable for this stitch and a contrasting or metallic thread can be used for the lacing. A foundation row of evenly spaced vertical stitches is made first. A second thread is then laced through the foundation stitches at the lower edge; do not pick up any ground fabric. Use a blunt-ended tapestry needle for the lacing to avoid splitting the foundation stitches.

Lock stitch band is a simple variation of lock stitch. The foundation row is made in the same way but then laced in two journeys instead of one to cover both ends of the straight stitches. Make sure that the upper and lower loops of the lacing are worked over the same two foundation stitches.

110 Butterfly chain stitch ☆

Butterfly chain stitch is an ornamental composite line stitch used on common- and even-weave fabrics. Each row is worked in two journeys, using either the same thread for both journeys, or two contrasting weights or colors. First work a foundation row of groups of three vertical straight stitches. The spaces between the groups of stitches should be approximately the same width as the area covered by the three stitches. On the second journey, bunch each group of stitches together with a twisted chain stitch *(see page 21)*: pull each twisted

chain stitch tightly before proceeding to the next one. On the second journey, do not allow the needle to enter the ground fabric except at the beginning and end of the row.

Butterfly chain stitch should be worked with the fabric stretched in an embroidery hoop or frame to prevent it from puckering or pulling out of shape. The stitch can also be used as a light, decorative filling by working the groups of straight stitches on the second row between the groups on the first row.

111 Threaded treble running stitch ☆

Threaded treble running stitch is a wide, composite line stitch used on common- and even-weave fabrics. A wider version of interlaced running stitch *(see page 25)*, it makes an attractive threaded line which is best used as a border. A heavier thread is normally used for the interlacing, and a round, twisted thread, such as pearl cotton, gives a slightly raised line. The stitch can be monochrome, or contrasting colors can be used for the interlacing. A foundation of three parallel rows of ordinary running stitch *(see page 12)* is made first, and then the interlacing is worked in two journeys. This stitch can also be used in multiple rows to fill a shape, provided that a small space is left between each row.

112 Doubled herringbone stitch ☆

Doubled herringbone stitch is a wide, decorative line stitch used on common- and even-weave fabrics. It has an attractive, lacy, zig-zag pattern, which is usually worked in a straight line. Guidelines may need to be marked on the fabric, if the threads cannot be counted, to keep the row an even width. It can also be worked in multiple rows to make a light filling; the rows should touch each other at the tips of the crosses. First work a row of herringbone stitch *(see page 8)* for a foundation. Then, work a second row of this stitch over the top and through the fabric, flattening the stitches so that only the tips of the crosses in the foundation row are still visible.

113 Battlement stitch ☆
Battlement stitch is a composite line stitch made up of four or more rows of evenly spaced blanket stitch (see page 13). The blanket stitch rows overlap and form a heavy border with a crenellated top edge. This stitch is used on common-weave fabrics and can be worked in more than one color to create a more decorative border. A deeper border can be made by working two rows of parallel stitching with the straight edges facing one another. Spacing this stitch evenly is essential in order to keep the notches along the top edge an identical size and shape.

114 Threaded running stitch ☆
Threaded running stitch is a composite line stitch used on common- and even-weave fabrics. It makes a lacy line with loops along the lower edge, and can be used alone or in multiple rows to fill a shape. A wider line can be made by working two parallel rows of the stitch with the looped edges on the outside and the inside stitches touching. This stitch does not follow curves well and should be used on the straight. It is a variation of ordinary running stitch (see page 12) worked on a foundation of two parallel rows. A second thread is then laced up and down each pair of stitches, linking the pairs together along the lower edge. The second thread, which enters the fabric only at the beginning and end of the row, can be of a contrasting weight, color or texture for a more interesting effect. Use a blunt-ended tapestry needle for the second thread to avoid splitting the stitches on the foundation rows.

115 Stepped and threaded running stitch ☆
also known as laced double stitch
Stepped and threaded running stitch is a composite border stitch used on common- and even-weave fabrics. It makes a pretty lacy line, which can also be worked solidly to fill a shape. This stitch is normally worked in straight rows as it does not follow curves well. It is a variation of ordinary running stitch (see page 12) and is worked on a foundation of two parallel rows of that stitch. The stitches are set alternately on the second row. A second thread is then laced from row to row without picking up the ground fabric. Use a blunt-ended tapestry needle for the threading to avoid splitting the running stitches. The second thread can be of a contrasting weight, texture and color, or a metallic thread can be used to create a luxurious effect.

116 Siennese stitch ☆
Siennese stitch is a wide line stitch used on common- and even-weave fabrics. It makes a pretty looped line which can be used alone as a border, or can be worked in multiple rows to fill a shape. The stitch is worked from left to right along two parallel lines, and guidelines may need to be marked on the fabric if the threads cannot be counted to keep the row of an even width. Each stitch consists of a vertical straight stitch with a second stitch worked at the right and looped around the first stitch. The stitch can be worked with an open or closed finish, depending on the effect required and on the type of thread being used. A heavy thread, such as pearl cotton, gives this stitch a raised appearance along the central row of loops.

117 Laced double running stitch and laced treble running stitch ☆
Laced double running stitch is a composite border or filling stitch used on common- and even-weave fabrics. It makes a simple, wide threaded line, which is normally used on the straight, although it also follows a gradual curve well. This stitch is a variation of ordinary running stitch (see page 12) and looks very decorative if a metallic thread is used for the lacing.

First work a foundation of two rows of evenly spaced running stitches, making sure that the stitches and the spaces between them are all of an even length. Then lace a second thread up and down the rows. The second thread can be of a heavier weight and a contrasting color and texture to the first. Use a blunt-ended tapestry needle for the lacing to avoid picking up the ground fabric and splitting the running stitches. This stitch makes an attractive filling when worked solidly row on row. A heavier version can be worked by adding an extra foundation row. The stitch is then known as laced treble running stitch.

118 Eskimo edging stitch ☆
also known as Eskimo laced edge
Eskimo edging stitch is a composite line stitch used on common- and even-weave fabrics. It is an adaptation of a reversible edging stitch, used by Eskimos to bind the edges of their sealskin clothing to make it waterproof. A simply constructed stitch, Eskimo edging stitch is worked on a foundation of running stitch (see page 12) and makes a looped line, which follows gradual curves well. Work evenly spaced running stitch first, from right to left. Then lace a second thread alternately through the running stitches and the ground fabric. The second thread can be of a contrasting weight and color. This stitch looks very effective when worked as a double line, with the looped edges of each row touching.

119 Double chain stitch ☆
also known as Turkmen stitch
Double chain stitch is a line stitch and filling used on common- and even-weave fabrics. It makes an attractive wide border when worked along two parallel lines; alternatively, the size of the stitches can be altered to fill shapes of varying widths. It can also be worked solidly, row on row, to fill larger shapes. Double chain stitch works best when used in straight lines, but it will follow a gentle curve. A simple variation of chain stitch (see page 12), any type of embroidery thread can be used. The stitch consists of a fairly wide chain stitch worked downward alternately to the left and then to the right of the line. If working double chain stitch in a straight line, guidelines may need to be marked on the fabric to keep the width of the stitches even. The rows can be made more decorative by the addition of an isolated stitch, such as a French knot (see page 96) or dot stitch (see page 92), worked in the center of each chain.

107 Laced buttonhole stitch ☆

109/1 Lock stitch and lock stitch band ☆

110 Butterfly chain stitch ☆

108/1 Two-sided plaited Spanish stitch ☆

109/2 Lock stitch and lock stitch band ☆

111 Threaded treble running stitch ☆

108/2 Two-sided plaited Spanish stitch ☆

109/3 Lock stitch and lock stitch band ☆

112 Doubled herringbone stitch ☆

113 Battlement stitch ☆

114 Threaded running stitch ☆

115 Stepped and threaded running stitch ☆

116/1 Siennese stitch ☆

116/2 Siennese stitch ☆

116/3 Siennese stitch ☆

117 Laced double running stitch ☆

118 Eskimo edging stitch ☆

119 Double edging stitch ☆

120 *Zig-zag stitch* ☆

Zig-zag stitch is a line stitch or filling used on common- and even-weave fabrics. It makes a decorative outline stitch or border and has a delicate geometric pattern. Each horizontal row is worked in two journeys. Beginning at the right, work a row of alternate vertical and diagonal straight stitches. On the return journey, the vertical stitches share the same holes as the first vertical stitches, while the diagonal stitches cross each other. Guidelines may need to be marked on the fabric if the threads cannot be counted to keep the rows straight. A fine embroidery thread such as fine crochet cotton accentuates the pattern if the stitches are worked fairly small. When used as a filling, the rows of zig-zag stitch are worked close together, the vertical stitches touching, to make a lattice pattern. A different pattern can be created by arranging the rows so that the vertical stitches lie under the crossed diagonals.

121 *One-sided insertion stitch* ☆

Despite its name, one-sided insertion stitch is an attractive border stitch, and not a stitch to join two pieces of fabric. It can be worked on common-weave fabrics, but a neater effect is achieved when it is used on an even-weave fabric. A decorative and intricate variation of cross stitch, it is always used in a straight line, working from right to left. One-sided insertion stitch consists of a combination of ordinary cross stitch *(see page 14)* and long-armed cross stitch *(see page 141)* and is quite easy to work; follow carefully the sequence of stitches shown.

122 *Buttonholed herringbone stitch* ☆ ☆

Buttonholed herringbone stitch is a heavy, composite line stitch used on common- and even-weave fabrics. It makes a bold zig-zag line and can be worked in multiple rows to fill a shape. Guidelines may need to be marked on the fabric if the thread cannot be counted to keep the rows straight. This stitch should be worked on fabric stretched in an embroidery hoop or frame, otherwise the buttonhole stitch tightens the foundation row and may pucker the fabric. A foundation row of ordinary herringbone stitch *(see page 8)* is worked first and then a finer thread is used to work a row of buttonhole stitch *(see page 13)* over the foundation. At the top and bottom of the herringbone stitches, the working thread must be taken under the cross, without picking up the ground fabric. Use a blunt-ended tapestry needle for the second thread to avoid splitting the stitches on the foundation row.

123 *Guilloche stitch* ☆ ☆

Guilloche stitch is a wide, composite border stitch used on common- and even-weave fabrics. The name is derived from an architectural term for an ornamental band containing two or more interwoven wavy lines. The stitch makes a very decorative band, which is used singly to make a border and is often worked in several colors and weights of thread. To keep these lines parallel, guidelines may need to be marked on the fabric, unless the threads can be counted. The outer lines are worked in stem stitch *(see page 9)*, and groups of three horizontal satin stitches *(see page 24)* are then worked at regular intervals between the stem stitch lines. These groups of stitches are then threaded in two journeys, without picking up the ground fabric. Use a blunt-ended tapestry needle for the threading to avoid splitting the satin stitches. Finally, a French knot *(see page 96)* is worked at the center of each circle.

124 *Twisted lattice band* ☆ ☆

Twisted lattice band is a composite border stitch used on common- and even-weave fabrics. A pretty lattice band is made by this stitch and it can be used alone to make a light border, worked in two colors or two weights of thread. Alternatively, the rows can be arranged solidly as a filling when they create an extremely decorative effect if a metallic thread is used for the lacing.

A row of double herringbone stitch *(see page 53)* is worked first, using the second method described. The foundation row should be worked qute loosely, with the fabric stretched in an embroidery hoop or frame, as the lacing will tighten the stitches. Make sure that the formation of the double herringbone stitches is correct before proceeding with the lacing. The lacing is worked in two journeys, from left to right of the area then back again; be careful not to pick up any ground fabric.

125 *Raised chain band* ☆ ☆
Raised chain band is a composite line stitch worked downward on common- and even-weave fabrics. It can be given a more raised appearance by working a padding of laid threads underneath the foundation stitches. The foundation of evenly spaced, short, horizontal stitches is worked first. These can vary in width to accommodate one, two or three bands of the top stitch, depending on the width of line required. The chain-like stitching is worked over the foundation threads, without picking up any of the ground fabric. Any type of thread can be used for this stitch but a blunt-ended tapestry needle should be used for the second thread to avoid splitting the foundation threads.

126 *Double herringbone stitch* ☆ ☆
also known as Indian herringbone stitch
and Triple herringbone stitch
also known as criss-cross herringbone stitch
Double herringbone stitch is a line stitch used on common- and even-weave fabrics. It consists of a foundation row of ordinary herringbone stitch *(see page 8)* with a second row worked over it, so that the stitches interlace. This stitch has two distinct uses, for which the stitches are interlaced differently.

When the stitch is used as a decorative line on its own, it is often worked in two colors. Both rows are worked in the same way as herringbone stitch, interlacing only where they cross each other. This version of the stitch can be composed of three rows instead of two, all spaced evenly along the line; it is then known as triple herringbone

stitch. The second method of interlacing is slightly more complicated and is used as a foundation row for other stitches, such as interlaced herringbone stitch *(see page 65)*. The sequence of "unders" and "overs" should be followed carefully, or the interlacing will be incorrect. When used as a foundation row, this stitch is usually worked in only one color. With both these methods, guidelines may need to be marked on the fabric if the threads cannot be counted, to keep the rows of an even width.

127 *Striped woven band* ☆ ☆
A striped woven band is a composite border stitch used on common- and even-weave fabrics. It is a simply worked variation of a diagonal woven band *(see page 56)*, but in this case the stripes are horizontal rather than diagonal. The foundation stitches and the weaving are worked in the same way, but by beginning each row of weaving with the same color of thread, the formation of the stripes is changed. The preliminary padding can be worked to give a raised band.

128 *Interlaced chain stitch* ☆ ☆
Interlaced chain stitch is a composite line stitch used on common- and even-weave fabrics. A relatively little-known variation of chain stitch *(see page 12)*, it makes a rich, ornamental line, especially if a metallic thread is used for the interlacing. It is an old stitch, probably of French origin, and examples of it have been found on several sixteenth-century embroideries. Once the sequence of loops has been mastered it is deceptively simple to work.

Work a foundation row of fairly large chain stitch first and then

interlace a second, contrasting thread through each side of the row, following the sequence shown. Always work the interlacing in two journeys, starting from the top of the foundation row each time, and without picking up any ground fabric. To avoid splitting the stitches on the foundation row, use a blunt-ended tapestry needle for the interlacing. The interlacing thread should be left fairly loose but may need to be anchored to the fabric by tiny horizontal stitches at regular intervals along the row.

This stitch should always be worked with the fabric stretched in an embroidery hoop or frame to prevent the fabric from distorting when the interfacing is worked. Rows of interlaced chain stitch alternating with ordinary chain stitch make a wide, heavy border: alternately interlaced chain stitch can be edged on both sides with one or more rows of chain stitch.

129 *Belgian cross stitch* ☆ ☆
Belgian cross stitch is a variation of ordinary cross stitch *(see page 14)* and can be used on even-weave fabrics and canvas for borders or textured fillings. It is worked in rows from left to right, and consists of elongated diagonal stitches that cross each other. A row of horizontal straight stitches is formed along the lower edge of the stitch. When working this stitch on canvas, care should be taken when matching the weight of the thread to the gauge of the canvas to make sure that the canvas is completely covered by the stitching. On an even-weave fabric, any type of embroidery thread can be used, and the stitch can be worked with an open or closed finish, depending on the effect required.

120/1 Zig-zag stitch ☆

121/2 One-sided insertion stitch ☆

122 Buttonhole herringbone stitch ☆ ☆

120/2 Zig-zag stitch ☆

121/3 One-sided insertion stitch ☆

123 Guilloche stitch ☆ ☆

121/1 One-sided insertion stitch ☆

121/4 One-sided insertion stitch ☆

124 Twisted lattice band ☆ ☆

125 **Raised chain band** ☆ ☆

127/1 **Striped woven band** ☆ ☆

128/2 **Interlaced chain stitch** ☆ ☆

126/1 **Double herringbone stitch** ☆ ☆

127/2 **Striped woven band** ☆ ☆

129/1 **Belgian cross stitch** ☆ ☆

26/2 **Double herringbone stitch** ☆ ☆

128/1 **Interlaced chain stitch** ☆ ☆

129/2 **Belgian cross stitch** ☆ ☆

130 French knot border ☆☆

French knot border is a composite line stitch used on common- and even-weave fabrics. It makes an attractive knotted line, which is often used in conjunction with a plain line stitch, such as chain stitch *(see page 12)*, to make a multiple border. It is a combination of French knot *(see page 96)* and fly stitch *(see page 93)* and is easy to work once the technique of making French knots has been mastered. Each stitch consists of a fly stitch loop with a French knot instead of a straight stitch worked to anchor it. The stitches are placed close together to form a row and the rows are worked horizontally, from left to right, in one journey.

131 Step stitch ☆☆
also known as ladder stitch

Step stitch is a composite border stitch used on common- and even-weave fabrics. It makes a very decorative wide border which looks like a ladder, and it can be worked in two colors. A fine thread should be used. Step stitch should be worked with the fabric stretched in an embroidery hoop or frame, and is always worked vertically between two parallel lines. These lines may need to be marked on the fabric if the threads cannot be counted to keep the edges of the stitch even.

First, work a foundation of two vertical rows of chain stitch *(see page 12)*, taking care to make each chain the same size, so that the chains lie directly opposite one another on the two rows. Next, work a row of horizontal straight stitches from one side of the row to the other, threading into the centers of the chains. Work these stitches through

every alternate chain stitch right down the border to make the rungs of the ladder. Then use a second thread to whip along each rung, making a loop to link two rungs at the center. The second thread should not pick up the ground fabric, and a blunt-ended tapestry needle should be used. The row of loops should lie neatly along the exact center of the border.

132 Diagonal woven band ☆☆

A diagonal woven band is a composite border stitch used on common- and even-weave fabrics. It is worked in two colors and makes a solid band with an attractive diagonal stripe. The stitch is worked downward over a foundation row of evenly spaced, horizontal straight stitches. Two needles threaded with contrasting colored threads are used for the weaving, and both threads are brought to the front of the work at the top left-hand corner of the foundation row. The threads are used alternately to weave over and under the foundation stitches. Each row of weaving begins at the top of the foundation, using the alternate color to begin each journey. Such rows will form the diagonal stripes. The rows of weaving should be worked close together in order to cover the foundation stitches completely. The band can have a preliminary padding of long, vertical straight stitches if a raised effect is required.

133 Feather stitch raised band ☆☆

Feather stitch raised band is a composite, wide line stitch used on common- and even-weave fabrics. It consists of a row of feather stitch *(see page 12)* worked over a padded foundation, and makes a heavy,

textured line, which is always used on the straight. It can also be used as a solid filling by working it row on row over a shape. A round, twisted thread such as pearl cotton gives the best results for this stitch, which is worked in three journeys. On the first journey, the padding is made of five long vertical straight stitches worked close together. A foundation of short, horizontal straight stitches is then worked over the padding, with the stitches arranged at regular intervals. The last journey consists of a row of feather stitch worked over the foundation stitches. The needle enters the fabric only at the beginning and end of each row. Feather stitch raised band should be worked on fabric stretched in an embroidery hoop or frame to keep the padding stitches parallel.

134 Russian cross stitch ☆☆
see also herringbone stitch

Russian cross stitch is a canvas stitch used on mono and Penelope canvas. It makes a richly plaited surface and is used for borders and for filling large shapes and backgrounds. It is rather similar in construction to long-armed cross stitch *(see page 141)*, but the stitches are longer and Russian cross stitch is slightly more complicated to work. Follow carefully the arrangement of stitches shown. Any type of embroidery thread can be used, but care should be taken to match the weight of the thread to the gauge of the canvas to make sure that the canvas is completely covered by the stitching. Russian cross stitch can also be worked on an even-weave fabric using fine crochet or a fine pearl cotton for the best results.

135 *Vandyke stitch* ☆ ☆

Vandyke stitch is a border stitch and filling used on common- and even-weave fabrics. It makes a wide line with a raised plait in the center, and looks very attractive worked in multiple rows to create a heavy border. By graduating the length of the stitches on each side of the plait, it is also used to fill narrow shapes. It is worked downward between two parallel lines, and guidelines may need to be marked on the fabric if the threads cannot be counted to keep the stitch an even width. The top stitch picks up a tiny amount of fabric at the center to anchor the whole row. The second and subsequent stitches cross the line from left to right, passing behind the preceding stitch at the center; no ground fabric is picked up. The stitches should be worked close together to make a solidly stitched row that covers the fabric completely. A lustrous embroidery thread, such as stranded silk or cotton floss, shows Vandyke stitch to its best advantage and accentuates the central plait.

136 *Singhalese chain stitch* ☆ ☆

Singhalese chain stitch is a wide, composite line stitch worked downward on common- and even-weave fabrics. It looks most effective when worked in straight lines to form a border, and can be used as a narrow casing for ribbon, tape or flat cord. It is worked in the same way as open chain stitch *(see page 17)* but with contrasting threads added at the sides. Before working the open chain stitch, mark two parallel guidelines on the fabric and pull through a contrasting thread at the top of each line. Let these threads lie loosely on the fabric, following the lines. Then work the open chain stitch over these two threads. The contrasting threads should be tightened at the end of each row and then taken to the back of the work and secured. The two extra threads give a pretty, twisted edge to the stitch.

Singhalese chain stitch is found on the traditional embroideries of Sri Lanka, and the stitch is equally effective worked with an open or closed finish. Any type of embroidery thread is suitable, but a rounded thread such as pearl cotton makes the stitch stand out from the background.

137 *Fancy couching* ☆ ☆

Fancy couching is the term used to describe several variations of ordinary couching stitch *(see page 8)*. Its uses are the same: outlining; linear details; covering the edges of an appliquéd shape; and making a solid filling. The variations are worked in the same way as ordinary couching, but instead of using the straight stitches, other embroidery stitches hold down the laid threads to give a more decorative effect. A number of these are suggested here, but many of the stitches which form broad bands are suitable. Fancy couching is often more striking when worked over a group of laid threads, rather than a single thick one. Narrow ribbons, tapes or flat cords can be used instead of the laid threads, but care must be taken to secure the edges of these neatly, to prevent fraying. Buttonhole stitch *(see page 13)* and open chain stitch *(see page 17)*, arranged in a continuous row and spaced quite widely, work well as couching stitches over a single line of laid threads. Blocks of satin stitch *(see page 24)*, or a row of cross stitch *(see page 14)*, fly stitch *(see page 93)* or daisy stitch *(see page 92)* worked across the laid threads at regular intervals are also effective. Where a wide band of couching is needed, feather stitch *(see page 12)* can couch down two rows of laid threads simultaneously. The threads are arranged in parallel rows with a small gap between them.

138 *Two-sided insertion stitch* ☆ ☆

Two-sided insertion stitch is, despite its name, a decorative border stitch. Similar to one-sided insertion stitch *(see page 52)*, this stitch should be worked on an even-weave fabric to give it regularity, an essential feature of the stitch. A reversible stitch, the front of thestitch builds up plaited borders consisting of two interwoven rows of zig-zag stitches of different size. On the reverse of the fabric, a lattice-work of diamond shapes is made. Each stitch is worked in five stages and the sequence of straight stitches, which are worked from left to right, should be followed carefully.

130 French knot border ☆ ☆

132/1 Diagonal woven band ☆ ☆

133/2 Feather stitch raised band ☆ ☆

131/1 Step stitch ☆ ☆

132/2 Diagonal woven band ☆ ☆

134/1 Russian cross stitch ☆ ☆

131/2 Step stitch ☆ ☆

133/1 Feather stitch raised band ☆ ☆

134/2 Russian cross stitch ☆ ☆

135 Vandyke stitch ☆ ☆

136 Singhalese chain stitch ☆ ☆

137 Fancy couching ☆ ☆

139 Closed herringbone stitch ☆ ☆
also known as shadow stitch
Closed herringbone stitch is a dual-purpose line stitch used on common- and even-weave fabrics. It can be worked as a border stitch when it makes a wide plaited line. It is also used for shadow work on semi-transparent fabrics, such as organdy or voile, when it becomes an alternate way of forming double backstitch *(see page 60)*, which appears on the reverse of closed herringbone stitch. It is worked in exactly the same way as herringbone stitch *(see page 8)* but it is closed up so that the diagonal stitches touch at the top and bottom. To keep the row an even width, guidelines may need to be marked on the fabric if the threads cannot be counted. Closed herringbone stitch is also an attractive stitch for couching down a narrow ribbon, flat cord or a group of laid threads.

140 Tied herringbone stitch ☆ ☆
also known as coral knotted herringbone stitch
Tied herringbone stitch is a composite line stitch used on common- and even-weave fabrics. It makes a knotted zig-zag line which is usually worked in two contrasting colors of thread. This stitch is used as a light border, or in multiple rows to make a lacy, knotted filling for a shape. First, work a row of ordinary herringbone stitch *(see page 8)*, and then use a second thread to make a row of coral stitch *(see page 9)*. Work the knots over each intersection of the foundation stitches to tie them together; do not pick up any ground fabric. Use a blunt-ended tapestry needle for the coral stitch to avoid splitting the foundation threads. When used as a filling, the foundation rows should touch at the tips of the crosses. The colors of the thread used for the coral stitch can be graduated to give a subtle color change over the area.

141 Double backstitch ☆ ☆
also known as crossed backstitch
Double backstitch is used particularly for shadow embroidery. On the front of the fabric it forms a double row of backstitch worked simultaneously along two lines, while on the reverse of the work, a row of closed herringbone stitch *(see page 60)* appears. Shadow embroidery is always worked on a semi-transparent fabric, such as organdy or voile, with silk or stranded cotton floss. The rows of backstitch form the outline of the design, while the herringbone showing through the fabric forms the shadow. The two lines on the front of the fabric need not be parallel, and double backstitch is often used for leaf and petal shapes. Care should be taken with the spaces between the lines so that the herringbone on the reverse lies flat and does not sag.

142 Ladder stitch ☆ ☆
see also open chain stitch, ladder hem stitch and step stitch
Ladder stitch is a wide line stitch used on common- and even-weave fabrics. It has a ladder-like appearance, hence the name, and it is used as a border stitch or to fill a long, narrow shape of varying width. This stitch should always be worked on fabric stretched in an embroidery hoop or frame to prevent it from tightening and distorting the fabric. When the stitch is worked in a straight line, guidelines may need to be drawn on the fabric, unless the fabric threads can be counted, to keep the line straight. The rungs of the ladder can be placed close together to achieve a solid effect, or can be spaced apart to give the stitch a more lacy appearance. It is worked downward along two parallel lines and consists of a sequence of crossing stitches, which forms the rungs, and loops which build up to create a plaited edge on each side of the row. A rounded thread, such as pearl or matte embroidery cotton, gives a raised appearance to the plaited edges.

143 Triple Cretan stitch ☆ ☆ ☆
also known as French Cretan stitch
Triple Cretan stitch is a decorative line stitch used on common- and even-weave fabrics. It makes an attractive lacy line and can be worked with any type of embroidery thread, the choice depending on the effect required. Similar to open Cretan stitch *(see page 20)*, it has additional loops, and looks most effective when worked in a straight line; it does not follow curves well. Follow the sequence of stitches shown and be sure to tension each loop before proceeding to the next one. Triple Cretan stitch can also be worked solidly row on row to fill a regular shape with a very unusual lacy pattern.

144 Raised lattice band ☆ ☆ ☆
also known as raised lace band
Raised lattice band is a composite border stitch used on common- and even-weave fabrics. It makes a rich padded line, which can be worked in more than one color; a metallic thread can be used for the lacing. This stitch needs to be worked with the fabric stretched in an embroidery hoop or frame to prevent distortion.

A padding is made first: long, horizontal surface satin stitches *(see page 72)* are worked along the whole length of the row; then extra stitches are worked along the center of the line to give a rounder effect. The padding is then covered by a foundation of closely worked, vertical satin stitches *(see page 24)* to cover the padding completely. A flat thread, such as stranded cotton or silk floss, gives better coverage. Care should be taken to make all the vertical stitches exactly the same length. To make the lattice pattern, a row of threaded herringbone stitch *(see page 45)* is worked over the satin stitches. The tips of the herringbones should enter the fabric just above and below the foundation line. Use a blunt-ended tapestry needle for the lacing to avoid disturbing the foundation stitches. Raised lattice band can be worked in multiple rows for a heavier border.

145 Checkered chain band ☆ ☆ ☆
Checkered chain band is a composite stitch worked downward on common and even-weave fabrics. It is used as a heavy line stitch, and as a solid filling, making a chessboard pattern. A foundation of evenly spaced, short, horizontal stitches is made first, using the thread singly. Chain stitch *(see page 12)* is embroidered over these stitches, without picking up the ground fabric. They are worked in two colors of thread, using the two needles alternately on the same journey. The thread is doubled in each needle, rather than having two separate lengths threaded through it; this makes the two threads easier to manage and less likely to tangle. Blunt-ended tapestry needles should be used to avoid splitting the threads on the foundation row. The stitched examples show where to insert the two threads to begin the stitching, and how the stitches are made alternately by using one doubled thread at a time.

The horizontal bars can be made wider to accommodate three or four rows of chain stitch to make a heavier line. When this stitch is used for filling an area, lines of single checkered chain band are worked solidly side by side. When the colors at the top of each row alternate, a chessboard pattern emerges. A horizontal striped version is worked by making the top stitch on each row the same color.

146 Diamond stitch ☆ ☆ ☆
Diamond stitch is a wide, knotted line stitch used as a border on common- and even-weave fabrics. It is worked downward between two parallel lines and, to keep the width of the stitch even, guidelines may need to be marked on the fabric if the threads cannot be counted. It makes an attractive lacy line with a diamond pattern and can also be worked in adjacent rows to make a trellis filling. The stitch consists of straight, horizontal stitches placed one below the other with a knot at each end, which is worked over each straight stitch and through the fabric. A knot is also made in the center of the row to link the straight stitches, without picking up the ground fabric. The arrangement of straight stitches and knots is shown. After completion, the line can be decorated by working an isolated stitch such as a French knot *(see page 92)* in the diamond-shaped spaces. Diamond stitch should be worked in a straight line, since it does not follow curves well.

139 *Closed herringbone stitch* ☆ ☆

142/1 *Ladder stitch* ☆ ☆

142/4 *Ladder stitch* ☆ ☆

140 *Tied herringbone stitch* ☆ ☆

142/2 *Ladder stitch* ☆ ☆

142/5 *Ladder stitch* ☆ ☆

141 *Double backstitch* ☆ ☆

142/3 *Ladder stitch* ☆ ☆

142/6 *Ladder stitch* ☆ ☆

143/1 Triple Cretan stitch ☆ ☆ ☆

143/4 Triple Cretan stitch ☆ ☆ ☆

145/1 Checkered chain band ☆ ☆ ☆

143/2 Triple Cretan stitch ☆ ☆ ☆

144/1 Raised lattice band ☆ ☆ ☆

145/2 Checkered chain band ☆ ☆ ☆

143/3 Triple Cretan stitch ☆ ☆ ☆

144/2 Raised lattice band ☆ ☆ ☆

146 Diamond stitch ☆ ☆ ☆

147 *Scottish Cretan stitch* ☆ ☆ ☆

Scottish Cretan stitch is an ornamental line stitch used on common- and even-weave fabrics. A variation of open Cretan stitch *(see page 20)*, it makes a rich, bold line, best used in a straight row to make a band or border. Any type of thread can be used, but a rounded thread, such as pearl cotton, will be easier to work with. It consists of blocks of open Cretan stitch worked close together and linked to form a row. After each block has been worked, the thread is passed upward through the edge of the stitches on the left, taken over the top of the block and threaded downward through the stitches on the right. The thread must be carefully tensioned before proceeding to the next block, and should not be pulled too tightly or the Cretan stitches will be distorted. Scottish Cretan stitch can also be worked as a motif stitch. To do this, secure the thread on the back of the fabric after each block has been threaded. The blocks can then be used to powder an area; they will look best if they are worked quite small.

148 *Sheaf stitch* ☆ ☆ ☆

Sheaf stitch is a composite border stitch used on common- and even-weave fabrics. It makes a dramatic, heavy line and is always used on the straight. Sheaf stitch is a complicated stitch to work and requires some practice to master, but the end result is well worthwhile. The stitch is always worked vertically, from the bottom to the top, and three stages are needed to complete one row.

First make a foundation of pairs of horizontal straight stitches, spacing each pair evenly at a distance that matches the proposed length of the finished sheaves. (Guidelines may need to be marked on the fabric if the threads cannot be counted.) Then bring the thread through at the bottom right-hand corner of the border, and link together the bottom two pairs of foundation stitches with a block of seven satin stitches *(see page 24)*; be careful not to pick up any ground fabric. Working upward, link every two pairs of foundation stitches in this way, making sure that the satin stitches interlock. Then make a third journey, tying each sheaf around the center with two satin stitches, and making rows of simple knots where the sheaves interlock. A fairly firm thread which does not slip is essential for working sheaf stitch successfully.

149 *Spanish knotted feather stitch* ☆ ☆ ☆

also known as **twisted zig-zag chain stitch**

Spanish knotted feather stitch is an ornamental line stitch used on common- and even-weave fabrics. It makes a wide, decorative line with a braided appearance and is used for bands and borders. It is worked downward, along three parellel lines and, to keep the line straight, guidelines may need to be marked on the fabric if the threads cannot be counted. This stitch is rather difficult to keep even at first, so some practice will be needed to achieve a good result. It consists of a series of twisted loops worked from the center line alternately to the left and to the right. The loops create a knotted effect at the edges of the row. A round, twisted thread such as pearl cotton will give a bolder effect than a flat, stranded cotton or silk floss.

150 *Raised stem stitch band* ☆ ☆ ☆

Raised stem stitch band is a composite border stitch used on common- and even-weave fabrics. It makes a wide, heavily stitched raised band, and is more successful if the fabric is stretched in an embroidery hoop or frame to prevent puckering and to keep the foundation threads parallel. A foundation is made by working long surface satin stitches *(see page 72)* along the border to the required width. Extra stitches are then added over the central portion of the row to give a more raised effect in the middle. Next, single short straight stitches are worked at regular intervals at a right angle to the long stitches. Rows of stem stitches *(see page 9)* are then worked over the short stitches, without picking up the long threads underneath. Use a blunt-ended tapestry needle for the stem stitch rows to avoid disturbing the long threads. All the stem stitch rows should share a common hole at each end of the band to give a neat, rounded finish. The stem stitch rows should be packed as tightly as possible, so that none of the foundation thread shows through, and a flat, stranded thread gives good coverage.

151 *Portuguese border stitch* ☆ ☆ ☆

Portuguese border stitch is a composite stitch used on common- and even-weave fabrics. It makes a wide, ornamental line with a raised effect, which can either be used alone as a straight border, or worked solidly to make a heavy filling. This stitch should always be worked with the fabric stretched in an embroidery hoop or frame to prevent the ground fabric from puckering. A firm thread should be used, especially for the foundation stitches so that they keep their shape. The foundation consists of horizontal straight stitches, which are evenly spaced between two parallel vertical lines. If the threads cannot be counted, guidelines may need to be marked on the fabric to keep the foundation stitches an even length. The left-hand side of the foundation row is then threaded. Without picking up the ground fabric, a group of two satin stitches *(see page 24)* is worked over the bottom two foundation stitches; pairs of foundation stitches are then joined together by a group of two satin stitches, keeping the thread at the right. After two satin stitches have been worked, the thread is taken around the top foundation stitch of the pair to secure it before moving upward to the next pair of satin stitches. The right-hand side of the line is worked in the same way, starting at the bottom, but this time the thread is kept to the left of the satin stitches. The tension of the satin stitches is very important and the foundation stitches should not be pulled out of line.

---

152 *Interlaced herringbone stitch* ☆ ☆ ☆

also known as **interlacing stitch** *and* **Armenian cross stitch**

Interlaced herringbone stitch is a wide, composite line stitch used on common- and even-weave fabrics. It makes a rich, interlaced line, which is always used on the straight. The interlacing thread is usually of a contrasting weight, texture and color to the thread of the foundation row. This stitch looks very attractive when a metallic thread is used for the interlacing.

To keep the row an even width, guidelines may need to be marked on the fabric if the threads cannot be counted. A foundation row of double herringbone stitch *(see page 53)* is worked first, using the second method described. The foundation should be worked quite loosely, with the fabric stretched in an embroidery hoop or frame, as the interlacing will tighten the stitches considerably. Make sure that the formation of this row is correct before proceeding further. The interlacing is threaded in two rows, beginning at the left and completing one side before returning in the opposite direction. Follow the sequence of "unders" and "overs" carefully, and do not pick up the ground fabric. Use a blunt-ended tapestry needle for the interlacing to avoid splitting the foundation stitches.

---

153 *Laced herringbone stitch* ☆ ☆ ☆

also known as **woven herringbone stitch** *and* **German interlacing stitch**

Laced herringbone stitch is a decorative, composite line stitch used on common- and even-weave fabrics. It makes an attractive border stitch and has an unusual circular threading. If the threads cannot be counted, guidelines may need to be drawn on the fabric to keep the rows an even width. This stitch can be worked in one or two colors: a contrasting color, weight or texture of thread can be used for the lacing. A metallic lacing thread will also look attractive.

A foundation row of herringbone stitch *(see page 8)* is worked first, and should be at least ³/₄ inch wide to show the lacing to its best advantage. The work is then turned upside-down before the lacing is begun. This will ensure that the "unders" and "overs" of the herringbone stitch follow the correct sequence. The circular threading is quite complicated, so follow the sequence shown very carefully. Laced herringbone stitch should be worked with the fabric stretched in an embroidery hoop or frame, otherwise the lacing will tighten the stitch and pucker the fabric.

147/1 Scottish Cretan stitch ☆ ☆ ☆

148/1 Sheaf stitch ☆ ☆ ☆

149 Spanish knotted feather stitch ☆ ☆ ☆

147/2 Scottish Cretan stitch ☆ ☆ ☆

148/2 Sheaf stitch ☆ ☆ ☆

150/1 Raised stem stitch band ☆ ☆ ☆

148/3 Sheaf stitch ☆ ☆ ☆

150/2 Raised stem stitch band ☆ ☆ ☆

151/1 Portuguese border stitch ☆ ☆ ☆

152/2 Interlaced herringbone stitch ☆ ☆ ☆

153/2 Laced herringbone stitch ☆ ☆ ☆

151/2 Portuguese border stitch ☆ ☆ ☆

153/1 Laced herringbone stitch ☆ ☆ ☆

153/3 Laced herringbone stitch ☆ ☆ ☆

152/1 Interlaced herringbone stitch ☆ ☆ ☆

Filling stitches

154 Spaced buttonhole filling ☆
Spaced buttonhole filling is a quick and easy way of filling areas of common- and even-weave fabrics. It consists of rows of buttonhole stitch (see page 13) in which the individual stitches are grouped together, often in pairs, with spaces in between. The first row is always worked from left to right, and the spaces on that row filled by the stitches on the next row, which is worked in the opposite direction. The number of stitches in the group can vary, as can the size of the spacing between the groups. This stitch can be worked as a detached filling, anchored through the fabric around the edges of the shape.

---

155 Encroaching satin stitch ☆
Encroaching satin stitch is a filling stitch used on common- and even-weave fabrics. It can be used over a shape of any size and is especially useful for shading and blending colors. It is worked in horizontal rows and consists of closely worked vertical satin stitches (see page 24). On the second and subsequent rows, the head of each stitch is worked between the bases of the two stitches on the row immediately above. The rows of satin stitches blend into each other without a pronounced dividing line. Colors can be shaded very effectively using this stitch, and for really subtle effects the color should be changed on every row — the colors chosen must be very similar for this to work well. Any type of embroidery thread can be used, but a lustrous thread, such as stranded floss or silk, shows off the closely worked surface to its best advantage. Encroaching satin stitch should be worked with the fabric stretched in an embroidery hoop or frame to prevent the fabric from puckering.

---

156 Fly stitch filling ☆
also known as **flowing fly stitch** and **crossed fly stitch**
Fly stitch filling is used on common- and even-weave fabrics for filling a shape of any size. A variation of ordinary fly stitch (see page 93), it makes an attractive trellis pattern. It is worked in horizontal rows, and the tying-down stitches of each fly are very short. A row of fly stitch is worked with the "V" shapes touching. In the second row, the fly stitches are inverted and the tying-down stitches are placed alongside those of the previous row, linking the two fly stitches to make an elongated cross. The two rows are then repeated over the space, with the rows touching. The trellis can be decorated by working a small, isolated stitch, such as a Chinese knot (see page 96), or daisy stitch (see page 92), in the spaces.

---

157 Double Algerian eye stitch ☆
Double Algerian eye stitch is a variation of Algerian eye stitch (see page 168). Although it is worked in the same sequence, each stitch is drawn twice through the same hole, resulting in a heavier appearance. This effect is very useful when a textured appearance is required on a fine, even-weave fabric. This stitch is often worked in a self-colored thread.

---

158 Star filling stitch ☆
Star filling stitch is used on common- and even-weave fabrics. It has a variety of uses: as a light filling stitch, arranged either in formal rows or scattered at random over a shape; worked in a straight line to make a simple border; or used alone as an accent stitch. It is worked by making a large St George cross stitch (see page 68), which is first covered by an ordinary cross stitch (see page 14) of about the same size. A tiny ordinary cross stitch is then worked at the center to anchor both the larger crosses firmly to the fabric. Star filling stitch can be worked in one color, or a different color can be used for each cross, and the tiny central cross can be worked in a finer thread.

---

159 Seed stitch ☆
also known as **seeding stitch, seed filling stitch, speckling stitch** and **isolated backstitch;** see also **dot stitch**
Seed stitch is a filling stitch used on common- and even-weave fabrics. It makes a light speckled powdering for an area, and is extremely quick and easy to work. Work tiny backstitches (see page 14) in any direction over the area to be filled. They should all be of even length, but should be scattered irregularly and should not make a pattern. The size and spacing of the backstitches can be varied, depending on the type of thread used and the effect required. To make a similar but slightly heavier filling, use dot stitch (see page 92) instead of seed stitch.

---

160 Brick and cross filling ☆
Brick and cross filling is a simple yet attractive way of decorating an area of common- or even-weave fabric. It is constructed by alternating square blocks of four horizontal or vertical satin stitches (see page 24) with single cross stitches (see page 14) to form a chessboard pattern; it is usually worked in vertical rows, beginning at the top and working downward. Two or more shades of thread can be used, or it can be monochrome in appearance. A variation of this filling alternates square blocks of three vertical satin stitches with St George cross stitches (see page 68) worked in the center of the spaces.

---

161 St George cross stitch ☆
St George cross stitch is a filling stitch used on common- and even-weave fabrics. It is an upright cross stitch worked in two journeys. On the first journey, make a row of horizontal stitches; on the second, cross them with vertical stitches of the same length. It makes a neat, geometric filling when worked regularly over an area, and the density can be varied by altering the spaces between each cross and between the rows. Any type of embroidery thread can be used for this stitch, but a rounded thread, such as pearl cotton, will make the stitches stand out from the ground fabric better than a flat, stranded floss or silk. St George cross stitch can also be worked individually, in the same way as ordinary cross stitch (see page 14). It can then be scattered at random over a shape to make an attractive powdering, or it can be used as an accent stitch.

162 Double darning ☆
also known as pessante
Double darning is a filling stitch best worked on an even-weave fabric, as complete regularity is essential. It makes a flat solidly stitched surface of vertical rows; no ground fabric should show through the stitching. The method of working this stitch is identical to that of Holbein stitch *(see page 9)* but double darning is always used as a filling rather than an outline stitch. Each row is worked in two journeys. On the first journey, the stitches and the spaces between them should be of equal size. On the return journey, the spaces are filled in by stitches, and the needle must enter and emerge from the fabric through the holes made on the first journey.

163 Roman filling stitch ☆
Roman filling stitch is used on common- and even-weave fabrics and makes an attractive and unusual filling for shapes of any size. A variation of Roman stitch *(see page 44)*, it consists of groups of seven vertical stitches of graduated length, tied down individually by tiny crossing stitches. Each group of stitches is arranged alternately over the shape with spaces between them. The groups can be worked alternately in two colors and placed with the edges touching to give a more solid effect, or they can be arranged in horizontal rows. Another variation is to work the groups so that the longest stitches touch each other at the top and bottom. Diamond shaped areas of ground fabric then show through to add interest to the stitching.

164 Link filling stitch ☆
also known as link powdering stitch and detached chain filling
Link filling stitch is used to fill shapes on common- and even-weave fabrics. It is a simply worked filling, which can look extremely attractive, and consists of an arrangement of daisy stitches *(see page 92)* across an area. The arrangement should be very formal and the stitches worked in horizontal rows and placed so that, vertically, every other stitch aligns. This stitch is often used on crewel

work, and its effect can be varied by spacing the stitches closer together or further apart. The size of the stitch depends to a large extent on the thread used. A fine crewel yarn makes a smaller stitch than a heavy thread, such as pearl cotton or tapestry yarn.

165 Trellis stitch ☆
Trellis stitch is a filling stitch used on common- and even-weave fabrics. It makes a delicate trellis pattern of laid threads, and it should be worked on fabric stretched in an embroidery hoop or frame. A foundation grid is made first, consisting of long, horizontal straight stitches, crossed by vertical stitches set at a right angle. Long, diagonal stitches are then worked from top left to bottom right, crossing each intersection of the grid. The diagonal stitches are then couched down by working a tiny diagonal stitch over every intersection. Trellis stitch can be worked in one color, or different colors can be used for each type of stitch to create a more interesting effect.

166 Cloud filling stitch ☆
also known as Mexican stitch
Cloud filling stitch is a composite filling stitch used on common- and even-weave fabrics. It is a quick and effective way of filling a shape, and it has an attractive, lacy appearance. Any type of embroidery thread can be used, the choice depending on the effect desired. A foundation of regularly spaced, vertical darning stitches *(see page 14)* is worked over the entire area to be filled. The stitches can be placed close together or be widely spaced, but they should be worked perfectly evenly. If a common-weave fabric is used, the position of these stitches will need to be marked on the fabric before they are worked. A second thread of contrasting color or weight is then laced through these stitches in rows. The needle enters the fabric only at the beginning and end of each row. Use a blunt-ended tapestry needle for the second thread to avoid splitting the stitches on the foundation row. The delicate trellis pattern that is made can be

decorated by working an isolated knot stitch, such as French knot *(see page 96)* or Chinese knot *(see page 96)*, in the spaces. This stitch can be shaded easily by working the second and subsequent rows of threading in carefully graduated shades across the whole area.

167 Closed wave stitch ☆
also known as looped shading stitch
Closed wave stitch is a solid filling stitch used on common- and even-weave fabrics. It is an economical way of covering a shape, since nearly all the thread lies on the surface of the fabric. It is also excellent for shading, as each row, or part of a row, can be worked in a different shade. Closely packed vertical satin stitches *(see page 24)* form the top row. Then, on each subsequent row, looped stitches are taken around the bases of the stitches on the preceding row. The stitches should be worked close together so that no ground fabric is visible. Stranded cotton or silk floss give better coverage of the fabric than a twisted thread.

168 Stem stitch filling and stem stitch shading ☆
Stem stitch filling is a way of using rows of stem stitch *(see page 9)* to make a very useful solid filling for a shape of any size on common- and even-weave fabrics. It makes a closely packed filling with a woven appearance, and any type of embroidery thread can be used, from a fine crewel yarn to a heavy pearl cotton. The lines of this stitch should follow the contours of the shape quite carefully, and the stem stitches should be of an even size on each row. The first stem stitch of each row should be a little shorter than the first stitch of the preceding row in order to give the effect of a pattern of diagonal lines across the surface.

Stem stitch shading is worked in exactly the same way by following the contours of the shape carefully. The colors should be evenly shaded and changed on every second or third row.

154 Spaced buttonhole filling ☆

157 Double Algerian eye stitch ☆

159 Seed stitch ☆

155 Encroaching satin stitch ☆

158/1 Star filling stitch ☆

160 Brick and cross filling ☆

156 Fly stitch filling ☆

158/2 Star filling stitch ☆

161 St George cross stitch ☆

162 *Double darning* ☆

165/1 *Trellis stitch* ☆

167 *Closed wave stitch* ☆

163 *Roman filling stitch* ☆

165/2 *Trellis stitch* ☆

168 *Stem stitch filling and stem stitch shading* ☆

164 *Link filling stitch* ☆

166 *Cloud filling stitch* ☆

169 Colcha stitch ☆

Colcha stitch is a type of couching used on common-weave fabrics. The stitch has its origins in New Mexico and the name refers to the "colchas" or embroidered woolen hangings and bedspreads worked by the Spanish settlers in this country.

The stitch is similar in construction to Roumanian couching *(see page 81)* and is most effective when worked with tapestry or crewel yarn. Two lengths of the thread are used in the needle at the same time. A line of thread is laid across the shape and anchored at irregular intervals with slanting stitches before the next line of thread is laid. Colcha stitch gives a rough, almost woven, effect and can be used for covering large shapes, where a solid area of stitching is required.

170 Long and short stitch ☆

also known as embroidery stitch, shading stitch, tapestry shading stitch, brick stitch, leaf stitch, Irish stitch, plumage stitch, feather-work, long and short satin stitch *and* opus plumarium

Long and short stitch is a variation of satin stitch *(see page 24)* which gives a gradually shaded effect and is much used in naturalistic embroidery. It is also used to fill an area that is too large or irregularly shaped to be covered neatly by satin stitch. It can be worked on all types of fabric and on mono canvas. The first row is made up of alternately long and short stitches which follow closely the outline of the shape to be filled. The subsequent rows are worked in satin stitches of equal length. The stitches should lie closely together and cover the ground fabric.

171 Fancy stitch ☆

Fancy stitch is a modern filling stitch used on common- and even-weave fabrics. It is worked on horizontal foundation rows, which are then threaded to make a decorative lacy filling which allows the ground fabric to show through. To keep the foundation rows straight, guidelines may need to be marked on the fabric if the threads cannot be counted. The foundation consists of alternate rows of running stitch *(see page 12)* and short vertical stitches, commencing with a row of vertical stitches. A second thread, which can be of a contrasting weight and color, is then threaded downward through the foundation rows, without picking up the fabric. Each row of threading is worked separately, one row to the right and one to the left of each vertical foundation stitch. Use a blunt-ended tapestry needle for the threading to avoid splitting the stitches on the foundation rows.

172 Surface satin stitch ☆

Surface satin stitch is a way of working ordinary satin stitch *(see page 24)* on fabric, which gives the same smooth surface but is much more economical with the thread. The standard way of working satin stitch means that as much thread lies underneath the work as on the surface, which is rather wasteful, especially if an expensive silk is being used. In surface satin stitch, the needle picks up only a tiny amount of fabric at the edge of the shape, wasting very little thread. It is rather difficult to keep the stitches closely worked and even, so the shape is often covered in two journeys instead of one. On the first journey, a small space is left between each stitch, which is then filled on the return journey. This method of working satin stitch is used to make a foundation for laid-work *(see page 84)* and, except on canvas, it can be substituted for ordinary satin stitch when a large area is being worked.

173 Sheaf filling stitch ☆

also known as faggot filling stitch

Sheaf filling stitch is used to fill a shape of any size on common- and even-weave fabrics. It makes an extremely attractive light filling when worked in a regular pattern, and each stitch looks like a tiny sheaf of corn. The sheaves are usually arranged in rather formal rows but they can also be scattered in all directions. Each sheaf consists of three vertical satin stitches *(see page 24)* bunched and tied around the center by two overcast stitches *(see page 28)*. The needle should emerge from the fabric behind the satin stitches to work the overcasting, without picking up any ground fabric, before taking the needle to the back of the work. Any type of embroidery thread can be used, the choice depending on the size of sheaves required.

174 Basket filling stitch ☆

also known as basket satin stitch

Basket filling stitch provides a simple but effective way of filling an area of common- or even-weave fabric with a flat, geometric pattern. It is worked in alternate blocks of four horizontal and four vertical satin stitches *(see page 24)*; the blocks should be evenly spaced and regular. Although basket filling stitch is normally worked in one color, it looks very attractive when a second color is used for each alternate block. This stitch can also be worked on mono canvas, using either yarn or stranded floss. The number of stitches in each block can vary between three stitches worked over four canvas threads, and five stitches worked over six threads, depending on the gauge of the canvas and the weight of the thread chosen.

175 Tête de boeuf filling stitch ☆

Tête de boeuf filling stitch is used on common- and even-weave fabrics. It looks like a bull's head, complete with the horns. A fly stitch *(see page 93)* makes the horns, and a daisy stitch *(see page 92)* anchors the fly stitch and makes the head. It is usually worked in formal rows to make an attractive light filling but the stitch can also be worked in horizontal rows to form a border.

There appears to be some confusion about exactly which embroidery stitch is called tête de boeuf filling stitch. In some modern books tête de boeuf filing stitch appears under the name of detached wheatear stitch even though it looks exactly like a bull's head. However, the stitch described above can be found in many 19th-century needlework books, including Caulfield and Saward's 1887 edition of *The Dictionary of Needlework: An Encyclopedia of Artistic, Plain and Fancy Needlework*, where a wood engraving of it and the reference "Tête de boeuf stitch" can be seen .

176 Arrowhead stitch ☆

Arrowhead stitch is primarily used as a filling stitch, preferably on an even-weave fabric, as the regularity of the stitch is part of its character. It also makes a pretty line stitch when worked in pairs along a row. It can be worked horizontally or vertically, and is formed by working two straight stitches at a right angle to each other. When used as a filling stitch, each row should touch the previous one. Arrowhead stitch can also be scattered in pairs at random on a common-weave fabric for a light, powdered effect.

177 Chessboard filling stitch no.1 ☆

Although chessboard filling stitch no.1 and chessboard filling stitch no.2 (see page 120) share the same name, they create entirely different effects. Chessboard filling stitch no.1 is used on common- and even-weave fabrics. It makes a light, decorative filling of textured squares, and any type of embroidery thread can be used. The chessboard pattern is made by alternating stitched squares with unstitched squares. The stitched squares are usually worked in two journeys, and can be worked in two colors. Groups of four straight stitches arranged in the chessboard pattern are worked on the first journey. These groups are then overstitched on the second journey by a large cross stitch (see page 14), extending from corner to corner of the group. The cross stitch is anchored in the center by a short vertical stitch.

178 Croatian stitch ☆

Croatian stitch is a composite filling stitch used for covering small shapes on common- and even-weave fabrics. It looks most effective worked on a small scale and using two colors which contrast boldly with the ground fabric. A thick embroidery thread, such as matte embroidery cotton, tapestry yarn or the heaviest available weight of pearl cotton, accentuates the beauty of this stitch. It is extremely simple to work, but the foundation stitches must be neatly worked, and of even length. Outline the shape with a row of running stitches (see page 12). Then lace a second thread of a different color across the shape and through the running stitches to make parallel lines. Use a blunt-ended tapestry needle for the lacing to avoid picking up any ground fabric.

179 Trellis backstitch ☆
also known as square stitch

This trellis pattern makes an attractive filling stitch that is simple and quick to work, and can be used on both common- and even-weave fabrics. Guidelines need to be drawn on the surface of the fabric if the threads cannot be counted in order to keep the stitched lines evenly spaced. A totally regular grid is the main characteristic of this stitch, so care must be taken in ruling the guidelines, which may be worked diagonally, or horizontally and vertically. To stitch the trellis, first work all the parallel lines in one direction, stitching up one and down the adjacent line. Then work the parallel lines at a right angle to the first set in the same way. The trellis can be decorated in the squares with a small cross stitch (see page 14), French knot (see page 96) or dot stitch (see page 92).

180 Japanese darning ☆

Japanese darning is a light filling stitch used on common- and even-weave fabrics. To keep the rows even, guidelines may need to be marked on the fabric if the threads cannot be counted. Japanese darning makes an attractive geometric filling, which allows the ground fabric to show through, and it can be used for any size of shape. Spaced horizontal rows of ordinary darning stitch (see page 14) are worked over the shape with the stitches arranged alternately on every row. The thread is then brought through to the right of the second row to link the two rows with slanting stitches. This process is repeated over the entire shape; the linking rows should be worked from right to left. Make sure that the needle enters and emerges from the fabric through the holes made by the darning stitches; in this way the stitches are kept perfectly regular.

181 Open wave stitch ☆

Open wave stitch is a filling stitch used on common- and even-weave fabrics. It makes a delicate, lacy filling and is worked in the same way as closed wave stitch (see page 69), but the stitches on each row allow the ground fabric to show through. Any type of embroidery thread can be used, providing that it is compatible with the size of the stitch and the weight of the ground fabric.

182 Herringbone ladder filling stitch ☆
also known as interlaced band stitch, double Pekinese stitch and laced Cretan stitch

Herringbone ladder filling stitch is used on common- and even-weave fabrics as both a border and a filling stitch. It has an attractive, lacy appearance and can be worked in two colors. The stitch is worked on a foundation of two parallel rows of backstitch (see page 14) arranged so that the stitches are placed alternately on each row. Guidelines may need to be marked on the fabric if the threads cannot be counted to keep the rows parallel. A second thread of contrasting weight or color is then interlaced between the two rows. The ground fabric is not picked up and a blunt-ended tapestry needle should be used for the interlacing. To use this stitch as a filling, work further parallel rows of backstitch to cross the fabric and interlace adjacent rows. This stitch can be made into a reversible border by using Holbein stitch (see page 9) for the foundation.

183 Brick stitch no.1 ☆

Although both this and brick stitch no.2 (see page 120) bear the same name, they give different effects. Brick stitch no.1 is a filling stitch used on all types of fabric and on mono canvas. It is constructed very simply and consists of vertical and horizontal straight stitches of an even length, fitted together to form a brickwork pattern. Any spaces left uncovered at the edge of the shape are filled in using shorter straight stitches, keeping the pattern even. It is worked in horizontal rows alternately from left to right and right to left.

169 *Colcha stitch* ☆

171 *Fancy stitch* ☆

173 *Sheaf filling stitch* ☆

170/1 *Long and short stitch* ☆

172/1 *Surface satin stitch* ☆

174 *Basket filling stitch* ☆

170/2 *Long and short stitch* ☆

172/2 *Surface satin stitch* ☆

175 *Tête de boeuf filling stitch* ☆

176 **Arrowhead stitch** ☆

179 **Trellis backstitch** ☆

181 **Open wave stitch** ☆

177 **Chessboard filling stitch no. 1** ☆

180/1 **Japanese darning** ☆

182 **Herringbone ladder filling stitch** ☆

178 **Croatian stitch** ☆

180/2 **Japanese darning** ☆

183 **Brick stitch no. 1** ☆

184 Bosnia stitch ☆
also known as Bosnian stitch, fence
stitch *and* barrier stitch
and Yugoslav border stitch
also known as zig-zag Holbein stitch
These two stitches are grouped
together because they are very
similar to create and Yugoslav border
stitch is probably no more than a
variation of Bosnia stitch — or the
other way around! Bosnia stitch is
indigenous to Yugoslavia and is
frequently used as a filling stitch on
common- and even-weave fabrics. It
is a simply constructed stitch,
worked in two journeys. On the first
journey, the upright stitches are
made and on the second, the spaces
are filled in from bottom left to top
right with slanting stitches. When it is
used as a filling, the uprights of the
second and subsequent rows are
placed above each other in straight
lines, and regularity of spacing is
essential. Bosnia stitch is also found
on French embroideries but the
slanting stitches run from the bottom
right-hand corner to the top left-hand
corner and it is then known as fence
or barrier stitch.

Yugoslav border stitch is probably a
variation of Bosnia stitch but is
always used as a line stitch rather
than a filling. It is also worked in two
journeys but both rows of stitches
slant to form a zig-zag line. This stitch
is often used to decorate the national
costumes of south-eastern Europe,
when it is worked in multiple rows to
form deep borders. It is often
threaded with a second color, in the
same way as threaded herringbone
stitch *(see page 45)*. The traditional
colors chosen vary from village to
village, although the use of a red line
threaded with blue on white linen is
widespread. Sometimes gold or
silver threads are used, giving a rich
appearance to this very simple stitch.

185 New England laid stitch ☆ ☆
also known as Deerfield stitch *and*
self couching
New England laid stitch is a filling
stitch used on common- and even-
weave fabrics. This stitch is an
attractive variation of Roumanian
stitch *(see page 77)*, worked with a
longer crossing stitch, and is used for
making solidly filled lines and narrow

shapes. Very little thread is wasted
on the back of the fabric and it is
thought that the stitch was devised
by the thrifty colonial settlers when
supplies of embroidery threads were
extremely scarce and also
expensive. New England laid stitch
was used extensively on the blue
and white Deerfield embroideries
worked by the settlers of New
England, hence its alternative name.
It is very simple to work and consists
of a long, horizontal straight stitch
couched down by a long, slanting
stitch on the return journey. The
stitches should be worked close
together to cover the ground fabric
completely.

186 Japanese stitch ☆ ☆
Japanese stitch is a solid stitch used
on common- and even-weave
fabrics. Found on old Japanese
embroideries, it is a traditional way of
arranging satin stitch *(see page 24)* to
form a wide, diagonal line. It consists
of equal-sized satin stitches ranged
one below another. The stitches are
packed closely together so that no
ground fabric shows through, and the
line slants from top left to bottom
right. This stitch looks most effective
when worked in a lustrous thread,
such as stranded floss or, as in
Japan, an untwisted silk thread.
Japanese stitch is especially suitable
for use on an even-weave fabric, and
guidelines may need to be marked
on a fabric where the threads cannot
be counted to keep the line even.

187 Open fishbone stitch ☆ ☆
Open fishbone stitch is a filling stitch
used on common- and even-weave
fabrics. It is a variation of fishbone
stitch no.1 *(see page 80)* and is
worked with an open finish to allow
the ground fabric to show through. It
is used to fill petal and leaf shapes
where a light, open filling is needed.
The stitches are worked downward,
following the outlines of the shape.
The thread is taken from the left-
hand side and a slanting stitch is
made at the center before the thread
is taken through at the right-hand
side. A lustrous embroidery thread
such as stranded floss will show off
this stitch to best advantage,
although any other type of thread can

be used. Leaf stitch *(see page 80)*
makes a similar open filling for a
small shape.

188 Squared filling stitch no.1 ☆ ☆
This and the two following stitches
are all composite fillings for shapes
or backgrounds, suitable for
common- and even-weave fabrics.
Any type of embroidery thread and
color combinations can be used, the
choice depending on personal
preference. All three stitches should
be worked with the fabric stretched
in an embroidery hoop or frame to
keep the foundation threads stable.
Unless an even-weave fabric is being
used, where the threads can be
counted, guidelines may need to be
marked on the fabric to keep the
foundation stitches evenly spaced.

Squared filling stitch no.1 is
worked on a vertical and horizontal
foundation. The long vertical stitches
are made first across the whole area
to be covered. Then the long
horizontal stitches are interwoven at
a right angle, exactly in the manner
of darning; avoid picking up the
ground fabric. A second thread is
then wound around the intersections
of the grid on diagonal journeys from
the top left to the bottom right and
then back again, without picking up
any ground fabric. Use a blunt-ended
tapestry needle for the second
thread to avoid splitting the
foundation stitches.

189 Squared filling stitch no.2 ☆ ☆
Squared filling stitch no.2 is worked
on a foundation grid of vertical and
horizontal straight stitches which,
unlike the preceding stitch, are not
interwoven. First, work the horizontal
stitches over the whole area to be
covered, and then cross these with
the vertical stitches. Couch down
each intersection with a tiny diagonal
stitch, before working a second
diagonal grid over the entire area.
The intersections of the second grid
must fall over the squares of fabric
showing through the first grid. Short,
vertical stitches are used to couch
down the second grid and anchor the
filling securely.

190 Squared filling stitch no. 3 ☆ ☆

Squared filling stitch no. 3 is very simple to work. The diagonal foundation uses pairs of stitches to give a heavier effect. Work the diagonals that run from the bottom left to the top right first, and then cross these with a second set running in the opposite direction. Anchor each intersection to the fabric with a St George cross stitch *(see page 68)* and work a French knot *(see page 96)* or a Chinese knot *(see page 96)* in each of the diamond shapes of fabric which show through the grid.

191 Bokhara couching ☆ ☆

Bokhara couching is a solid filling stitch used on common- and even-weave fabrics. Like Roumanian couching *(see page 81)*, it is a couching stitch which uses a continuous thread for both the laid and the couching stitches. It will fill any size and shape of space well and it looks best when worked with a lustrous stranded thread, either cotton or silk, to catch the light. Adjoining areas of Bokhara couching can be worked with the laid threads running in alternate directions to enhance the light and shade effect the stitch makes. It is straightforward to work but a little practice will be needed to keep the couching stitches even. This stitch should always be worked with the fabric stretched in an embroidery hoop or frame to keep the laid threads parallel. The thread is laid across the shape from left to right and then couched down on the return journey with small, slanting stitches placed at regular intervals. The slanting stitches can be arranged to form lines across the laid threads, or they can be set alternately to give a woven effect.

192 Underside couching ☆ ☆
also known as **invisible stitch**

Underside couching is a filling stitch used on common- and even-weave fabrics. A very old stitch, it has been used for centuries to attach gold and silver threads to ecclesiastical vestments and church furnishings and was used extensively for this purpose during the Middle Ages. Many examples of "Opus Anglicanum," as English embroidery from this period is known, still survive with much of the underside couching still intact; pieces can be seen in the Victoria and Albert Museum in London.

Underside couching is ideally suited to metal thread embroidery, as the couching stitches do not show and therefore do not conceal the metallic surface of the couched thread but it is also worked successfully with other, less precious, threads. Underside couching should be worked on a strong, finely woven ground fabric, which has been stretched tautly in an embroidery hoop or frame. The couching thread must be extremely strong and supple and should be waxed before use. This thread lies underneath the work, and the laid thread on the surface. At regular intervals the couched thread is brought through the fabric, taken over the laid thread and then threaded back through the same hole in the fabric, when it is given a gentle pull, so that a fraction of the laid thread is taken through the fabric and secured. This stitch can be used to fill small shapes or to cover backgrounds.

193 Roumanian stitch ☆ ☆
also known as **Oriental stitch, antique stitch, Indian filling stitch** and **lanina stitch**; see also **Holbein stitch**

Roumanian stitch is a line and filling stitch used on common- and even-weave fabrics. It makes an attractive wide boder when worked between parallel lines and is also used to fill long, narrow shapes by graduating the width of the stitches. In either case, the tying-down stitches in the center must be kept perfectly even and be placed in a neat line.

A long stitch is made across the line or shape to be worked and is tied down on the return journey. The construction of the stitch is similar to that of Roman stitch *(see page 44)* but the tying-down stitches are longer and slanted. The stitches should be worked closely together to cover the fabric completely and they look very effective when worked in stranded floss or silk. A wide shape can be filled by using Roumanian couching *(see page 81)* to give a similar effect.

194 Overlapping herringbone stitch ☆ ☆
also known as **raised herringbone stitch** and **self-padded herringbone stitch**

Overlapping herringbone stitch is a raised stitch used on common- and even-weave fabrics. It makes a closely stitched padded surface and is used for filling leaf and petal shapes and small geometric shapes where a raised effect is needed. Any type of embroidery thread can be used but a stranded floss or silk gives a better fabric coverage. This stitch benefits from being worked in an embroidery hoop or frame although it is not essential to do so. The stitch is worked over a central straight stitch at the top of the shape and is built up with overlapping diagonal straight stitches worked from side to side and crossing in the center. The stitches should be evenly worked and placed as close together as possible to give a smooth surface to the raised area and complete coverage of the fabric.

195 Plaid filling stitch ☆ ☆
also known as **tartan stitch**

Plaid filling stitch is a composite filling stitch used on common- and even-weave fabrics. It is usually worked in three contrasting colors to give a tartan effect. It can be used to fill shapes of any size and the fabric should be stretched in an embroidery hoop or frame to keep the foundation grid perfectly even. The grid is made by working long, vertical straight stitches across the shape, which are then crossed by long, horizontal stitches; the horizontal stitches are interwoven with the verticals in exactly the same way as for darning a sock. The foundation grid should be evenly spaced and make a pattern of squares on the fabric. Two horizontal straight stitches are then worked over each square, using a second color. Finally, two vertical stitches worked in a third color are sewn across these to make a double cross. The crosses are placed in alternate squares to accentuate the plaid pattern.

184 Bosnia stitch ☆

187 Open fishbone stitch ☆ ☆

188/3 Squared filling stitch no. 1 ☆ ☆

185 New England laid stitch ☆ ☆

188/1 Squared filling stitch no. 1 ☆ ☆

189/1 Squared filling stitch no. 2 ☆ ☆

186 Japanese stitch ☆ ☆

188/2 Squared filling stitch no. 1 ☆ ☆

189/2 Squared filling stitch no. 2 ☆ ☆

190 **Squared filling stitch no. 3** ☆ ☆

193 **Roumanian stitch** ☆ ☆

195/1 **Plaid filling stitch** ☆ ☆

191 **Bokhara couching** ☆ ☆

194/1 **Overlapping herringbone stitch** ☆ ☆

195/2 **Plaid filling stitch** ☆ ☆

192 **Underside couching** ☆ ☆

194/2 **Overlapping herringbone stitch** ☆ ☆

196 Couched filling stitch   ☆ ☆
also known as Jacobean couching
Couched filling stitch is a composite stitch used for filling shapes on common- and even-weave fabrics. It has a pretty, lattice appearance and can be worked in two or more colors. It should always be worked with the fabric stretched in an embroidery hoop or frame to keep the foundation grid perfectly regular. The grid is worked first and consists of long horizontal stitches placed at regular intervals across the shape. Long vertical stitches are then worked to cross the first set of stitches at right angles. Keep the foundation grid as even as possible or the beauty of the stitch will be lost. These long stitches are then anchored or ''couched down'' at each intersection by a tiny cross stitch *(see page 14)*, usually in a contrasting color of thread.

197 Torocko stitch   ☆ ☆
also known as cross couched filling stitch and Hungarian cross stitch
Torocko stitch is a quickly worked filling stitch used only on common-weave fabrics. First a foundation grid of evenly spaced long stitches is worked to cover the whole shape. This grid is then overstitched with diagonal rows of upright crosses, and a short, diagonal stitch is worked from bottom left to top right to finish. The crosses can be worked in a second color, with a third color used for the anchoring diagonal stitches. Torocko stitch is most successful if worked on a closely woven ground fabric stretched in a hoop or on a frame during stitching.

198 Leaf stitch   ☆ ☆
see also fir stitch and long and short stitch
Leaf stitch is a filling stitch used on common- and finely woven, even-weave fabrics. It is a light, open stitch suitable for filling small areas, such as oval or leaf shapes. It is always worked upward and consists of slanting straight stitches, which pass from one side of the shape to the other and make a loose plait down the center. An outline stitch, such as backstitch *(see page 14)* or stem stitch *(see page 9)*, is worked around the edge to define the shape more

distinctly. Leaf stitch can also be worked between parallel lines to make a border and the length of the stitches can be varied to give an undulating line. A lustrous embroidery thread, such as stranded floss, shows this stitch off to its best advantage, although any type of thread can be used. Open fishbone stitch *(see page 76)* makes a similar open filling for a small shape.

199 Honeycomb filling stitch   ☆ ☆
also known as net passing stitch
Honeycomb filling stitch is used on common- and even-weave fabrics and has a lacy, geometric appearance. It is essential to work this stitch with the fabric stretched in an embroidery hoop or frame to keep the tension even. The three sets of stitches can be worked in more than one color and a round thread, such as pearl cotton, makes the stitch easier to work. Honeycomb filling stitch consists of long, horizontal and diagonal straight stitches worked so that they interlock, forming triangles. Even spacing of these stitches is crucial. The horizontal stitches are worked first across the whole shape; then one set of diagonal stitches is worked over these, from bottom left to top right. A second set of diagonal stitches is worked at right angles to the first set, passing under the horizontal and over the first diagonal stitches and interlocking all the threads, as shown.

200 Fishbone stitch no.1   ☆ ☆
Although fishbone stitch no.1 and fishbone stitch no.2 *(see page 137)* share the same name, the effect produced from each is quite different.
   Fishbone stitch no.1 is a filling stitch used on common- and even-weave fabrics. It is often used to fill petal and leaf shapes when the stitch lengths are graduated to follow the outline of the shape. It also makes an attractive solid border when the stitches are of equal length, and it makes a flat, solidly stitched surface in which the stitches cross one another at the center. A central vertical straight stitch is worked at the top and then slanting straight stitches are worked alternately from the center to each side of the shape.

The stitches should be worked evenly and very close together so that no ground fabric is visible. A lustrous embroidery thread, such as stranded floss or silk, will emphasize the different directions of the stitches. Fishbone stitch no.1 can be striped by threading two needles with different colors and using each color alternately.

201 Faggot filling stitch   ☆ ☆
see also sheaf filling stitch
Faggot filling stitch is a composite stitch used on common- and even-weave fabrics. It is a variation of a canvas stitch called shell stitch *(see page 160)* adapted from use on fabric. It makes a decorative row of groups of vertical stitches linked together, and it can be used as a border or to make a filling. Each row is worked in two journeys and two different threads can be used, depending on the effect required. To keep the rows even, guidelines may need to be marked on the fabric if the threads cannot be counted. A foundation group of three vertical straight stitches is made first. Then, before proceeding to the next group, these stitches are tied down and bunched together by two short crossing stitches. After a row of bunched stitches has been made, a second thread is used to lace them together. A round, twisted thread, such as pearl cotton, shows this stitch to its best advantage.

202 Basket stitch no.2   ☆ ☆
Basket stitch no.2 is a laid filling. It is used for covering areas of ground fabric and should always be worked in an embroidery hoop or frame to prevent the fabric from puckering. The effect is like that of a woven basket and the stitch can be used on common- or even-weave fabrics. It consists of a foundation grid of single, verticle straight stitches overlaid by double, horizontal ones. The horizonal stitches are then tied down at intervals by short, vertical stitches. The basket weave appearance of this stitch can be made more pronounced by selecting threads in three tones of one color.

203 Flat stitch ☆ ☆
also known as Croatian flat stitch
Flat stitch is a filling stitch used on common- and even-weave fabrics. It makes a flat, solidly stitched shape and is used for filling small shapes, such as leaves and petals. It can also be worked in a line to give a heavy outline to a shape, or in multiple rows to fill a large shape. It is worked downward in slanting straight stitches, which cross the center of the shape. The stitches should be placed close together so that the ground fabric is completely covered. A fairly thick thread, such as matte embroidery cotton or the heaviest weight of pearl cotton, works best with this stitch.

204 Damask darning ☆ ☆
Damask darning is a solid filling stitch used on even-weave fabrics. Perfect regularity is essential for this stitch, so a common-weave fabrics is not suitable. Its appearance is of a woven fabric with a diagonal pattern and the stitch looks best when worked with a lustrous thread, such as stranded floss or silk. The use of this type of thread will enhance the light and shade effect created by the different directions on which the thread lies. In spite of its name, this stitch is not formed by rows of darning stitches. Each diagonal row, which starts from the top left to the bottom right, is worked separately by making short, horizontal stitches. The stitch should cover the surface, allowing no ground fabric to show through, and it makes an attractive filling when used over a large area.

205 Burden stitch ☆ ☆
Burden stitch is named after Elizabeth Burden, the sister-in-law of the nineteenth-century English designer, William Morris. Miss Burden taught at The Royal School of Needlework and revived a type of couching which dates back to the Middle Ages, when it was used as a grounding stitch, particularly in Italy and Germany, and used mainly on the large ecclesiastical pieces of that period. She worked this type of couching to cover large areas in the figurative pieces she embroidered to the designs of William Morris and Walter Crane.

The stitch consists of rounded, fairly thick threads laid horizontally across the area to be covered, with an even space between each one. These laid threads are then attached to the background fabric (common- or even-weave) by vertical straight stitches which cross them. These vertical stitches can be worked close together or spaced out to let the color of the fabric show through. When completed, the stitch makes a brick-like pattern, which can be shaded by the use of different colors of thread and is very effective when the laid threads are metallic. It is often used for ecclesiastical embroidery when either silk or lengths of gold and silver purl are used for the vertical stitches. The name Burden stitch is also sometimes applied to a type of darning (see page 14), which makes the same brick-like pattern.

206 Buttonhole stitch shading ☆ ☆
A filling of closely worked rows of buttonhole stitch (see page 13) is ideal for shading an area when a solidly embroidered shape is required. Work the rows of buttonhole stitch from left to right, beginning at the top of the shape to be filled. The second and subsequent rows should encroach on the loops of the preceding row. The shading is effected by changing the color of the thread very gradually row by row or once every two rows. An alternative way of shading with this stitch is to work pairs of long, horizonal stitches across the area in different colors. Then work the buttonhole stitch over each pair of laid threads, leaving spaces between the stitches. The amount of color showing from the contrasting laid threads is controlled by the extent of the spaces between the buttonhole stitches; vary the size of the spaces until you achieve the amount of shading required. The laid threads can be all of the same color and the buttonhole stitch worked in graduating colors to provide the shading; alternatively, the buttonhole stitch can be monochrome, with the shading created by the different colors of the laid threads.

207 Roumanian couching ☆ ☆
also known as antique couching, Oriental couching, laid Oriental stitch and figure stitch
Roumanian couching is a solid filling stitch used on common- and even-weave fabrics. It has a continuous thread for both the laid and the couching stitches, in the same way as Bokhara couching (see page 77). Roumanian couching makes a flat area of stitching without an apparent pattern and is used for filling large spaces and backgrounds. This stitch looks very effective when worked with a lustrous thread, such as stranded floss or silk, and can be shaded over the area by choosing graduated colors. This stitch should always be worked in an embroidery hoop or frame to keep the laid threads well tensioned. The thread is laid across the area from left to right and then couched down, using loose slanting stitches arranged evenly along the row. It is straightforward to work but a little practice will be needed to achieve the correct slant and tension on the couching stitches, which should be sufficiently long and angled to be almost indistinguishable from the laid stitches.

208 Triangular Turkish stitch ☆ ☆
also known as two-sided triangular Turkish stitch
Triangular Turkish stitch is a filling stitch used on even-weave fabrics. It makes a neat, triangular pattern on both sides of the fabric. If the stitches are pulled quite tightly, the effect of a drawn fabric stitch is achieved. A fine thread, such as fine crochet cotton or the lightest available weight of pearl cotton, is best suited to this stitch, which is worked in diagonal rows. Two journeys are necessary to complete one row and the sequence of stitches shown should be followed very carefully. Each stitch can cover three, four or five fabric threads, depending on the weight of the fabric and the effect desired, but triangular Turkish stitch does benefit from being worked on a fairly small scale.

196 Couched filling stitch ☆ ☆

198 Leaf stitch ☆ ☆

200 Fishbone stitch no. 1 ☆ ☆

197/1 Torocko stitch ☆ ☆

199/1 Honeycomb filling stitch ☆ ☆

201 Faggot filling stitch ☆ ☆

197/2 Torocko stitch ☆ ☆

199/2 Honeycomb filling stitch ☆ ☆

202 Basket stitch no. 2 ☆ ☆

203 Flat stitch ☆ ☆

206 Buttonhole stitch shading ☆ ☆

208/2 Triangular Turkish stitch ☆ ☆

204 Damask darning ☆ ☆

207 Roumanian couching ☆ ☆

208/3 Triangular Turkish stitch ☆ ☆

205 Burden stitch ☆ ☆

208/1 Triangular Turkish stitch ☆ ☆

208/4 Triangular Turkish stitch ☆ ☆

209 *Valerian stitch* ☆

Valerian stitch is a filling stitch used on common- and even-weave fabrics. It makes a trellis pattern of laid threads in the same way as trellis stitch *(see page 69)* but texture is added in the form of bullion knots *(see page 97)*. This stitch should be worked on fabric stretched in an embroidery hoop or frame to keep the foundation threads stable.

First make a grid consisting of long, horizontal straight stitches worked across the whole shape to be filled. Work vertical stitches at right angles across the horizontal stitches. Then work long, diagonal stitches from the top left to the bottom right of the shape, across each intersection of the grid. Then anchor the diagonal stitches to the fabric by working a diagonal bullion knot across every intersection. Valerian stitch can be monochrome, or a thread of contrasting color can be used for the bullion knots.

210 *Cretan open filling stitch* ☆ ☆

Cretan open filling stitch is used on common- and even-weave fabrics. Any type of embroidery thread can be used for this Cretan stitch. However, the foundation stitches must be worked in a firm, rather stiff thread, and the fabric should be stretched in an embroidery hoop or frame. A variation of Cretan stitch *(see page 13)*, it makes an attractive chessboard pattern. First work a foundation of evenly spaced straight vertical stitches across the shape. Then take a second thread to work blocks of Cretan stitch over the foundation, without picking up any ground fabric. Work the blocks in diagonal lines, from the top right-hand corner to the bottom left-hand corner on each journey. The tension of the Cretan stitch blocks is important as they should make a neat, perfectly regular chessboard pattern.

211 *Griffin stitch* ☆ ☆ ☆

Griffin stitch is a laid stitch used on common- and even-weave fabrics. It has an attractive, lacy appearance and can be used for filling shapes of any size. It is essential to work the foundation grids accurately and the fabric should be stretched in an embroidery hoop or frame to keep the stitches stable. First, cover the shape with long, vertical and horizontal straight stitches to form a squared grid. Then work a diagonal grid over the squared grid. Use vertical rows of running stitch *(see page 12)* to couch down the diagonal grid at alternate intersections, where the diagonal grid does not cross the first grid. Where the two grids cross, interlace a second thread around the intersections to make a circular shape. Do not pick up the ground fabric during the interlacing. Then, take the thread through to the back of the work so that it emerges close to the next intersection to be threaded. Use a blunt-ended tapestry needle for the interlacing to avoid splitting the stitches of the two grids.

212 *Trellis couching* ☆ ☆ ☆

Trellis couching is a laid-work stitch used for filling areas on common- and even-weave fabrics. It makes a solid filling of stitches secured by a trellis pattern and is often worked in two colors. Any type of embroidery thread can be used but the stitch will look more effective if worked in a lustrous thread, such as silk. The shape is filled by a foundation of laid stitches worked in two journeys. These stitches should be worked evenly and should completely cover the ground fabric. It is essential to work this stitch in an embroidery hoop or frame, keeping the fabric stretched rather tightly. This will ensure that the foundation and trellis threads remain stable while the couching is in progress. The trellis threads are also worked in two journeys and should be placed at an angle to the foundation stitches. The trellis threads are then couched down at the intersections using a tiny straight stitch.

213 *Eyelet stitch* ☆ ☆ ☆

Eyelet stitch is a filling stitch used on common-weave fabrics. It makes an attractive, lacy pattern and the fabric chosen should be fairly fine. Small interlocking circles are marked on the fabric and then pairs of backstitches *(see page 14)* are worked alternately along the circumference and into the center of each circle; twelve pairs of stitches are worked into the center and twelve pairs around the edge. The stitches should be pulled quite firmly during the embroidery, so that small holes are created at the center of the circles. Two stitches on one eyelet double as two stitches on an adjoining one. Eyelet stitch is often used to fill the background area, while the design itself is left unworked. A fine cotton embroidery thread should be used for this stitch.

214 *Laid-work* ☆ ☆ ☆

Laid-work is an extension of couching *(see page 8)* and is used for covering large and small areas of common- or even-weave fabric. The shape is completely covered with a foundation of long threads (or laid threads), which are then anchored by a second, often contrasting, thread, which is then couched down in a pattern. It is a technique which is often used in metal thread embroidery, when the gold or silver thread is couched down over a foundation of silk or cotton laid threads. Laid-work should always be worked on fabric stretched in an embroidery hoop or frame to keep the foundation stitches even during the couching.

The simplest form of laid-work is shown. The shape is filled with vertical surface satin stitch *(see page 2)*, worked in two journeys, with the threads laid closely and evenly together. Horizontal satin stitches are worked over this foundation at regular intervals and are then couched down by a finer thread to make a simple, striped pattern. A more decorative form of laid-work is described under trellis couching *(see above)*, which makes a pretty trellis pattern. A great many different patterns can be made by the couching thread, such as swirls, scales and chevrons, but the couched threads should lie at an angle to the laid threads to ensure that they are firmly anchored.

215 *Twisted lattice stitch* ☆ ☆ ☆

Twisted lattice stitch is a composite filling stitch used on common- and even-weave fabrics. It makes an attractive lattice pattern and is often worked in two contrasting colors or weights of thread. Twisted lattice stitch should be worked with the fabric stretched in an embroidery hoop or frame, as the lacing will tighten the stitches and pucker the fabric if it is not. Worked on the same principle as twisted lattice band (see page 52), the foundation is formed in a different way. A grid is made first by working evenly spaced, long diagonal stitches in one direction over the shape to be filled. A second set of stitches is then worked at right angles to the first set of stitches. The second set interlaces with the first, by passing over and under them in the same way as darning. Finally, a second thread is laced through the lattice grid in the same way as for twisted lattice band.

216 Maltese cross filling stitch ☆ ☆ ☆

Maltese cross filling stitch is a complex, interlaced filling used on common- and even-weave fabrics. It is rather similar to Maltese cross (see page 105) but its construction is slightly different.

A foundation grid of interlocking, diagonal straight stitches is worked first to cover the entire shape. First complete the diagonal stitches running in one direction and then work those running in the opposite direction, passing them over and under the first set in the same way as for old-fashioned darning. The spacing of the grid is important, pairs of diagonal stitches should be worked close together, making a plaid pattern on the fabric of large and small squares and rectangles. Alternatively, the foundation can be made of horizontal and vertical stitches, if preferred. The Maltese crosses are made by interlacing around the corners of the large squares and then repeating the journey, in the same sequence, to make a double interlacing. The interlacing thread can be of a contrasting weight, color and texture to that used for the foundation, or a metallic thread can be effective. A blunt-ended tapestry needle should be used for the interlacing to avoid splitting the foundation stitches. After each square is interlaced, the

needle is taken through the fabric to emerge at the next large square. The crosses can be worked on alternate squares to give a more open effect.

217 Diamond filling stitch ☆ ☆ ☆

Diamond filling stitch makes a pretty, knotted filling and is used on common- and even-weave fabrics. It is worked on a foundation of long horizontal stitches and can be used as a detached filling. However, this stitch is difficult to keep even and a better effect is achieved if the fabric is picked up when each knot is made. To keep the rows even, guidelines may need to be marked on the fabric if the threads cannot be counted. Each row of the filling is made in two journeys. On the first, work a horizontal foundation stitch from the right to the left of the shape, bringing the thread through the fabric just below the left-hand corner to begin the return journey. Make a coral knot (see coral stitch, page 9) at the corner of the shape, leaving a loop of thread; then make a second coral knot over the foundation stitch. Continue along the row, working knots at regular intervals and leaving loops between them. Then repeat the process to fill the shape, anchoring the loops of the previous row with the knots. Diamond filling stitch is a little tricky to work at first, as regularity is very important, but it is a stitch well worth practising.

218 Battlement couching ☆ ☆ ☆

Battlement couching is a type of couching used for filling areas of common- and even-weave fabrics. The complex arrangement of different colored laid threads makes a bold filling for simple shapes but it should not be attempted if the shape has an intricate or sharply curved outline. It consists of a foundation of alternate vertical and horizontal threads laid on the fabric to make an overlapping lattice. Follow the sequence shown very carefully. The foundation is worked in four contrasting or harmonizing colors of thread; a fifth thread is used to couch down the top rows of laid threads with a short diagonal stitch.

At first sight, battlement couching looks rather complicated but once

the sequence of the foundation has been mastered, it will prove quite easy to effect. This stitch should always be worked with the fabric stretched tautly in an embroidery hoop or frame to keep the laid threads stable. Any type of embroidery thread can be used but the stitch will be simpler to work if the thread is twisted, rather than stranded. The secret of good battlement couching is to spend considerable time laying the foundation threads; they should have an even tension and cross each other at perfect right angles.

219 Chevron stem stitch ☆ ☆ ☆

Chevron stem stitch is a composite filling stitch used on common- and even-weave fabrics. It is essential to work this stitch with the fabric stretched tautly in an embroidery hoop or frame to ensure that the foundation threads do not move. The foundation consists of threads laid horizontally and evenly right across the space to be covered. Stem stitch (see page 9) is then worked in a zig-zag pattern over these threads (the needle should enter the fabric at only the beginning and end of each row). Use a blunt-ended tapestry needle for the stem stitch threading to avoid splitting the stitches on the foundation row. The rows of stem stitch should be packed close together to cover the foundation threads completely. The pattern is made more apparent if two tones of thread are used for the zig-zags. A firm thread must be used for the foundation but any type of thread can be used for the stem stitch. The small "V" shapes at the top and bottom of the stitching should also be filled in with stem stitch, keeping the pattern correct. Chevron stem stitch can be used to fill any size shape. After the stitching is completed, the edge should be finished by outlining the shape with another line stitch: twisted chain stitch (see page 21), double knot stitch (see page 36) or pearl stitch (see page 21) would all make a neat edge.

209 *Valerian stitch* ★ ☆

211/2 *Griffin stitch* ★ ★ ☆

213 *Eyelet stitch* ★ ★ ☆

210 *Cretan open filling stitch* ★ ☆

212/1 *Trellis couching* ★ ★ ☆

214/1 *Laid-work* ★ ★ ☆

211/1 *Griffin stitch* ★ ★ ☆

212/2 *Trellis couching* ★ ★ ☆

214/2 *Laid-work* ★ ★ ☆

215 Twisted lattice stitch ☆ ☆ ☆

218/1 Battlement couching ☆ ☆ ☆

218/4 Battlement couching ☆ ☆ ☆

216 Maltese cross filling stitch ☆ ☆ ☆

218/2 Battlement couching ☆ ☆ ☆

218/5 Battlement couching ☆ ☆ ☆

217 Diamond filling stitch ☆ ☆ ☆

218/3 Battlement couching ☆ ☆ ☆

219 Chevron stem stitch ☆ ☆ ☆

Detached filling stitches

220 Hollie stitch ☆
also known as *holy stitch* and
holy point
Hollie stitch is a detached filling stitch
used on the surface of common- and
even-weave fabrics. Outline the
shape to be filled with a row of chain
stitch *(see page 12)* worked quite
small; this makes a foundation to
anchor the filling to the fabric. Work
the filling rows in alternate directions,
working a long, horizontal straight
stitch from chain to chain from right
to left across the shape. Then bring
the thread through the next chain on
the left-hand side to make a row of
looped knotted stitches over both the
thread and the chain stitch. The
ground fabric should not be picked
up. Continue in this way with
alternate long stitches and rows of
loops, working the second and
subsequent rows of loops over both
the long stitch and the previous row
of loops. Secure the last row by
working the loops through the chain
stitch row at the lower edge of the
shape.

221 Ceylon stitch ☆
Ceylon stitch is a detached filling
stitch used on common- and even-
weave fabrics. It can be worked to
give two different effects: if the
stitches are spaced widely apart, the
filling appears light and lacy; if the
stitches are placed close together,
the filling looks like a piece of
stockinette stitch knitting. A
horizontal straight stitch worked right
across the top of the shape forms
the anchoring foundation. Rows of
looped stitches are then worked from
left to right without picking up any
fabric. At the end of each row of
loops, the needle must be taken
through the fabric to emerge again at
the beginning of the next row; this is
always at the left-hand side of the
shape. This process keeps the filling
anchored to the fabric at the sides.
Ceylon stitch is often worked in
bands of two or more colors. A
round, twisted thread works well
with this stitch although a stranded
thread can also look attractive.

222 Rich buttonhole stitch ☆☆
also known as *loop buttonhole
filling stitch*
Rich buttonhole stitch is a detached
filling stitch with a honeycomb
pattern used on common- and even-
weave fabrics. A foundation of
parallel horizontal straight stitch rows
is worked right across the area to be
covered. A row of closely packed
buttonhole stitch *(see page 13)* is
then worked over the first horizontal
stitch. The ground fabric must not be
picked up. Buttonhole stitch is then
worked over the subsequent straight
stitches, and, at intervals along the
rows, a longer, vertical stitch
connects the row being worked to
the row above. These long verticals
give a honeycomb effect.

223 Fancy buttonhole filling ☆☆☆
also known as *fancy buttonhole
stitch*
Fancy buttonhole filling is used as a
detached filling on the surface of
common- and even-weave fabrics
and also to fill a space in cutwork.
When worked on the surface of the
fabric, the shape must first be
outlined with a row of backstitch
(see page 14) to form a foundation
to anchor the filling. The area is then
covered with rows of mirrored
buttonhole stitch *(see page 32)*.
Work the first row of the filling from
left to right into the foundation
stitches without picking up any
ground fabric. Then work the
second and subsequent rows in
alternate directions, catching each
pair of stitches into the loops lying
between the pairs of stitches on the
first row; do not enter the fabric.
When the last row is reached, the
loops should be worked through the
line of backstitch to anchor the
filling; the filling is also anchored at
the sides. When used for filling a
shape in cutwork, buttonhole edging
stitch *(see page 108)* serves as the
anchoring foundation.

224 Knotted buttonhole filling ☆☆
also known as *knotted buttonhole
filling stitch*
Knotted buttonhole filling is used as a
detached filling on common- and
even-weave fabrics and to fill spaces
in cutwork. When used as a
detached filling, the shape is outlined
by a row of backstitch *(see page 14)*
to anchor the filling. The filling rows
are worked in alternate directions
and consist of buttonhole stitches
(see page 13) overcast individually on
the same journey by a second
buttonhole stitch worked at an angle
to the first. This second stitch forms
a knot and should be pulled tight
before proceeding to the next stitch.
After the first row, which is worked
into the backstitch foundation, the
subsequent rows are worked into the
loops of the previous rows. The
needle should enter the fabric only at
the beginning and end of the
stitching. The last row is secured by
working the loops through the
backstitch line at the bottom. When
this filling is used for cutwork,
buttonhole edging stitch *(see page
108)*, worked round the raw edges,
forms the anchoring foundation.

225 Trellis filling stitch ☆☆
Trellis filling stitch is a detached filling
used on common- and even-weave
fabrics; it has a lacy, knotted
appearance. Outline the shape first
with a row of evenly spaced chain
stitch *(see page 12)* to make a
foundation to anchor the filling. Work
the first row of the filling into the
chain stitch at the top of the shape by
making alternate loops and knots
from left to right. Tighten the knots
before proceeding to the next loop by
pulling the working thread to the
right. When the edge is reached, and
without entering the fabric, take the
thread down to the next chain stitch
and continue the knots and loops in
the opposite direction. This row and
all subsequent rows are worked into
the loops on the preceding row.
When the lower edge is reached,
work the last row of loops through
the chain stitch edge to anchor it.

226 Venetian filling stitch ☆☆
Venetian filling stitch is a detached
filling used on common- and even-
weave fabrics. A firm, twisted
thread, such as pearl cotton, is most
suitable. First, outline the shape with
a row of backstitch *(see page 14)*,
working each stitch quite large. Work
the first row of filling from left to right

over the outline. Make a loose buttonhole loop and then work a group of four buttonhole stitches (see page 13) into it. Continue in this way until the right-hand side of the shape is reached. Then take the thread behind the outline row to anchor it before working the return journey. On this journey, make loose loops between each group of buttonhole stitches on the preceding row by working a row of open buttonhole filling (see below). These two rows alternate to form the filling, and the thread must be taken behind the outline stitches at the end of every row to anchor the filling firmly. When the lower edge of the shape is reached, pick up the outline stitches with the last row of loops.

227 *Lace filling stitch*   ☆ ☆
also known as **honeycomb stitch**
Lace filling stitch makes a detached filling and is used on common- and even-weave fabrics. It makes a twisted, lacy pattern and benefits from being worked in an embroidery frame or hoop, as it is rather unstable. Work the stitch with a round, twisted thread, such as pearl cotton.

Each row is worked in two journeys. On the first journey, a series of twists and loops are worked from left to right, picking up the fabric only at the right-hand side of the area to anchor the filling. On the second journey, the working thread is brought back across the shape to enter the fabric just below the point where the previous row began. This thread is then wound around each loop on the completed row. When the bottom of the shape is reached, a little fabric is picked up to secure the filling. An outline of stem stitch (see page 9) or backstitch (see page 14) is worked to define the shape.

228 *Surface darning*   ☆ ☆
Surface darning is a detached filling stitch used on common- and even-weave fabrics. It makes a closely woven surface best suited to small shapes. The fabric should be stretched in an embroidery hoop or frame to keep the foundation stitches taut while the darning is being worked. First work a foundation of surface satin stitch (see page 72) over the shape, placing the stitches evenly and very close together. Then weave a second thread regularly in and out of these stitches in exactly the same way as a stocking darn. With the second thread, pick up the fabric only at the sides of the shape, so that the filling is quite detached except at the edges. Any type of embroidery thread can be used but, for the foundation stitches, a round, twisted thread such as pearl cotton is less likely to split during the darning. The satin stitches can be darned in groups of three by working three horizontal rows below one another before changing the sequence of "unders" and "overs" and working the next three rows. This method gives a heavier effect and makes a close basket-work pattern.

229 *Open buttonhole filling* ☆ ☆ ☆
Open buttonhole filling is used as a detached filling stitch on common- and even-weave fabrics. It can be used to fill a space in cutwork, although it is less even and stable than fancy buttonhole filling (see page 88) or knotted buttonhole filling (see page 88). This stitch gives a very open, lacy effect and, even when worked as a surface stitch, it requires some practice to keep an even tension between the stitches. The filling consists of rows of ordinary buttonhole stitch (see page 13) worked in alternate directions into the loops of the previous rows. The needle enters the fabric only at the outline of the shape.

230 *Detached buttonhole stitch*   ☆ ☆ ☆
Detached buttonhole stitch is a detached filling stitch with a rather heavy, solid appearance. It is worked on common-weave fabrics and is useful when a raised, closely embroidered shape is needed. Work two horizontal straight stitches across the top of the area to be covered. Next, work a row of buttonhole stitch (see page 13) over these strands from left to right, without entering the ground fabric. The stitches should be worked close together and a firm, quite stiff thread is needed. Work the subsequent rows of buttonhole stitch into the loops of each preceding row, alternately from side to side of the shape, with only the edge stitches passing through the fabric. The shaping is worked by increasing or decreasing stitches at the end of each row, the edge stitches should be worked with a slightly tighter tension than the detached stitches. This stitch can be made more raised by working it over a padding of felt. The felt is cut slightly smaller than the shape, but following the same contours, and then basted in position on the ground fabric before the embroidery is started.

231 *Raised honeycomb filling stitch*   ☆ ☆ ☆
Raised honeycomb filling stitch is a detached filling stitch used on common- and even-weave fabrics and should be worked in an embroidery hoop or frame. It makes a very raised trellis pattern and looks best when worked with a fine thread. A trellis of long vertical and horizontal straight stitches is worked over the shape first. These stitches are then overcast (see overcast stitch, page 28), covering first the vertical and then the horizontal stitches. The thread is then taken around each long stitch on the trellis in a crossed spiral shape, beginning with the vertical stitches. The spirals are worked around the horizontal stitches and then overcast with a fine thread.

232 *Filet stitch*   ☆ ☆ ☆
Filet stitch is a detached filling stitch worked on common- and even-weave fabrics. It makes a geometric, lacy filling with raised knots and is best used for filling small shapes. It is a difficult stitch to work evenly and care must be taken to tighten each knot after it is worked. The needle enters the fabric only around the edges of the shape. Loops are made in diagonal rows from right to left and then back again, beginning at the top left-hand corner of the shape. They are then linked together by a knotted stitch. The loops can be pinned to the fabric to keep them even while the knots are being made, or held down by the thumb.

220 Hollie stitch ☆

223 Fancy buttonhole filling ☆ ☆

226 Venetian filling stitch ☆ ☆

221 Ceylon stitch ☆

224 Knotted buttonhole filling ☆ ☆

227 Lace filling stitch ☆ ☆

222 Rich buttonhole stitch ☆ ☆

225 Trellis filling stitch ☆ ☆

228 Surface darning ☆ ☆

229 *Open buttonhole filling* ☆ ☆ ☆

231/1 *Raised honeycomb filling stitch* ☆ ☆ ☆

231/3 *Raised honeycomb filling stitch* ☆ ☆ ☆

230/1 *Detached buttonhole stitch* ☆ ☆ ☆

231/2 *Raised honeycomb filling stitch* ☆ ☆ ☆

232 *Filet stitch* ☆ ☆ ☆

230/2 *Detached buttonhole stitch* ☆ ☆ ☆

Isolated stitches

233 Daisy stitch ☆
also known as **detached chain stitch, lazy daisy stitch, tail chain stitch, loop stitch, tied loop stitch, picot stitch** and **knotted knot stitch**

Daisy stitch is a useful isolated stitch used on common- and even-weave fabrics. It is actually a single chain stitch (see page 12) and is often known by the name of detached chain stitch. This stitch is commonly used in groups to make leaf and flower shapes, hence the name "daisy," but it also makes a pretty powdering when the stitches are scattered at random over a shape. It also makes the foundation row for threaded chain stitch (see page 44). It is formed in exactly the same way as chain stitch but each loop is anchored to the fabric by a small vertical stitch before the next loop is made. The size of the stitch is determined by the weight of embroidery thread used and any type of thread will work well. An isolated knot stitch, such as a French knot (see page 96) or a Chinese knot (see page 96) can be worked in the center of each stitch in a contrasting color for a more decorative effect. Daisy stitch can also be worked on top of an area of flat needlepoint where an accent stitch is needed.

234 Four-legged knot stitch ☆
Four-legged knot stitch is an isolated stitch used on common- and even-weave fabrics. It is an attractive small stitch and resembles an upright cross with a knot at the center. It is used as an accent stitch, worked closely in a row for a narrow border, and as a powdering. The stitches can be arranged in a regular all-over pattern, or they can be scattered at random for a less formal effect. The size of the stitch varies according to the weight of the thread used but it is equally effective on any scale. First,

make a vertical straight stitch; then loop a horizontal stitch around the vertical to form the knot, before making the last arm of the cross. The knot should not pick up any ground fabric.

235 Straight stitch ☆
also known as **stroke stitch**

Straight stitch is an isolated stitch which is used on common- and even-weave fabrics. Individual satin stitches (see page 24) are worked to any length and in any direction to create a textured area. This stitch is particularly useful for depicting grass and other landscape details, and any type of embroidery thread can be used, depending on the weight of the ground fabric. Straight stitch should not be worked too large as the stitches then look loose and untidy. This stitch can easily be shaded and blended by using close shades of one color, or two or three fine, contrasting threads can be used in the same needle. Lengths of different colored stranded thread can be split into strands and then rearranged to give a subtle blending of colors.

236 Cross and twist stitch ☆
also known as **moss stitch**

Cross and twist stitch is an isolated stitch used on common- and even-weave fabrics. It is most effective when worked on a small scale with a fine, rounded thread, such as fine crochet cotton, and can be used as an accent stitch or as a powdering to decorate a shape. This stitch can also be placed side by side to form a border and the top stitch can be worked in a contrasting color or different weight of thread. An ordinary cross stitch (see page 14) is worked as a foundation and is then crossed by a longer vertical stitch. The vertical stitch enters the ground

fabric only at the top and bottom and is looped around the center of the cross stitch, making a twisted chain stitch (see page 21) with a long tail. As a variation, the vertical stitch can be made shorter.

237 Dot stitch ☆
also known as **simple knot stitch, rice grain** and **seed stitch**

Dot stitch is an isolated stitch used on common- and even-weave fabrics. As the name suggests, it makes a small, raised dot, which can be used individually as an accent stitch, worked in rows as a dotted outline, or scattered at random to make a powdering. It is very simple to work and any type of thread can be used, the choice depending on the weight of the ground fabric and the size of dot required. It is made by working two backstitches (see page 14) into the same holes. When used as an outline, a tiny space of fabric is left between each pair of stitches. Dot stitch is often used as an accent stitch when line stitches or fillings need extra decorative spots of color.

238 Square boss ☆
also known as **raised knot**

A square boss is a simply worked isolated stitch used on common- or even-weave fabrics. It can be used individually, where extra color or texture is needed, or several can be scattered over a shape to make a pretty knotted powdering.

First work a cross stitch (see page 14) and then cover each arm with a backstitch (see page 14) worked through the fabric. A round, twisted thread, such as pearl cotton, makes this stitch appear more raised than a flat, stranded thread. When used as a powdering, the crosses can all be worked on one journey and a contrasting thread can then be used for the backstitch.

239 Long-tailed daisy stitch ☆
Long-tailed daisy stitch is a simple variation of daisy stitch (see above) and is used on common- and even-weave fabrics. It is worked in the same way as daisy stitch but the loop is made smaller and the anchoring stitch is elongated to form a "tail." It is often worked in circular groups, with either the tails or the loops at the center. It also looks attractive as a powdering, or worked closely together in rows with the loops alternately at the top and bottom of the rows. As with daisy stitch, any type of embroidery thread can be worked easily.

240 Ermine stitch ☆
Ermine stitch is a useful isolated stitch used on common- and even-weave fabrics. It earned its name from the ermine tail effect it makes when worked in black thread on a white fabric ground and it is often used as a filling stitch in blackwork. The stitch can be used as an accent stitch or it can be worked in rows to make a delicate border. When used as a filling, it is worked regularly, often on an even-weave fabric, and it also makes a pretty powdering when scattered at random on common-weave fabrics. It is simple to work and consists of a long, vertical straight stitch, which is then covered by an elongated cross stitch (see page 14) about one-third of the size of the straight stitch. The cross stitch should be placed slightly above the base of the vertical stitch.

241 Berry stitch ☆
Berry stitch can be used on any type of fabric. It can act as an accent stitch on canvas: scatter berry stitch on top of a smoothly stitched background of tent stitch (see page 121) or Gobelin stitch (see page 125). On fabric, berry stitch can be used as a powdering, worked close together in a line, or massed together to fill a solid area. It is a very simple stitch, consisting of one large daisy stitch (see page 92) and one small daisy stitch worked inside the first one. A twisted thread, such as pearl or matte embroidery cotton will help keep the circular shape of each berry stitch intact.

242 Fly stitch ☆
also known as "Y" stitch and open loop stitch
Fly stitch is an isolated stitch often worked in rows and used on common- and even-weave fabrics. Each stitch is worked very easily: a V-shaped loop is made and then tied down by a vertical straight stitch. The tying stitch can vary in length to produce different effects. The fly stitches can be arranged side by side to make a horizontal row, or can be worked underneath each other to make a vertical row. The stitches can touch one another or be spaced apart at a regular interval. Isolated fly stitches can be used to make a pretty powdering, either spaced evenly or scattered at random over a shape. Each stitch can be decorated by the addition of a French knot (see page 96) or a Danish knot (see page 97) in a contrasting thread. Any type of thread can be used for this stitch although the size of the stitch and the weight of the ground fabric must be taken into account.

243 Twisted satin stitch ☆
Twisted satin stitch is a useful isolated stitch worked on common- and even-weave fabrics. It can be used alone as an accent stitch, sprinkled over a shape; worked in close rows where texture is needed in a satin stitched area; or worked solidly as a filling. Twisted satin stitches can also be arranged to make a motif, such as a flower or wheel shape. It is very simple to work and consists of an individual vertical satin stitch (see page 24) and a second stitch that twists around it and shares the same holes in the fabric. The second stitch passes through the fabric only at the top and bottom. Any type of embroidery thread can be used but, when the stitch is used alone, a coarse thread highlights the twists more effectively. An interesting two-color effect can be made by working the stitches underneath first in one color, then adding the twisted stitches in a contrasting color on a second journey. The two-colored effect is only possible when the stitches are spaced apart.

244 Crown stitch ☆
Crown stitch is an isolated stitch used on common- and even-weave fabrics. It can be used as a powdering, to give a delicate texture to an area, or it can be arranged in rows, possibly combined with a line stitch to make a border. Any type of embroidery thread can be used for this stitch; the choice depends on the size of stitch required and the weight of the ground fabric. Crown stitch can be worked in two ways. The first method is to work a fly stitch (see above) and then add two slanting straight stitches at the base. The slanting stitches are placed at each side of the vertical line of the fly stitch and pass over the loop. The second method is to work the three bottom straight stitches, radiating from the same hole, and then work the top stitch to pass under them, without picking up any ground fabric. Whichever method you choose, the finished stitch will look exactly the same.

233 Daisy stitch ☆

235 Straight stitch ☆

237 Dot stitch ☆

234/1 Four-legged knot stitch ☆

236/1 Cross and twist stitch ☆

238/1 Square boss ☆

234/2 Four-legged knot stitch ☆

236/2 Cross and twist stitch ☆

238/2 Square boss ☆

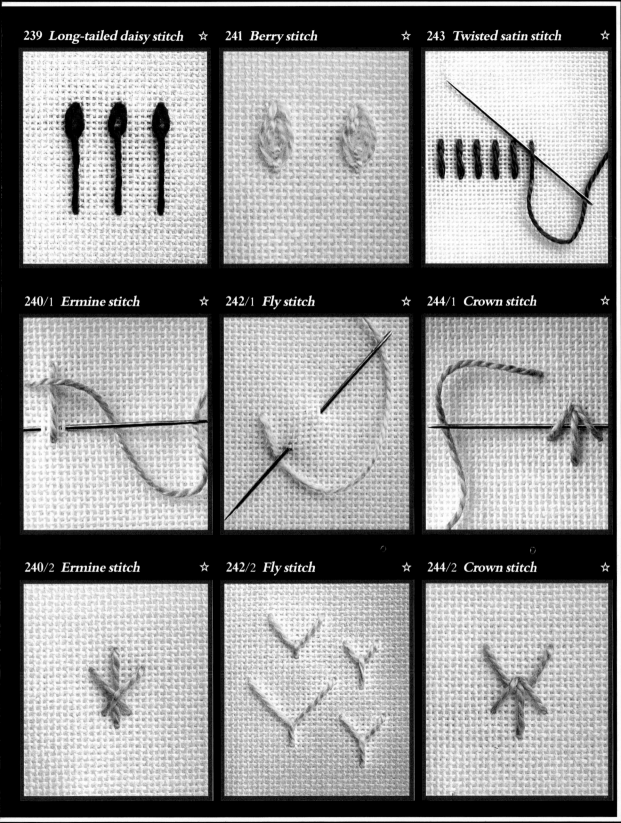

239 Long-tailed daisy stitch ☆

241 Berry stitch ☆

243 Twisted satin stitch ☆

240/1 Ermine stitch ☆

242/1 Fly stitch ☆

244/1 Crown stitch ☆

240/2 Ermine stitch ☆

242/2 Fly stitch ☆

244/2 Crown stitch ☆

245 God's eye stitch ☆ ☆

God's eye stitch is an isolated stitch used on common- and even-weave fabrics. It is similar in construction to ribbed spider's web *(see page 100)* and makes a bold, raised diamond shape with a long tail. It is used as an accent stitch where extra color or texture is needed and it can be scattered over a shape to make a heavy powdering. Any type of thread can be used but a round, twisted thread such as pearl cotton makes the raised effect more pronounced. A foundation cross with a long lower arm is made first and then the thread is brought through at the center where the stitches cross. A spiral line of backstitch *(see page 14)* is then worked over the four arms of the cross until they are completely covered, without picking up the ground fabric.

---

246 French knot ☆ ☆

also known as French dot, knotted stitch, twisted knot stitch and wound stitch

and long-tailed French knot

also known as long tack knot stitch and Italian knot stitch

A French knot is an isolated stitch used on common- and even-weave fabrics. It is a neat, raised knot, which has many uses. It can be used as an accent stitch, as a powdering, massed together to make a solidly textured area, and worked closely in rows to make an outline. It can also be used over an area of canvas stitching, where extra texture or dots of contrasting colors are needed. Any type of thread can be used and the weight of the thread will determine the size of the finished stitch. Interesting effects can be made when French knots are massed

together. To achieve this, work each knot with three or four contrasting threads placed through the needle at the same time.

A French knot is a little tricky to work and some practice will be needed to perfect the stitch. Work the knot with the fabric stretched in an embroidery hoop or frame to leave both hands free for the working. Bring the thread through the fabric and, if you are right-handed, hold it taut with the left hand, while twisting the needle around it two or three times with the right hand. Then tighten the twists, turn the needle and insert it back into the same place in the fabric, still keeping the thread taut, and pull the needle through. The thread slides through the twists to make the knot.

A long-tailed French knot is made in a similar way. The needle is held down a short distance away from the place where the thread emerges and the twists are made around it. The needle is then inserted into the fabric at the spot where it has been held; the twists are pushed down the needle, and the needle is then taken through the fabric, leaving a knot with a long tail.

---

247 Chinese knot ☆ ☆

also known as Pekin knot, forbidden knot and blind knot

The Chinese knot is an isolated stitch used on common- and even-weave fabrics. It can also be used to accent areas of canvas by stitching it onto an area already covered by embroidery. This stitch closely resembles the French knot *(see above)* but the Chinese knot is flatter and more shapely.

Chinese knots are characteristic of the rich silk embroideries of China,

where they were worked very small and massed together to texture large areas. They were often worked in rows to create beautiful borders, with each row set close to the next one. Subtle color variations in the silk thread resulted in a delicate shading. The name blind knot reputedly derives from the fact that Chinese embroiderers stitched this knot on such a minute scale over large areas of fabric that eventually their eyesight was affected.

The Chinese knot is easy to work, especially if the fabric is stretched in an embroidery hoop or frame. A simple, loose loop is made around the needle and tightened after the needle has entered the fabric but before it is pulled right through. Hold the loop down on the fabric with the left thumb, while pulling the needle through the fabric. This stitch works well with any type of embroidery thread; choose the thread according to the effect required. A stranded floss or silk will give a flatter knot, while a rounded thread, such as pearl cotton or tapestry yarn, will make a raised knot.

---

248 Sword-edging stitch ☆ ☆

Sword-edging stitch is an isolated stitch used on common- and even-weave fabrics. It makes an elongated cross and is used as a powdering or worked close together to make a soft outline stitch. It is very quick and easy to work and consists of a loose straight stitch, which is pulled into a "V" shape by a second stitch. The choice of thread depends on the size of the stitch and the effect desired. A round thread, such as pearl cotton, makes sword-edging stitch stand out more from the background than a flat, stranded thread.

249 Swedish split stitch ☆ ☆
also known as **detached split stitch**
Swedish split stitch is an isolated stitch used on common- and even-weave fabrics. It can be used in different ways: as an accent stitch, arranged to form a flower shape; scattered over a shape to make a powdering; or used as a solid filling stitch in the same way as long and short stitch *(see page 72)*. It is like split stitch *(see page 9)* in construction but two threads are used at once in the needle, so the same thread restrictions do not apply. A long straight stitch is made, which is then split with the needle between the two threads, and a downward slanting stitch anchors it to the fabric. Different effects can be created by using two contrasting threads in the needle, or by working the straight stitches on one journey and using a second color for the splitting stitches.

250 Danish knot ☆ ☆
also known as **Danish knotted stitch** *and* **double knot**
A Danish knot is an isolated stitch used on common- and even-weave fabrics. It is made by first working a foundation of short diagonal stitches from bottom right to top left; the knot will be made over this. The needle is then brought through the fabric close to the diagonal stitch and two looped stitches are made over the foundation, without picking up any ground fabric. The needle then re-enters the fabric before the next stitch is made. This stitch makes quite a raised, robust knot, which is accentuated by the use of a round,

twisted thread, such as pearl cotton. It can be worked as an accent stitch, as a powdering or massed together to create a densely textured area. When it is worked solidly, different weights and colors of thread can be used to make an interesting surface.

251 Bullion knot ☆ ☆ ☆
also known as **bullion knot stitch, caterpillar stitch, coil stitch, knot stitch, post stitch, worm stitch, Porto Rico rose** *and* **grub knot**
A bullion knot is an isolated stitch used on common- and even-weave fabrics. It is a long, coiled knot which can be used as an accent stitch; as a powdering; massed together to make a densely textured filling; worked close together to make a heavy outline; or used on top of an area of flat needlepoint, where extra texture or splashes of color are needed. Any type of embroidery thread can be used; the weight of the thread determines the size of the finished knot. Three or four contrasting fine threads can be threaded through the needle at the same time to create some interesting effects with this stitch.

A bullion knot is a little tricky to work and some practice will be needed to perfect it. It is better to work bullion knots on fabric which is stretched in an embroidery hoop or frame, thus leaving both hands free to work the knot. Bring the thread to the surface and insert the needle a short distance away, so that the point emerges at the same place as the thread. The distance between the point where the needle is inserted and the place where the thread

emerges determines the length of the knot. Coil the thread around the needle six or seven times and then pull the needle carefully through the coil, which should be held down firmly on the fabric with the left thumb (if you are right-handed). Gently pull the working thread in the opposite direction to tighten the coils and insert the needle in exactly the same place as before. The coil of thread should now lie neatly on the surface. A rather thick needle with a small eye should be used so that it will pass easily through the coil. By coiling the thread many more times around the needle a different type of bullion knot can be created. The coil will be too long to lie flat on the fabric and will make a small hump instead of a long knot.

252 Turk's head knot ☆ ☆ ☆
A Turk's head knot is an isolated stitch used on common- and even-weave fabrics. It makes a large, complex knot, which should be worked as a firm, twisted thread for maximum effect. Bring the thread to the surface of the fabric and work the sequence of loops. Then pass the needle in and out of these loops in the order shown. Pull the working thread through gently to tighten the knot before returning through the fabric directly below the knot. Turk's head knots are normally worked alone where an accent of color and texture is needed but they can be massed together to fill a shape. They can also be used to decorate needlepoint by working them on top of previously stitched areas.

245/1 God's eye stitch ☆ ☆

246/1 French knot ☆ ☆

247/1 Chinese knot ☆ ☆

245/2 God's eye stitch ☆ ☆

246/2 French knot ☆ ☆

247/2 Chinese knot ☆ ☆

246/3 French knot ☆ ☆

248 Sword-edging stitch ☆ ☆

249 *Swedish split stitch* ☆ ☆

251/1 *Bullion knot* ☆ ☆ ☆

252/1 *Turk's head knot* ☆ ☆ ☆

250/1 *Danish knot* ☆ ☆

251/2 *Bullion knot* ☆ ☆ ☆

252/2 *Turk's head knot* ☆ ☆ ☆

250/2 *Danish knot* ☆ ☆

Motif stitches

253 Russian chain stitch ☆
also known as three chain stitch
Russian chain stitch is a motif stitch which can also be used as a lightweight border. Always used on common- and even-weave fabrics, it is suitable for use with any type of embroidery thread, depending on the size of the stitch and the weight of the background fabric. As indicated by its name, this stitch is found on Russian embroideries, often in conjunction with rows of ordinary chain stitch. The stitch is composed of three daisy stitches *(see page 92)* grouped together. Work the top daisy stitch first and then work the bottom stitches at an angle into the first stitch. When worked as a horizontal border, the Russian chain stitches are worked side by side, with the top daisy stitch pointing upward. When used vertically, they are placed underneath each other, the top daisy stitch again pointing upward.

254 Spider's web ☆
also known as woven wheel, woven spot and woven spoke stitch
A spider's web is a motif stitch used on common- and even-weave fabrics. It makes a raised, circular shape like a spider's web and can be used alone as an accent stitch, or worked in a number of different sizes to powder a shape. A foundation of spokes is made first: these should be of an odd number and should radiate from the central point of the circle. The stitched example shows how to make a five-spoke wheel by using a fly stitch *(see page 93)* combined with two straight stitches. A seven- or nine-spoke wheel can be made by working evenly spaced straight stitches from the circumference of the circle to the center point. After

completion of the foundation, a second thread is woven under and over the spokes, beginning at the center and working outward; be careful not to pick up any ground fabric. The second thread can be of a contrasting color and a round thread, such as pearl cotton, makes the spider's web stand out more from the background than a flat, stranded thread. Use a blunt-ended tapestry needle for the second thread to avoid splitting the foundation stitches.

255 Ribbed spider's web ☆
also known as ribbed wheel and backstitched spider's web
A ribbed spider's web is a motif stitch used on common- and even-weave fabrics. It makes a ribbed, circular shape, which is heavier in appearance than an ordinary spider's web *(see above)*. It can be used alone as an accent stitch of color or texture, or can be scattered over a shape to make a powdering. First, a foundation of spokes is made and these should be of an even number. The stitched example shows how to make a foundation of eight spokes by working a cross stitch *(see page 14)* over a St George cross stitch *(see page 68)*. A larger or smaller number of spokes can be made by working evenly spaced straight stitches from the circumference of the circle to the center point. After the foundation has been completed, a spiral of backstitch *(see page 14)* is worked over the spokes from the center outward. The second thread passes through the fabric only at the beginning and end of the spiral, and a blunt-ended tapestry needle should be used to avoid splitting the foundation stitches. A round thread, such as pearl or matte embroidery

cotton, accentuates the ribbed appearance better than a flat, stranded thread.

256 Vell stitch ☆
Vell stitch is a motif stitch used on common- and even-weave fabrics. It makes an attractive barred cross which can be used in a variety of ways. The stitch can be used individually to provide an accent of color; it can be worked as a border, either horizontally or vertically; or it can be scattered over an area to make an unusual powdering. It is extremely quick and simple to work and consists of a vertical straight stitch crossed by three shorter, horizontal straight stitches. Any type of embroidery thread can be used, providing that it is compatible with the size of stitch required and the weight of the ground fabric.

257 Point Russe stitch ☆
Point Russe stitch is a motif stitch used on common- and even-weave fabrics. It is a quick and simple stitch to work and makes a pretty fan-shaped pattern. It can be used individually as an accent stitch, or be arranged in vertical or horizontal rows to make a filling over shapes of any size. Any type of embroidery thread can be used, the choice depending on the weight of the ground fabric and the size of the stitch required. The stitch consists of four diagonal straight stitches arranged in pairs at both sides of a vertical straight stitch. These stitches should touch at the bottom and fan out evenly at the top. Point Russe stitch looks very attractive when worked in a color which contrasts strongly with that of the background fabric.

258 Buttonhole wheel ☆
also known as **wheel stitch**
A buttonhole wheel is a circular form of buttonhole stitch *(see page 13)*. Stitched on common- and even-weave fabrics, it works best on a fabric with quite a loose weave. Work buttonhole stitches in a circle, passing each vertical stitch through the same central space. The fabric threads are pulled back by the stitching and a neat circular hole forms at the center. If the fabric weave is too close for this to happen easily, the hole may have to be started with the help of a small awl.

A variation of this wheel, used on a very open, heavy fabric, is worked in the same way but a pair of crossed threads are left in the center of the hole, forming a cross at the center of the wheel.

259 Cup stitch ☆
Cup stitch is a raised motif stitch used on common- and even-weave fabrics. It can also be used to decorate and add depth to an area of canvas which has already been covered by a flatter stitch. It makes a circular, raised band rather like a cup and is best worked in a fairly firm thread to make it stand out well from the background. A foundation of three straight stitches which form a triangle is worked first — this can vary in size depending on the size of cup being worked. The thread is then brought back to the surface of the fabric just outside the triangle and looped stitches are made over the foundation, without entering the ground fabric. The looped stitches are worked close together right around the triangle and the more closely they are packed, the more

three-dimensional the effect will be. A second row of looped stitches can be worked into the loops on the first round to make a higher cup.

260 Point à la minute ☆
Point à la minute is a motif stitch used on common- and even-weave fabrics. It makes a heavy, raised upright cross, which can be used as an accent stitch where extra color or texture is needed, or scattered at random over a shape to make an impressive powdering. A rounded thread, such as pearl cotton, shows this stitch off to its best advantage; a stranded thread, however, gives a flatter appearance. This stitch should be worked with the fabric stretched in an embroidery hoop or frame to prevent puckering.

A foundation of four vertical and four horizontal straight stitches is made, forming a cross. Each of these stitches is then whipped very closely using the same thread and without picking up any ground fabric *(see whipped back stitch, page 16)*. For added emphasis, point à la minute can also be worked on top of an area of smoothly stitched needlepoint.

261 Star of David ☆
Similar to star darn *(see below)*, Star of David is an interwoven six-pointed star. Used on plain- and even-weave fabrics, the star can be used alone where an accent of color or a different weight of thread is needed, or several stars can be scattered over an area to make a light powdering. It consists of two interlocking triangles made of straight stitches. Any type of embroidery thread can be used to make a Star of David, providing that it is compatible with the size of the

stitch and the weight of the ground fabric. To emphasize the shape, the central hexagon could have a solid filling made of massed Chinese knots *(see page 96)* or closely worked satin stitches *(see page 24)* in a contrasting color or weight of thread.

262 Star darn ☆
also known as **woven star**
A star darn is a simple motif stitch used on common- and even-weave fabrics. It makes an interwoven five-pointed star shape which can be used alone or scattered over a shape to form an attractive powdering. It consists of five straight stitches, arranged as shown. Any type of embroidery thread can be used for a star darn, providing that it is compatible with the size of stitch and the weight of the ground fabric.

A star darn can be decorated by working an isolated stitch, such as a Danish knot *(see page 97)* or daisy stitch *(see page 92)*, in the center.

263 Tulip stitch ☆
Tulip stitch is a motif stitch used on common- and even-weave fabrics. The stitch makes a pretty floral motif, as its name suggests, and can be worked in any type of embroidery thread. The motifs can be used alone to add a splash of color; worked in a straight line to make a border; or scattered over a shape as a powdering. This stitch is quick and easy to work. First work a large daisy stitch *(see page 92)* with quite a long tail. Then make three stitches of different lengths from one side of the daisy stitch to the other, passing under the tail; do not pick up any fabric.

253 Russian chain stitch ☆

255/1 Ribbed spider's web ☆

256/2 Vell stitch ☆

254/1 Spider's web ☆

255/2 Ribbed spider's web ☆

257/1 Point Russe stitch ☆

254/2 Spider's web ☆

256/1 Vell stitch ☆

257/2 Point Russe stitch ☆

258 **Buttonhole wheel** ☆

260/1 **Point à la minute** ☆

262 **Star darn** ☆

259/1 **Cup stitch** ☆

260/2 **Point a la minute** ☆

263/1 **Tulip stitch** ☆

259/2 **Cup stitch** ☆

261 **Star of David** ☆

263/2 **Tulip stitch** ☆

264 Star   ☆ ☆
A star is, strictly speaking, a tailoring finish which is worked to strengthen a garment where there is a point of stress, for example, at the top of a pleat on a skirt. This stitch is, however, a highly decorative way of arranging satin stitches *(see page 24)* and it can be used in embroidery where a solidly stitched geometric motif is needed. Care should be taken to make the points of the star perfectly even. The stitches should cover the star shape completely: no ground fabric should show through. Any type of embroidery thread can be used for this stitch, but a lustrous thread such as stranded floss enhances the light and shade effect created by the positioning of the satin stitches. Similar stitches are the crow's foot *(see below)* and the sprat's head *(see below)*.

265 Rose stitch   ☆ ☆
Rose stitch is a motif stitch used on common- and even-weave fabrics. It makes a raised flower shape, which can be used as an accent stitch to provide extra color and texture in the same way as cup stitch *(see page 101)*, although the effect is flatter. This stitch can also be used to make an unusual powdering to decorate a shape. A round, twisted thread, such as pearl cotton, makes the flowers stand out more from the background than a flat, stranded floss.

First make a French knot *(see page 96)* to form the center of the flower.

Then work concentric circles of overlapping straight stitches around the French knot. The number of circles necessary depends on the size of rose stitch required; they can be in a different color from the central knot.

266 Wrapped cross stitch   ☆ ☆
Wrapped cross stitch is a motif stitch used on common- and even-weave fabrics. It is very simple to work and has a very raised, distinctive appearance. Interesting effects can be achieved by using a textured or heavy metallic thread for the wrapping. This stitch should be worked with the fabric stretched in an embroidery hoop or frame to prevent the wrapping from distorting and puckering the ground fabric. A large ordinary cross stitch *(see page 14)* forms the foundation, and this is then wrapped by the same or a second thread, without picking up the ground fabric. A fairly substantial thread should be used for the foundation cross but a supple thread is preferable for the wrapping.

267 Sprat's head   ☆ ☆
A sprat's head is, strictly speaking, a triangular tailoring finish which is worked to strengthen part of a garment where there is a point of stress; for example, at the top of a pleat on a skirt. This stitch is, however, highly decorative and can be used in embroidery where a small, heavily stretched, geometric

shape is needed. Follow the method of working shown, taking care to make the two outside stitches the same length. The remaining stitches should be worked close together and should completely cover the triangular shape. Any type of embroidery thread can be used to work a sprat's head but a lustrous thread, such as stranded floss, or a shiny one like pearl cotton, enhances the light and shade effect created by the positioning of the different slants of the stitches. A similar stitch is a crow's foot *(see below)*.

268 Crow's foot   ☆ ☆
A crow's foot is, strictly speaking, a triangular stitch used in dressmaking to strengthen a garment where there is a point of stress, for example, at the top of a pleat on a skirt. The stitch is, however, very decorative and can be used in embroidery where a small, heavily stitched geometric shape is needed. Care should be taken to make the three outside stitches equal in length. The remaining stitches should be worked close together and should completely cover the triangular shape without revealing the fabric beneath. Any type of embroidery thread can be used to work a crow's foot but a lustrous thread, such as stranded floss, or a shiny one like pearl cotton, will enhance the light and shade effect made by the different directions of the stitches. A similar stitch is a sprat's head *(see above)*.

269 *Interlaced cross stitch* ☆ ☆ ☆
Interlaced cross stitch is a composite motif stitch used on common- and even-weave fabrics. It looks very attractive when worked adjacent to or combined with a simpler stitch, such as ordinary cross stitch *(see page 14)* or herringbone stitch *(see page 8)*, to make a border. A foundation of four interlocking straight stitches, which make a diamond shape, is worked first. A second thread, often of a contrasting weight or color, is then interlaced through the foundation, without picking up any ground fabric. A blunt-ended tapestry needle should be used for the second thread to avoid splitting the foundation stitches. A rounded embroidery thread such as pearl cotton should be used for the straight stitches, but any type of thread can be used for the interlacing stitches. Use a metallic thread for the interlacing to make this stitch look rich and decorative.

270 *Catherine wheel* ☆ ☆ ☆
This stitch is a modern interpretation of an open needlepoint filling used during the nineteenth century for whitework, particularly on Ayrshire embroidery. The stitch was originally used as an open filling but is now used as a surface stitch on common- and even-weave fabrics. The appearance of the new stitch is similar to the nineteenth-century version, but the structure is rather different. A circle of blanket stitch *(see page 13)*, with the loops facing inward, is worked first in a heavy thread. A second row is then worked inside the first in a thinner thread through the loops of the first circle; this row is detached from the ground fabric. Four straight stitches are then worked through the fabric and span the center space to make eight "spokes." Finally, two rings of backstitch *(see page 14)* are worked over the spokes to form the "hub" of the wheel, without picking up the ground fabric. The central portion of the wheel is anchored to the fabric at the beginning and end of the backstitch. This stitch needs a firm thread to make it stand out from the fabric. Two thicknesses should be used: a heavy thread for the outside circle, and a lighter one for the remainder of the stitching.

271 *Square-laced herringbone stitch* ☆ ☆ ☆
Square-laced herringbone stitch is a large, isolated stitch used on common- and even-weave fabrics. It is used as a heavy accent stitch, worked side by side for a border, or worked solidly to fill a rectangular shape. It is a development of interlaced cross stitch *(see above)* although the finished effect is much heavier. This stitch should be worked with the fabric stretched in an embroidery hoop or frame to avoid puckering. It is worked in one color and weight of thread throughout but the needle should be changed to a blunt-ended tapestry needle for the lacing to avoid picking up any threads of ground fabric. First, work a square foundation of herringbone stitch *(see page 8)*: bring the thread through at the bottom left-hand corner of the area and lace the square together tightly. This tightening gives the stitch quite a different look from interlaced cross stitch. After the lacing is completed, take two vertical stitches over the center, without picking up the fabric, and then cross these with two horizontal stitches. Pass the thread through the fabric behind the interlacing to anchor the stitch to the fabric at the center.

272 *Maltese cross* ☆ ☆ ☆
Maltese cross is a motif stitch used on common- and even-weave fabrics. It makes an intricate, interlaced cross shape, which can be used alone or as a rich, heavy border. When used as a border, the motifs can be joined at the corners or placed edge-to-edge for a more solid effect.

A foundation grid of crossed straight stitches is made first; the stitches must pass over and under each other in the sequence shown. The interlacing tightens up the grid, so work the stitches quite loosely on fabric that has been stretched in an embroidery hoop or frame and make sure that the grid is correctly worked before proceeding to the interlacing. The interlacing is worked in a similar way to interlaced herringbone stitch *(see page 65)*, and either the same thread or one of a contrasting weight, color or texture is used; a metallic thread also looks very decorative. Use a blunt-ended tapestry needle for the interlacing to avoid splitting the foundation stitches. The motif can also be worked as a square by making the foundation stitches run vertically and horizontally, rather than diagonally.

264 Star ☆ ☆

266/1 Wrapped cross stitch ☆ ☆

267/2 Sprat's head ☆ ☆

265/1 Rose stitch ☆ ☆

266/2 Wrapped cross stitch ☆ ☆

268/1 Crow's foot ☆ ☆

265/2 Rose stitch ☆ ☆

267/1 Sprat's head ☆ ☆

268/2 Crow's foot ☆ ☆

269/1 **Interlaced cross stitch** ★ ☆ ☆

271/1 **Square-laced herringbone stitch** ★ ☆ ☆

272/1 **Maltese cross** ★ ☆ ☆

269/2 **Interlaced cross stitch** ★ ☆ ☆

271/2 **Square-laced herringbone stitch** ★ ☆ ☆

272/2 **Maltese cross** ★ ☆ ☆

270 **Catherine wheel** ☆ ☆ ☆

271/3 **Square-laced herringbone stitch** ★ ☆ ☆

272/3 **Maltese cross** ★ ☆ ☆

Edging stitches

273 Looped edging stitch no.1 ☆
Looped edging stitch no.1 is worked on common- and closely woven even-weave fabrics. It makes a neat, firm edging to a piece of fabric and is stronger than buttonhole edging stitch *(see below)*, although the appearance of both stitches is similar. It is often used in cutwork as it makes a good anchoring foundation for a lace filling stitch. Work from left to right over a tiny turned edge. Make a simple looped stitch along the edge and tighten each stitch by pulling the thread away from the body; this movement ensures that the loops fit neatly along the edge. Work the stitches close together. Any cotton embroidery thread can be used, providing that the weight of the thread is compatible with the fabric.

274 Loop picot ☆
also known as pinned picot
Loop picot is one of the simplest forms of picot and a firm, rounded thread should be used. It is worked from right to left of the area, which makes the buttonhole edging stitch *(see below)* to which it is usually attached a little more difficult to work but the picots much easier to effect. Once the place where the picot is to be worked is reached, insert a dressmaking pin into the fabric close to the last buttonhole stitch. Loop the thread under the pin, take a stitch into the fabric and adjust the loop for size. Secure the loop by passing the needle under it. Then tighten the working thread and continue with the edging stitch. The pin can be removed at this stage.

275 Ring picot ☆
Ring picots are easy to work and have a heavier appearance than other picot stitches. Any type of embroidery thread can be used but a flat stranded floss gives a flatter picot than a rounded thread such as pearl cotton. Buttonhole edging stitch *(see below)* is worked from right to left, as the picot is easier to work in this direction. Once the place is reached where the picot is to be worked, make a loop of working thread through a buttonhole loop three or four stitches back along the edging. This loop should be made fairly tight as the subsequent buttonholing enlarges it considerably. Then work close buttonhole stitches over the loop of thread until the edge of the fabric is reached. The resulting ring is then secured by the next buttonhole edging stitch.

276 Buttonhole edging stitch ☆
Buttonhole edging stitch is used to finish the edges of all types of cutwork, particularly Renaissance and Richelieu embroidery. Traditionally executed in white thread on a white fabric, cutwork is the term applied to work which has portions of the background fabric cut away around the stitched motifs; strengthening bars are then worked across the created spaces. Three or four straight stitches span the gap and are then covered by a row of buttonhole edging stitch to form a bar. This type of embroidery was popular during the sixteenth and seventeenth centuries and is probably the forerunner of needlemade laces. Cutwork appears to have originated in Italy or Flanders and examples of the technique were exported to the rest of Europe during the sixteenth century. By the seventeenth century, cutwork was found on most of the whitework samplers being produced in England. Eyelet embroidery is another example of cutwork where buttonhole edging stitch can be used to make an edge before parts of the ground fabric are cut away. In this type of embroidery, the center of the motifs (usually small circles or ovals), rather than the background around them, is cut away.

Buttonhole edging stitch consists of a row of closely packed buttonhole stitch *(see page 13)*, worked with the looped edge of the stitch next to the area to be cut away. If the fabric shows no sign of fraying, the shape is first outlined with running stitch *(see page 12)*, the fabric cut away close to this stitched line, and then the buttonhole edging stitch worked over the raw edge. For a fabric which looks as though it will fray, work the running stitch line and buttonhole edging stitch before cutting away the surplus fabric; always use very sharp scissors and cut very carefully. This method is also used for working a scallop-shaped edging on a piece of fabric.

277 Armenian edging stitch ☆ ☆
Armenian edging stitch is used as a decoration on the plain, hemmed edge of a piece of common-weave fabric. Work from left to right and pull the working thread quite tight after each knot is completed. Like most edging stitches, Armenian edging stitch is most effective when the stitches are small and evenly spaced along the edge and when a smooth thread is used.

278 Plaited edge stitch ☆ ☆
Plaited edge stitch is worked on common- and even-weave fabrics. It makes a decorative finish on the hemmed edge of a piece of fabric and is often used to ornament items of household linen. It is worked from left to right and makes a neat, knotted edge which can be worked with an open or closed finish. It can also be used to finish a raw edge, if the stitches are worked close together. A rounded thread such as pearl cotton gives plaited edge stitch a heavier appearance than a flat, stranded thread.

279 *Buttonhole picot* ☆ ☆
also known as **Venetian picot**

Buttonhole picot makes a larger picot than bullion picot *(see below)* and a firm, rounded thread should be used. It is worked from right to left, which makes the buttonhole edging stitch *(see page 108)* which it usually decorates a little difficult to work but the picots themselves much easier to effect. When the place where the picot is to be worked is reached, insert a dressmaking pin into the fabric close to the last buttonhole stitch; this will anchor the next loop of thread while the buttonhole stitch is worked over it. Insert the needle through the loop and over the pin, making sure that the point of the needle passes over the working thread. Pull the needle through and tighten the resulting stitch well, as it forms the end of the picot. Then work closely packed buttonhole stitches along the loop until the edge of the fabric is reached, when buttonhole edging stitch is resumed. Remove the pin after the picot is completed.

280 *Bullion picot* ☆ ☆

Picot is an embroidery term referring to a small loop of twisted thread attached to an edging. This stitch and the following picots can be used in a variety of ways: to decorate a plain buttonhole stitch edge *(see page 13)*; for ornamenting a bar in cutwork and needlemade laces; or to add to a row of buttonhole stitch worked on the surface of the fabric, such as in appliqué. With the exception of woven picot *(see below)*, which is worked directly into the fabric, the picots are worked into the buttonhole stitch loops without entering the ground fabric.

Bullion picot is one of the easiest picots to work and a firm, rounded thread, such as pearl cotton, is very suitable. Work buttonhole stitches *(see page 13)* close together along the edge until the place where the picot is made is reached. Insert the needle into the upright of the previous buttonhole stitch and twist the thread five or six times around the point of the needle in exactly the same way as for a bullion knot *(see page 97)*. Place the left thumb over the coils (if you are right-handed) and pull the needle through completely before tightening the coils. The bullion is then secured by the next buttonhole stitch, which must be worked very close to the previous one.

281 *Antwerp edging stitch* ☆ ☆
also known as **knot stitch** *and* **knotted blanket stitch**

Antwerp edging stitch adds a decorative finish to the plain, hemmed edge of a piece of common-weave fabric and is often used to decorate items of household linen, such as tablecloths and napkins. Work the stitch from left to right along the turned edge, using a fairly heavy, smooth thread. Additional rows of the stitch can be added for a deeper, lacy edging, or the outer row of loops can be whipped with a contrasting color *(see whipped backstitch, page 16)*. Antwerp edging stitch can also be used as a lacy line stitch on the surface of the fabric.

282 *Braid edging stitch* ☆ ☆ ☆

Braid edging stitch makes a useful edging on the plain, hemmed edge of a piece of common-weave fabric. It can be used to finish the edges of items of household linen, such as a tablecloth or napkin. This stitch is more difficult to work than Antwerp edging stitch *(see above)* or Armenian edging stitch *(see page 108)*, as the stitch is worked from right to left along the edge, which is itself facing away from the stitcher. The secret of working this stitch well is to leave the knot slack while the size of the loop is adjusted. After this has been done, tighten the knot firmly by pulling the thread outward at a right angle to the edge of the fabric. As with the two edging stitches mentioned above, the knots and loops should be evenly spaced and of a regular size, and some practice will be needed to achieve this. Care should also be taken in selecting thread: a firm thread is needed to keep the loops in shape. A fringe can be attached to the loops after the edging has been worked *(see fringed Antwerp edging stitch, page 29)*.

283 *Woven picot* ☆ ☆ ☆

Woven picots are rather large and, unlike other picots, are worked directly into the fabric edge. A firm, quite stiff, thread should be used for this stitch. Hold the edge of the fabric away from the body and make a loop of thread. Then insert a dressmaking pin over the loop and into the fabric to keep the loop firm. Slip the thread through the loop and tighten it to form the top of the picot. Then make a series of weaving movements until the edge of the fabric is reached. Each stitch should be tightened quite firmly to make the picot solidly worked and rather stiff. The end of the thread should be finished off as invisibly as possible and the pin removed.

273 Looped edging stitch no.1 ☆

276 Buttonhole edging stitch ☆

278/1 Plaited edge stitch ☆ ☆

274 Loop picot ☆

277/1 Armenian edging stitch ☆ ☆

278/2 Plaited edge stitch ☆ ☆

275 Ring picot ☆

277/2 Armenian edging stitch ☆ ☆

279 Buttonhole picot ☆ ☆

280 Bullion picot ☆ ☆

282 Braid edging stitch ☆ ☆ ☆

283/3 Woven picot ☆ ☆ ☆

281/1 Antwerp edging stitch ☆ ☆

283/1 Woven picot ☆ ☆ ☆

283/4 Woven picot ☆ ☆ ☆

281/2 Antwerp edging stitch ☆ ☆

283/2 Woven picot ☆ ☆ ☆

283/5 Woven picot ☆ ☆ ☆

Hemstitches

284 Hemstitch ☆
Hemstitching is a technique used to decorate and secure a hem. It is used for items of household linen and decorative hems and borders on clothes. Ordinary hemstitch is used for this purpose and is traditionally worked in white thread on white fabric. This technique can only be worked on a fabric with a fairly loose weave, such as linen, since three or four of the horizontal threads are removed from the fabric before the embroidery takes place. The threads are withdrawn and then the hem is turned in, just up to the edge of the drawn threads, and basted in position. The embroidery stitches, which group the remaining vertical threads into clusters, are then worked. After the embroidery is completed, the basting thread is removed. Any type of fine embroidery thread can be used, provided that it is compatible with the weight of the fabric.

Ordinary hemstitch is the simplest and easiest to work of all the hemstitches. It is worked from left to right, the right side of the work facing the stitcher. The embroidery thread should be secured neatly inside the hem at the beginning and end of the length. Follow the sequence of stitches shown, grouping the threads into fours, and pull each stitch quite tightly to make the cluster. Care must be taken to make sure than the

needle picks up the hem at the back of the work on the downward stroke so that it is secured in position.

285 Antique hemstitch ☆
Antique hemstitch is a variation of ordinary hemstitch *(see above)*. It is worked on the wrong side of the fabric and gives a much neater finish than ordinary hemstitch, as only the horizontal stitches that secure the clusters are visible on the right side of the work. It is worked in the same way as ordinary hemstitch but the needle is slipped between the hem instead of picking it up.

286 Serpentine hemstitch ☆ ☆
also known as trellis hemstitch
Serpentine hemstitch is a variation of ladder hemstitch *(see below)* and makes a pretty zig-zag border. It is worked in the same way as ladder hemstitch and consists of a row of ordinary hemstitch *(see above)* worked at the top and bottom of the withdrawn threads. The vertical threads are bunched together in groups of four (or any even number) along the lower line and then divided and regrouped when the edge is worked.

287 Ladder hemstitch ☆ ☆
also known as ladder stitch
Ladder hemstitch is an attractive variation of ordinary hemstitch *(see above)* and makes a border with a ladder pattern. It consists of a single

row of hemstitch worked along the lower edge in the usual way, bunching three vertical threads into each cluster. The fabric is then inverted and another row is worked on the opposite side of the drawn out threads. Make sure that the same three vertical threads are bunched together as on the preceding row. The number of horizontal threads which are withdrawn can be greater than that for ordinary hemstitch.

288 Italian hemstitch ☆ ☆ ☆
also known as double hemstitch, Roumanian hemstitch and double-rowed open-work
Italian hemstitch is a wider, more decorative hemstitch than the preceding two and is worked in two journeys. Work a row of ordinary hemstitch *(see above)* just above the hem, grouping three threads into each cluster. Leave three or four horizontal threads intact and withdraw the next group of horizontal threads — these should be of the same number as the threads which were drawn out originally. Work the second row of embroidery along the band of intact horizontal threads to form the vertical threads above and below this band into clusters. Follow the sequence of stitches shown, making sure that the clusters are formed from the same three vertical threads which were grouped together by the ordinary hemstitch.

Insertion stitches

289 Buttonhole insertion stitch ☆
also known as buttonhole faggot stitch

Insertion stitches are used to make open-work seams; the technique is also known as faggoting. It was originally developed as a way of joining two pieces of narrow hand-woven fabric to make large items of household linen, such as sheets, and the effect is very decorative. Traditionally, insertion stitches were worked in white, on white. With the exception of one-sided insertion stitch *(see page 52)*, and two-sided insertion stitch *(see page 57)*, insertion stitches are all used for this purpose on common- and even-weave fabrics. The method of preparing the fabric is the same for each version, although the space left between the two pieces of fabric varies depending on the width of the stitch. The fabric pieces are hemmed first, and then basted onto a strip of firm brown paper, leaving a gap between them. The paper ensures that the gap remains even, and that the stitches are of equal size. The paper is removed after the insertion stitch has been completed. Any type of cotton thread can be used, providing it is fairly strong and compatible with the weight of the fabric.

Buttonhole insertion stitch is a simple insertion stitch, which is worked over a fairly narrow space. Groups of three buttonhole stitches *(see page 13)* are worked alternately from edge to edge. The stitch begins at the right-hand side of the row and the central stitch of each group is made slightly longer than the others.

290 Twisted insertion stitch ☆
also known as faggoting

Twisted insertion stitch is one of the simplest forms of insertion and it makes a pretty, twisted zig-zag line. Make a simple twisted stitch alternately from one edge of the fabric to the other, ensuring that the needle always emerges from the back of the fabric. *(See buttonhole insertion stitch for details on preparing the fabric.)*

291 Knotted insertion stitch ☆ ☆
also known as knotted faggot stitch

Knotted insertion stitch makes a fairly narrow insertion with an attractive knotted appearance. It is quite simple to work and consists of Antwerp edging stitch *(see page 109)* worked so that the stitches are made alternately on the top and bottom edges of the fabric, as shown. *(See buttonhole insertion stitch for advice on preparing the fabric.)*

292 Plaited insertion stitch ☆ ☆ ☆
also known as interlaced faggot stitch

Plaited insertion stitch is a wide, ornate insertion stitch and should be worked in a firm, heavy thread. Often used on Victorian bed linen and ecclesiastical vestments, this stitch makes a bold plaited zig-zag line across an area. The stitch consists of diagonal stitches taken from one side of the space to the other in sequence. The stitches are grouped to make a heavy line of three threads and each stitch is interwoven with the adjacent one. *(See buttonhole insertion stitch for details on preparing the fabric.)*

293 Interlacing insertion stitch ☆ ☆ ☆
also known as interlaced faggot stitch and interlaced insertion stitch

Interlacing insertion stitch makes a very decorative wide insertion and is worked in exactly the same way as interlaced herringbone stitch *(see page 65)*. Work a row of double herringbone stitch *(see page 53)* into the edges of the fabric, using the second method described. Make sure that the stitches pass over and under each other in the correct formation before beginning the interlacing; follow the sequence shown. *(See buttonhole insertion stitch for advice on preparing the fabric.)*

294 Laced insertion stitch ☆ ☆ ☆
also known as laced faggot stitch

Laced insertion stitch is a wide, lacy insertion stitch, often worked in two colors . Unlike the other insertion stitches, some of the embroidery is worked before the two pieces of fabric are basted to the brown paper. *(See buttonhole insertion stitch for advice on preparing the fabric.)* A row of braid edging stitch *(see page 109)* is worked along each edge of the fabric before the fabric is basted down; the loops on the top edge should alternate with those on the bottom. The two rows of loops are then laced together, as shown.

Although this stitch makes a very pretty join, it is not particularly stable and it is therefore not advisable to use it on an item that is to be laundered. However, instead of the lacing, a row of knotted insertion stitch *(see above)* can be worked to join the rows of loops; this makes the join much stronger.

284/1 *Hemstitch* ☆

285/1 *Antique hemstitch* ☆

287 *Ladder hemstitch* ☆ ☆

284/2 *Hemstitch* ☆

285/2 *Antique hemstitch* ☆

288/1 *Italian hemstitch* ☆ ☆ ☆

286 *Serpentine hemstitch* ☆ ☆

288/2 *Italian hemstitch* ☆ ☆ ☆

289 *Buttonhole insertion stitch* ☆

292/1 *Plaited insertion stitch* ☆ ☆ ☆

292/4 *Plaited insertion stitch* ☆ ☆ ☆

290 *Twisted insertion stitch* ☆

292/2 *Plaited insertion stitch* ☆ ☆ ☆

293 *Interlacing insertion stitch* ☆ ☆ ☆

291 *Knotted insertion stitch* ☆ ☆

292/3 *Plaited insertion stitch* ☆ ☆ ☆

294 *Laced insertion stitch* ☆ ☆ ☆

Other fabric stitches

295 Lazy squaw stitch ☆

Lazy squaw stitch is a stitch used to attach beads to a common-weave fabric. This stitch, as its name implies, is used extensively by North American Indians when they attach beads to items of clothing. It is a quick and easy way of beading an area, as several beads are attached at once, but a very strong thread should be used, possibly even a button thread. The thread should enter the bead easily and an embroidery hoop or frame should be used to keep the fabric taut.

This stitch is worked downward between two parallel lines, which should be marked on the fabric. Several beads are threaded and then a horizontal straight stitch is made from one side of the row to the other, as shown. A small stitch is taken through the fabric at one side to anchor the beads and the process is repeated until the bottom of the line is reached. Work several bands of this stitch to fill the required area. For an alternative method of attaching beads, refer to spot stitch (see below).

296 Spot stitch ☆

also known as **bead couching** *and* **overlay stitch**

Spot stitch provides a way of attaching beads to common- or even-weave fabrics which is much quicker than sewing each one on individually. It is a variation of couching (see page 8) used by the North American Indians, particularly those of the Blackfoot, Crow and Shoshone tribes, for decorating items of clothing.

The beads are threaded onto a fairly strong thread, which is also fine enough to pass easily through the hole in the beads. The end of this thread is secured and the threaded beads are laid along the line to be covered. A second thread is then used to couch the first thread by making a tiny slanting stitch after every group of four beads. This method can be used for outlines or to make a solid beaded shape, either worked in straight rows, or spiralling outward from the center of the shape. See lazy squaw stitch (above) for an alternative method of attaching beads.

297 Corded bar stitch ☆

Corded bar stitch is a detached stitch used on common- and even-weave fabrics. Simple to work, it is used as an accent stitch in conjunction with other stitches where a raised effect is needed. It can also be scattered over a wide area to make an unusual powdering. Stretch the fabric in an embroidery hoop or frame to prevent distortion when the stitch is whipped. A foundation bar is worked first, consisting of six horizontal threads packed closely together; this bar should be kept fairly small. When a line is needed, work several small bars with the ends touching. A second thread is used to whip these foundation threads together. The second thread enters the fabric at only the beginning and end of each bar and a blunt-ended tapestry needle should be used to avoid splitting the foundation stitches. Corded bar stitch will have a more raised appearance if a round twisted thread such as a heavy pearl cotton is used.

298 Victorian tufting ☆

Victorian tufting is a ridged pile stitch used on common- and even-weave fabrics. It can be worked in a straight line or in multiple rows to fill a shape. This stitch is simple to work and consists of rows of closed herringbone stitch (see page 60) worked one on top of the other. The first row, which makes the center of the line of pile, is quite narrow but the second and subsequent rows should gradually become wider. Each row should overlap the previous row by a tiny amount. Work as many overlapping rows as possible until the required depth of line is reached. Using an extremely sharp pair of embroidery scissors, cut through each row of stitches carefully along the center. The resulting pile will be quite short at the center of the line, becoming higher toward the edges. A soft wool thread, such as Persian yarn, gives the best pile but a stranded thread can also be used, or even a mixture of the two. The rows of closed herringbone stitch can be worked in alternate colors, creating an unusual striped pile.

299 Cord stitch ☆ ☆

Cord stitch is a decorative joining stitch used on common- and even-weave fabrics. It makes a neat, plaited line, which covers the fabric completely, and is often used to finish pillow edges. The raw edges of the two pieces of fabric to be joined are first turned in and pressed. The pieces are then placed with the wrong sides facing each other and are basted together to hold them in place. The thread is secured neatly between the two layers and then brought to the right side of the front piece of fabric. The stitch is worked with a forward and backward motion and builds up until the edges are covered with a plaited line. When the embroidery is completed, the thread should be removed and the join pressed open from the wrong side. Press carefully to avoid flattening the embroidery. Any type of thread can be used but a flat thread, such as stranded cotton floss, will give better cover.

300 Eyelet hole ☆ ☆

Eyelet holes are worked on finely woven, common-weave fabrics and are chiefly used for eyelet lace, worked in a white thread on a white fabric. They are normally circular but oval and triangular shapes can be made in the same way. The circle is first traced on the fabric and outlined by tiny running stitches *(see page 12)*. The center of the fabric is then snipped vertically and horizontally. The surplus fabric is turned to the back and a row of closely worked overcast stitches *(see page 28)* is worked around the circle. When forming a triangle, make the overcast stitches slightly longer at the points to prevent fraying. The surplus fabric is then trimmed away on the back of the work. Tiny eyelet holes are worked in the same way, although the fabric is pierced by an awl to make the hole.

301 Shisha stitch no. 1 ☆ ☆

Shisha embroidery is the ancient Indian technique of attaching discs of mirror or tin to a piece of fabric by means of an embroidery surround. The word "shisha" means "little glass." The origins of shisha embroidery are found in the seventeenth century: the Taj Mahal in Agra, India, was built by Shah Jahan as a permanent monument to his wife, Mumtaz Mahal, who is believed to have developed the use of mirrors in embroidery *circa* AD 1630. The technique is still in use today, notably in the provinces of Kutch and Sind in India, and also in Pakistan and Afghanistan; the modern methods are practically identical to the old ones. Indian embroiderers still use this technique for traditional purposes: to decorate skirts and bodices; as ceremonial trappings for animals; and on torans.

Torans are embroidered friezes using shisha mirrors, which hang over doorways or windows on festive occasions. They are richly embroidered and have a row of pointed pendant shapes along the lower edge. Shisha mirrors are made in India and Pakistan and are available in this country through specialist needlework suppliers. They are made in a variety of colors: silver, which is the traditional color, amber, green and blue. The mirrors are hand cut and have irregular edges, which are covered by the embroidery. An alternative to the genuine shisha mirror for this type of work is a large round sequin but use the type which has a hole near the edge, rather than in the center.

The three shisha stitches in this book not only give different effects, but they show alternative methods of making the basic framework of stitches that hold the mirror in place while the decorative edge is worked. A snug framework is essential to prevent the mirror from being dislodged. Take care when stitching the framework to insert the needle vertically as close to the mirror as possible and also to tighten the stitches during working.

Shisha stitch no. 1 shows the traditional method of attaching the mirror, probably similar to that devised by Mumtaz Mahal. The framework is made by four straight stitches, two horizontal and two vertical. The vertical stitches are threaded over and under the horizontal stitches where they cross. When the mirror is firmly attached, the decorative twisted edging is then worked, as shown. A variation of this technique uses the same framework, but a row of tightly packed buttonhole stitches *(see page 13)* is worked around the edge to give a

plainer effect. Any type of smooth, strong thread can be used but stranded floss with either six or twelve strands, depending on the size of the mirror, produces a good edge.

302 Shisha stitch no. 2 ☆ ☆

This method uses eight straight stitches, interwoven in pairs, to anchor the mirror to the fabric. If a large mirror is being used, twelve stitches spaced in groups of three may be needed for extra security. After the framework has been completed, a band of stitches is worked around the circumference. The stitches can be all the same length, or alternately long and short for a more decorative finish. Buttonhole stitch *(see page 13)* also works successfully as a border with this framework.

303 Shisha stitch no. 3 ☆ ☆

This method of attaching the mirror differs from the previous two in that the framework is left uncovered and forms part of the decoration. It is a modern American interpretation of the technique and is much simpler to work than the preceding stitches. It is only successful, however, if a regularly shaped mirror or large sequin is used, as the edges are not covered by the border. Three vertical straight stitches are worked across the mirror, and then three horizontal stitches are woven through them, creating a mesh across the surface of the mirror; four vertical and four horizontal stitches will be needed if the mirror is large. These stitches must be placed centrally across the mirror and worked firmly. To finish, an outline of chain stitch *(see page 12)* is then worked through the fabric as close to the mirror as possible.

295 Lazy squaw stitch ☆

298/1 Victorian tufting ☆

299/1 Cord stitch ☆☆

296 Spot stitch ☆

298/2 Victorian tufting ☆

299/2 Cord stitch ☆☆

297 Corded bar stitch ☆

298/3 Victorian tufting ☆

299/3 Cord stitch ☆☆

300/1 **Eyelet hole** ☆ ☆

301/2 **Shisha stitch no. 1** ☆ ☆

302/2 **Shisha stitch no. 2** ☆ ☆

300/2 **Eyelet hole** ☆ ☆

301/3 **Shisha stitch no. 1** ☆ ☆

302/3 **Shisha stitch no. 2** ☆ ☆

301/1 **Shisha stitch no. 1** ☆ ☆

302/1 **Shisha stitch no. 2** ☆ ☆

303 **Shisha stitch no. 3** ☆ ☆

Straight and slanted stitches

304 *Reversed cushion stitch* ☆
Reversed cushion stitch is a canvas stitch used on mono canvas. It is a variation of cushion stitch *(see page 152)* worked without the framing of tent stitch. It makes a small-scale squared pattern over the canvas and is used for filling shapes and for background areas. The stitch consists of blocks of graduated diagonal straight stitches worked over squares of three canvas threads. The directon of these stitches is reversed on every alternate block.

An attractive light and shade effect is made by the positioning of the stitches, and this effect can be enhanced by choosing an embroidery thread with a sheen, such as stranded floss. However, this stitch also looks attractive if it is worked with tapestry or Persian yarn. When used over a large area, reversed cushion stitch can be shaded by the use of several shades of thread.

305 *Algerian filling stitch and Algerian filling stitch with bar* ☆
Algerian filling stitch is worked on mono canvas in vertical blocks of three satin stitches taken over four canvas threads. The blocks are worked diagonally with a half drop from top left to bottom right of the area to be covered. The stitch covers the canvas ground quickly, giving an even, slightly textured effect and is primarily used for background areas.

Algerian filling stitch with bar is a variation of Algerian filling stitch, in which a horizontal satin stitch is worked at the base of each block of vertical stitches. This extra stitch is worked either in the same thread or in a thread of contrasting color or texture.

306 *Chessboard filling stitch no. 2* ☆
Chessboard filling stitch no. 2 is a canvas stitch adapted from a drawn fabric stitch. It is used on mono canvas and has a regular geometric pattern which fills a large area quickly. Care should be taken when using it, as the pattern produced can be rather dominant unless it is worked on a small scale. It looks most attractive when worked with a lustrous thread, such as stranded floss or silk, as the light and shade effect created by the different directions of the stitches are enhanced by these. Chessboard filling stitch no. 2 consists of blocks of horizontal or vertical straight stitches. Each block is composed of three bands of ten straight stitches over three threads of canvas. The blocks are usually worked in diagonal rows, from top left to bottom right of the canvas.

307 *Mosaic stitch* ☆
Mosaic stitch is a canvas stitch used on mono and Penelope canvas. It makes a tiny, squared pattern and can be used to build up intricate patterns by using many different colors for the tiny squares (mosaics are made in the same way). Any type of thread can be used for this stitch, providing that it is compatible with the gauge of the canvas selected, but a smooth, non-hairy thread is essential to keep the pattern crisp. The stitch can also be used to work a monochrome area, as the smooth surface makes a good foil for the more raised and textured canvas stitches. It is composed of short and long diagonal straight stitches, and two horizontal journeys are needed to complete a row of squares. When working a complicated, multicolor design, work all the areas in the main color first, and then go back and fill in the spaces with the other colors.

308 *Florentine stitch* ☆
also known as **bargello stitch, cushion stitch, flame stitch, Irish stitch** *and* **Hungary stitch**
Florentine stitch is a canvas stitch used on mono canvas. This stitch is used for a type of needlepoint called Florentine work or bargello and makes a characteristic flame-shaped pattern. This type of needlepoint is often used for pillow covers and upholstery, and should be worked in a hard-wearing thread, such as tapestry yarn. The stitch consists of vertical straight stitches, usually placed over four horizontal canvas threads, worked in a step sequence to form zig-zag rows. The stitches can be arranged in different formations to create curves and pinnacles as well as zig-zags. One row is worked across the canvas, and the following lines of stitches are worked in different colors to fill the canvas above and below the first line, always following its contours. The stitches are the same length on the second and subsequent rows. The stitch is always worked using different colors or different shades of one color and the pattern is created by the use of color.

309 *Brick stitch no. 2* ☆
Brick stitch no. 2 is used only as a canvas stitch. Again it takes its name from the brickwork pattern that it produces but is used mainly for filling background areas. It is a quick and easy stitch to work and looks equally effective worked in yarn or stranded floss, depending on the gauge of the canvas. It consists of blocks of three horizontal straight stitches worked over six vertical threads of the canvas, which run side by side across the canvas. Below this row of blocks are two rows of short horizontal stitches, which are worked over two threads. This stitch looks best when worked in monochrome or in two very close tones of one color; one tone for the blocks and the other for the small stitches.

310 *Long stitch* ☆
Long stitch is a canvas stitch used on mono canvas. It makes a triangular pattern and has the appearance of a brocaded fabric when worked in a lustrous embroidery thread, such as stranded cotton or silk floss. Each horizontal row is worked in two journeys, and consists of groups of graduated vertical straight stitches, arranged in triangles. On the second journey, the triangles are reversed and fill in the spaces left on the first journey. Each journey can be made using a different color and the stitch looks very effective when two shades of the same color are used. Each double row of triangles is worked over five horizontal threads but the stitch can be made deeper by adding extra graduated stitches to each triangular group.

311 *Parisian stitch* ☆
Parisian stitch is a canvas stitch used on mono canvas. It is quick and easy to work and makes a fairly smooth surface, which is ideal for filling large areas and backgrounds. Any type of embroidery thread can be used for this stitch, but care should be taken to match the weight of the thread to the gauge of the canvas to ensure complete coverage of the surface. It is composed of long, vertical straight stitches worked over six horizontal canvas threads and short straight stitches worked over two horizontal threads, alternating across the canvas. The second and subsequent rows overlap the row immediately preceding them by two horizontal threads. This stitch is very useful where a gradually shaded area is needed, as it can be attractively blended in bands by using very similar shades of color.

312 *Double Parisian stitch* ☆
also known as old Parisian stitch
Double Parisian stitch is a canvas stitch used on mono canvas. A simple variation of Parisian stitch *(see above)*, it is worked in a similar way, except that the stitches are longer and arranged in pairs. The long stitches are nine threads high and the short stitches cover three canvas threads. A fairly coarse thread, such as tapestry or Persian yarn, will probably be needed to cover the canvas adequately but a small sample can be stitched first to check if another thread would be suitable. This stitch is used for large areas and backgrounds, which can be shaded in bands, but it gives a less even blend of colors over an area than ordinary Parisian stitch.

313 *Moorish stitch* ☆
Moorish stitch is a canvas stitch used on Penelope canvas. The flat surface produced has an attractive zig-zag pattern, which is usually worked in two colors of thread and can be worked in a combination of wool thread and cotton thread. Any type of embroidery thread can be used but care should be taken when matching the weight of the thread to the gauge of the canvas selected to ensure complete coverage of the canvas.

The stitch is worked diagonally from the top left to the bottom right of the area, in alternate rows. One row consists of groups of four graduated diagonal stitches, which form squares, and the other is made up of tiny diagonal stitches running in the same direction as those on the preceding row.

314 *Tent stitch* ☆
*also known as **needlepoint stitch, petit point, canvas stitch, perlen stitch, cushon stitch** and **continental stitch** and reversed tent stitch*
Tent stitch is a tiny canvas stitch used on mono canvas. It is known to have existed as long ago as the sixteenth century and was probably in use much earlier than that. It is a stitch which appears never to have gone out of fashion, which is probably due to its versatility.

A small, diagonal stitch, it can be worked in vertical, horizontal or diagonal rows to give a fairly smooth, flat surface; the stitch should all be in the same direction. When filling large areas with this stitch, work the stitch diagonally, as this method is less likely to distort the canvas. The small size of the stitches allows figurative designs to be intricate and full of detail. The designs are often followed from a colored chart, or from a painting on the canvas itself. Commercial needlepoint kits are usually worked in this stitch.

Tent stitch combines well with the heavier, more textured canvas stitches and accentuates their raised appearance. It is used to fill in the gaps of unworked canvas when a larger stitch does not totally cover the shape; in this case a matching thread should be used. It also frames square blocks of stitches, using a contrasting color or weight of thread; Scottish stitch *(see page 156)* is a good example of this use. Tent stitch can be trammed to make a hard-wearing, slightly ridged surface which, when a durable thread is used, is ideal for covering chair seats. Trammed tent stitch is worked on Penelope canvas, so that the tramming stitches can be worked between the pairs of canvas threads.

Reversed tent stitch gives a slightly more textured surface. It is mainly used for covering a solid-colored shape, giving a contrasting area to a textured stitch. It is worked in the same way as tent stitch but in this case the rows are horizontal and the direction of the stitches is reversed on every alternate row.

315 *Jacquard stitch* ☆
Jacquard stitch is a canvas stitch used on mono or Penelope canvas. It is used for covering large shapes and background areas, and has the appearance of a woven or brocaded fabric. It is quick and easy to work and can be sewn in more than one color and weight of thread, when it makes a diagonal, striped zig-zag pattern. It is worked diagonally from the top left to the bottom right of the area to be covered. Rows of satin stitches *(see page 24)*, each covering two vertical and two horizontal canvas threads, are arranged in steps of six stitches, as shown. The satin stitch rows alternate with rows of tent stitch *(see above)*. Any type of embroidery thread can be used but a combination of wool for the satin stitch and stranded or pearl cotton for the tent stitch looks attractive.

316 *Knitting stitch* ☆
*also known as **tapestry stitch** and **kelim stitch***
Knitting stitch is a canvas stitch used on mono canvas. It has a close worked, almost woven, surface and the effect varies depending on the weight of the thread and the gauge of the canvas used. A fine thread on small-gauge canvas gives the stitch the appearance of woven tapestry and the stitch can be used for tiny shapes and fine details. A border effect like that of knitting is made by using a coarse thread, such as tapestry yarn, on a larger gauge of canvas; the stitch can then be used for large shapes and background areas. Knitting stitch is similar to chain stitch *(see page 12)* but each vertical row of knitting is worked in two journeys. Each row consists of slanting straight stitches, worked upward first and then downward, with a reverse slant.

304 **Reversed cushion stitch** ☆

307/1 **Mosaic stitch** ☆

308 **Florentine stitch** ☆

305 **Algerian filling stitch** ☆

307/2 **Mosaic stitch** ☆

309 **Brick stitch no. 2** ☆

306 **Chessboard filling stitch no. 2** ☆

307/3 **Mosaic stitch** ☆

310 **Long stitch** ☆

311 *Parisian stitch* ☆

314/1 *Tent stitch* ☆

315 *Jacquard stitch* ☆

312 *Double Parisian stitch* ☆

314/2 *Tent stitch* (back) ☆

316/1 *Knitting stitch* ☆

313 *Moorish stitch* ☆

314/3 *Tent stitch* (diagonal) ☆

316/2 *Knitting stitch* ☆

317 *Cashmere stitch* ☆
Cashmere stitch is a canvas stitch worked on mono canvas. Quick to work and with good covering power, it is useful for stitching large areas of background. It makes a small, neat pattern with a steep slant and consists of a series of groups of three diagonal stitches which form slanting rows. The stitching usually starts in the top left-hand corner of the area and the first row is worked downward to the bottom right-hand corner; the second row is then worked upward, parallel to the first; the third downward, and so on. Any type of thread is suitable for this stitch but the weight of the thread used must be compatible with the gauge of the canvas.

318 *Straight Cashmere stitch* ☆
Straight Cashmere stitch is a canvas stitch used on mono canvas for covering large background areas. It is a relatively easy stitch to work and quickly covers the canvas. A variation of Cashmere stitch *(see above)*, it forms neat, rectangular blocks of slanting stiches. The blocks are fairly small and consist of four diagonal straight stitches which fill an area comprising two vertical canvas threads by three horizontal threads. The blocks can be worked in either horizontal or vertical rows to cover the area and, if worked in two colors or shades of thread, will make a tiny chessboard pattern. As with Cashmere stitch, any type of embroidery thread is suitable but the weight of the thread must be compatible with the gauge of the canvas.

319 *Fancy brick stitch* ☆
also known as **fancy bricking**
Fancy brick stitch, as its name implies, is a more complicated version of brick stitch no. 2 *(see page 120)*. It is a canvas stitch used on mono canvas and has a textured appearance. The stitch is constructed in a similar way to brick stitch no. 2 but the blocks in the first strip are smaller since they are made up of three horizontal straight stitches over three canvas threads. In the next strip, the small straight stitches are interspersed with pairs of vertical

stitches. Fancy brick stitch is used for filling shapes and for a background of textured brick pattern.

320 *Twill stitch* ☆
Twill stitch is a canvas stitch used on mono canvas. It is quick and easy to work and makes a small woven pattern with a strong diagonal feel. It is used to fill a shape of any size and is ideal for a background area. It is worked in diagonal rows from the top left to the bottom right of the area to be covered. The rows consist of vertical straight stitches worked over three horizontal canvas threads. Wool or cotton embroidery threads are equally well suited to this stitch but a stranded cotton or silk floss enhances the smoothly stitched surface beautifully. The rows can be worked in two colors to give a diagonally striped effect.

321 *Hungarian stitch* ☆
Hungarian stitch is used on mono and Penelope canvas. It makes tiny diamond shapes, which can be worked alternately in two colors or used to create a more complex geometric design, using several colors. It also makes a good background stitch when worked in monochrome. When making a complicated pattern, first work all the stitches of one color, then all the stitches of the second color, and so on. Each stitch consists of three vertical straight stitches of different lengths to cover two, four and then two horizontal threads of the canvas.

322 *Diamond straight stitch* ☆
Diamond straight stitch is used on mono canvas. It is used for filling large or small shapes and for background areas and has a small, regular, diamond-shaped pattern. It consists of diamond shapes made of five vertical straight stitches of graduating length, surrounded by small vertical stitches worked over one canvas thread. Work the diamonds in horizontal rows over the area, so that each row fits neatly into the one above. With the same thread, fill the remaining spaces with the small stitches.

323 *Diagonal stitch* ☆
Diagonal stitch is used on mono canvas for filling large shapes and backgrounds. It makes a flat, patterned surface with the appearance of a woven or brocaded fabric, which can be made more striking by using a lustrous thread such as stranded floss. It is worked in diagonal rows from the top left-hand corner to the bottom right-hand corner of the shape and consists of graduated diagonal stitches. The stitches on each row fit neatly into the stitches on the preceding row and the largest stiches are worked on a line with the smallest stitches so that no gaps are created. Diagonal stitch can be worked in two or more colors to make a bold, diagonal striped pattern. Work backstitch *(see page 14)* in a different color between the rows of diagonal stitch to enhance the striped effect.

324 *Reversed mosaic stitch* ☆
Reversed mosaic stitch is used on mono and Penelope canvas. Like mosaic stitch *(see page 120)*, it makes a tiny squared pattern, although the diagonal stitches run in the opposite direction every alternate square. Each square is completed before moving on to the next one and they are worked in horizontal rows across the shape, and then back again. The light and shade effect created by the slanting stitches is enhanced by the use of a lustrous thread, such as stranded floss or pearl cotton.

325 *Linked stitch* ☆
Linked stitch is used on mono canvas and is extremely quick and simple to work. Suitable for backgrounds, it makes a brickwork pattern of square, barred blocks, worked in horizontal rows. The blocks can be worked in vertical rows with a half drop and the number of vertical stitches in each block can be altered to form a rectangle. Each block consists of five vertical straight stitches worked over six horizontal canvas threads and overstitched by one horizontal straight stitch over six vertical threads.

326 Double twill stitch ☆

Double twill stitch is a canvas stitch used on mono canvas. A simply worked variation of twill stitch (see page 124), it has a bold diagonal pattern useful for filling large shapes and background areas. It is worked in diagonal rows, from the top right to the bottom left of the area to be covered. Rows of large vertical straight stitches, worked over four horizontal canvas threads, alternate with rows of shorter vertical straight stitches, worked over two horizontal threads. The rows can be worked in two contrasting or harmonizing colors to give a diagonally striped effect. Any type of embroidery thread can be used but care should be taken to match the weight of the thread to the gauge of the canvas to make sure that the canvas is completely covered by the stitching.

327 Byzantine stitch ☆

Byzantine stitch is a canvas stitch used on mono canvas. It is useful for large background areas because it is easy to work and covers the canvas rapidly. The regular zig-zag pattern made by this stitch is similar to the formal geometric patterns found in Byzantine art and architecture; hence its name. The Byzantine Empire existed in Eastern Europe and parts of Africa and Asia during the period between AD 330 and AD 1453 when it was conquered by the Turks. The textiles of the Byzantines embodied the characteristic blend of classical traditions and Eastern influences found in all the visual arts of that civilization. In AD 552, the Emperor Justinian acquired the secrets of silk cultivation and Byzantium (present-day Istanbul) became the first center outside China to produce silk thread and fabrics. Byzantine pattern weaving became greatly admired for its stylized designs of animals and birds and for its complex geometric patterns. The technical skill of the weavers was also widely recognized. Silk production continued in Byzantium as a jealously guarded monopoly almost until the time of the Turkish conquest.

Byzantine stitch produces the effect of a woven or brocaded fabric, especially when worked on a small-gauge canvas with a stranded silk or cotton thread. The zig-zag pattern is made by arranging groups of five diagonal straight stitches in equal-sized steps. The rows are worked diagonally, beginning at the top left-hand corner of the area to be covered. Any small spaces at the edge of the shape that are not covered by the diagonal rows are filled in with shorter diagonal stitches, always keeping the pattern correct.

328 Gobelin stitch ☆ ☆

also known as oblique Gobelin stitch

Gobelin stitch is a canvas stitch used on mono canvas. It makes a smooth surface, which is useful where a flat area of needlepoint is needed to accentuate a more textured stitch. It is very similar to tent stitch (see page 121) in appearance and consists of horizontal rows of small slanting stitches. The rows are worked from the bottom of the area to be covered and run alternately from left to right and from right to left. The stitches are two canvas threads tall and slant diagonally over one thread. It is very important to follow this method closely in order to keep the "pull" of the stitch correct, otherwise the surface will become uneven.

329 Encroaching Gobelin stitch ☆ ☆

also known as interlocking Gobelin stitch

Encroaching Gobelin stitch is a canvas stitch used on mono canvas and is a variation of Gobelin stitch (see above). It makes a flat surface and is an ideal stitch to use if you wish to shade and blend colors over large areas. It is worked in close horizontal rows, starting at the top of the area to be covered, and the rows are worked in alternate directions. The stitches are longer than ordinary Gobelin stitches: they are worked over five horizontal canvas threads and slant diagonally over one thread. The stitches in each row overlap the stitches in each previous row by one horizontal thread, causing the rows to interlock. Any type of embroidery thread can be used but care should be taken to match the weight of the thread to the gauge of the canvas.

330 Gobelin filling stitch ☆ ☆

Gobelin filling stitch is used on mono canvas and is used both for filling shapes and for backgrounds. It makes a fairly flat surface, and it is important to match the weight of the thread to the gauge of the canvas to ensure that the canvas is completely covered by the stitching. A very quick stitch to work, it lends itself very well to shading and blending different colors, as the rows of stitches overlap each other by three canvas threads. To prevent an obvious break between rows, the shades of the colors used should not be dramatically different. The rows are worked horizontally in alternate directions, beginning from the left. Each row consists of spaced, vertical straight stitches worked over six horizontal canvas threads into alternate holes in the canvas. Each row overlaps the preceding row by three canvas threads and fills in the spaces.

331 Square satin stitch ☆ ☆

also known as flat square

Square satin stitch is a canvas stitch used on mono canvas primarily for filling large shapes and backgrounds. It makes a pattern of diamond shapes, which in turn makes a pattern of large squares when four diamonds are set together. Each diamond shape consists of eleven satin stitches (see page 24) of graduating lengths, with the satin stitches worked either vertically or horizontally. Follow the arrangement of the diamonds and the direction of the stitches shown carefully. This stitch looks extremely attractive when worked on a small scale, using a pearl cotton or stranded floss to accentuate the light and shade effect created by the different directions of the stitches. The diamonds can also be striped in alternating colors: this creates a strong bold pattern on the surface if two contrasting colors are used, or a much more subtle effect if two close shades of one color are used.

317 *Cashmere stitch* ☆

320 *Twill stitch* ☆

323 *Diagonal stitch* ☆

318 *Straight Cashmere stitch* ☆

321 *Hungarian stitch* ☆

324 *Reversed mosaic stitch* ☆

319 *Fancy brick stitch* ☆

322 *Diamond straight stitch* ☆

325 *Linked stitch* ☆

326 **Double twill stitch** ☆

329 **Encroaching Gobelin stitch** ☆ ☆

330/2 **Gobelin filling stitch** ☆ ☆

327 **Byzantine stitch** ☆

330/1 **Gobelin filling stitch** ☆ ☆

331 **Square satin stitch** ☆ ☆

328 **Gobelin stitch** ☆ ☆

332 Wide Gobelin stitch ☆ ☆
also known as oblique slav stitch
Wide Gobelin stitch is a canvas stitch used on mono canvas. A larger version of Gobelin stitch *(see page 125)*, it makes a flat surface, which is useful to contrast with the more textured canvas stitches. It is worked in horizontal rows in the same way as Gobelin stitch but the slanting straight stitches are larger and each cover three horizontal canvas threads. They also have a more angled slant, running across two vertical canvas threads instead of one. Wide Gobelin stitch looks very effective when worked in closely shaded bands and any type of embroidery thread can be used, provided that it is compatible with the gauge of the canvas.

333 Balloon satin stitch ☆ ☆
Balloon satin stitch is a canvas stitch used on mono canvas for filling large shapes and backgrounds. The pattern of balloon shapes is made with ordinary satin stitches. The horizontal stitches are worked in vertical rows from the top of the shape and the second and subsequent rows interlock closely. A lustrous thread, such as stranded floss or silk, is well suited to this stitch and enhances the smooth, even surface of each balloon shape, but a wool thread can also be used with good results. To add texture to this stitch, an isolated knot stitch, such as a small bullion knot *(see page 97)* or a French knot *(see page 96)*, can be worked between the balloons.

334 Upright Gobelin stitch ☆ ☆
also known as straight Gobelin stitch
Upright Gobelin stitch is a canvas

stitch used on mono canvas. It is simple and very quick to work and makes a close, ridged surface, which lends itself well to working small, intricate shapes, as well as backgrounds. The upright variation of Gobelin stitch *(see page 125)*, it is worked in horizontal rows, in alternate directions, from the top of the area to be covered. The rows consist of small vertical straight stitches, each worked over two horizontal canvas threads and worked close together, filling every hole along the rows. Upright Gobelin stitch can be trammed to give a hard-wearing surface suitable for upholstery.

335 Linen stitch ☆ ☆ ☆
Linen stitch is a canvas stitch used on mono and Penelope canvas. As its name suggests, this stitch creates a neatly woven surface reminiscent of linen fabric. It provides an unusual way of covering large areas and backgrounds and looks equally effective worked in tapestry yarn, matte embroidery cotton or stranded floss, provided that the gauge of the canvas is compatible with the weight of the thread. The rows are worked diagonally from bottom left to top right and then back again. A neatly interlocking pattern of straight stitches is made; each vertical and horizontal stitch covers two canvas threads.

336 Plaited Gobelin stitch ☆ ☆ ☆
Plaited Gobelin stitch is a canvas stitch worked on Penelope canvas. It makes an attractive plaited surface and is used for filling large areas and backgrounds. Quite quick to work, it covers the canvas well, provided that the weight of the thread used is

compatible with the gauge of the canvas chosen. It is a variation of Gobelin stitch *(see page 125)* and the stitches are all the same size, covering two double canvas threads and slanting diagonally over one thread. However, the rows are arranged in a different way from Gobelin stitch. They are worked in horizontal rows, from right to left and then back again, starting at the top right-hand corner of the area. The stitches on the first row slant to the left, while those on the second and every alternate row thereafter slant to the right and overlap the stitches on each preceding row by one horizontal double thread.

337 Rep stitch ☆ ☆ ☆
also known as Aubusson stitch
Rep stitch is a canvas stitch that must be worked on Penelope canvas. A very small diagonal stitch with a ridged texture, it is used for working finely detailed designs and tiny shapes. This stitch takes its name from the fabric, rep, which it resembles when worked closely, using a heavy thread. Rep stitch should cover the canvas completely, and a small sample should be worked to check the compatibility of the weight of the thread with the gauge of the canvas. It is worked in the same way as tent stitch *(see page 121)* but in this case the rows are always worked downward and the stitches are less slanted. Each vertical row covers one vertical double thread of the canvas, and the stitches are worked not only in the wider spaces but also between the double threads, giving a very closely stitched appearance.

338 *Milanese stitch* ☆ ☆ ☆
Milanese stitch is used on mono and Penelope canvas. It makes an attractive, triangular pattern, with a brocaded appearance and flat surface, and is excellent for backgrounds. This brocaded effect is enhanced when the stitch is worked in a lustrous thread, such as stranded floss or pearl cotton, and also looks effective when worked in a wool thread.

The triangles consist of four stitches of graduated lengths, arranged so that they point alternately up and down. Instead of working satin stitch blocks, as is usual when producing this type of pattern, Milanese stitch is worked entirely in backstitch *(see page 14)*. Begin at the top left of the area to be covered and work the rows diagonally up and down the shape, ensuring all the time that the triangular formation is retained.

339 *Straight Milanese stitch* ☆ ☆ ☆
Straight Milanese stitch is a canvas stitch used on mono and Penelope canvas. It is a simply worked variation of ordinary Milanese stitch *(see above)* but in this case the triangles are arranged in horizontal rather than diagonal rows. It is worked in backstitch *(see page 14)* in exactly the same way as Milanese stitch but the rows run alternately from left to right, and from right to left.

340 *Oriental stitch* ☆ ☆ ☆
see also *Roumanian stitch*
Oriental stitch is a canvas stitch used on mono and Penelope canvas. It is a variation of Milanese stitch *(see above)*, which makes a larger pattern with a definite zig-zag

look to the flat surface. It is quick and easy to work, and is used for large areas and backgrounds. This stitch is worked in the same way as Milanese stitch: backstitch *(see page 14)* is worked in diagonal rows across the shape from the bottom left-hand corner to the top right-hand corner of the shape and back in the opposite direction, keeping the pattern correct. Any type of embroidery thread can be used for this stitch but care should be taken when matching the weight of the thread to the gauge of the canvas selected to ensure complete coverage of the canvas

341 *Lozenge satin stitch* ☆ ☆ ☆
Lozenge satin stitch is used on mono canvas for filling large shapes and backgrounds. The bold, lozenge-shaped pattern is made by arranging ordinary satin stitches *(see page 24)* in the pattern shown. The vertical stitches are worked in horizontal rows, beginning at the left-hand side of the area to be covered. The central group of three stitches can be left unworked on the first journey, to be filled in later, using a contrasting color of thread. A lustrous thread, such as stranded floss or silk, enhances the smoothly stitched surface of the lozenges but tapestry or Persian yarn is also suitable.

342 *Renaissance stitch* ☆ ☆ ☆
Renaissance stitch is used on mono and Penelope canvas. It makes a flat, closely worked surface of tiny vertical stitches arranged in horizontal rows and is used for a shape of any size. This stitch can be used to work small details and complex geometric patterns can be built up using many different colors

of thread. This stitch makes a very hard-wearing surface when worked in a durable thread such as tapestry yarn, and it can be used for upholstery. It is similar in appearance to upright Gobelin stitch *(see page 128)* but the methods of working are entirely different.

Each Renaissance stitch consists of two vertical stitches worked over two canvas threads and a horizontal stitch of the same length. The stitch is worked in vertical rows, and each pair of vertical stitches is worked under the preceding pair; the rows should always be worked downward. Any type of embroidery thread can be used but care should be taken to make sure that the canvas is completely covered by the stitching, especially when using Penelope canvas.

343 *Web stitch* ☆ ☆ ☆
Web stitch is a canvas stitch used only on Penelope canvas. It has a closely woven surface and is used for filling shapes or backgrounds of any size. It is a form of couching *(see page 8)*, and consists of long, diagonal straight stitches tied down at regular intervals by short, diagonal straight stitches. The short stitches should lie at right angles to the long stitches and be set alternately on each row to create a woven surface. The long stitches are worked into the holes between the double threads but the short stitches pass into the tiny holes between the threads. Any type of embroidery thread can be used but care should be taken to match the weight of the thread to the gauge of the canvas to make sure that the canvas is completely covered by the stitching.

332 Wide Gobelin stitch ☆ ☆

334 Upright Gobelin stitch ☆ ☆

336/1 Plaited Gobelin stitch ☆ ☆ ☆

333 Balloon satin stitch ☆ ☆

335/1 Linen stitch ☆ ☆ ☆

336/2 Plaited Gobelin stitch ☆ ☆ ☆

335/2 Linen stitch ☆ ☆ ☆

337 Rep stitch ☆ ☆ ☆

338 *Milanese stitch* ☆ ☆ ☆   341 *Lozenge satin stitch* ☆ ☆ ☆   342/3 *Renaissance stitch* ☆ ☆ ☆

339 *Straight Milanese stitch* ☆ ☆ ☆   342/1 *Renaissance stitch* ☆ ☆ ☆   343 *Web stitch* ☆ ☆ ☆

340 *Oriental stitch* ☆ ☆ ☆   342/2 *Renaissance stitch* ☆ ☆ ☆

Crossed stitches

344 Canvas fern stitch ☆
Canvas fern stitch is used on Penelope canvas. It makes a striking ridged surface and is used for filling shapes and for backgrounds. It consists of vertical rows of top-heavy crosses which are worked downward to make ridges. The ridged effect can be accentuated by the use of two or more harmonizing or contrasting colors of thread. Any type of embroidery thread can be used but care should be taken to match the weight of the thread to the gauge of the canvas to make sure that the canvas is completely covered by the stitching. Rows of canvas fern stitch can be worked alternately with rows of broad stem stitch *(see page 9)* to make an attractive striped pattern.

345 Double stitch ☆
also known as alternating cross stitch; *see also* stepped and threaded running stitch
Double stitch is a composite canvas stitch and is used on mono canvas. It makes a good background stitch as it is quite quick to work and covers the canvas well. It can be worked in two colors by working the different-sized crosses on two journeys instead of one. It looks most attractive when the two threads chosen are close to each other in shade.

Double stitch consists of interlocking horizontal rows of cross stitch *(see page 14)* alternating with oblong cross stitch *(see page 133)*. The rows are arranged so that the oblong cross stitches fit neatly under the ordinary cross stitches of the previous row. The oblong cross is worked over two vertical and six horizontal threads, while the ordinary cross stitch covers a square of two threads. Any type of embroidery thread can be used but care should be taken to match the weight of the thread to the gauge of the canvas to ensure that the canvas is completely covered.

346 Cross stitch plus two ☆
Cross stitch plus two is primarily a canvas stitch used on mono canvas but it can also be worked successfully on an even-weave fabric. When worked on canvas, this stitch makes a distinctive woven surface and is useful for filling large shapes and background areas since it is quite quick to work. It consists of a large, slightly elongated cross stitch worked over four vertical and six horizontal canvas threads with the addition of a vertical straight stitch across the center of the cross. A horizontal straight stitch is then worked at the base of the cross. Any type of embroidery thread can be used, provided that it covers the canvas well, but the woven pattern will be most effective if a thick thread such as tapestry yarn is used. When working this stitch on an even-weave fabric, it makes a pretty, lacy pattern if a fine pearl cotton or crochet cotton is used.

347 Broad diagonal cross stitch ☆
also known as diagonal broad cross
Broad diagonal cross stitch is a canvas stitch used for filling large shapes and background areas and is usually worked on mono canvas. It is worked in the same way as broad cross stitch *(see page 133)* and makes a raised geometric pattern with a bold, diagonal appearance. Although worked in the same way as broad cross stitch, the blocks are arranged diagonally rather than straight. Each block consists of three straight stitches, slanting from the top right-hand corner to the bottom left-hand corner and crossed by three straight stitches, which slant in the opposite direction. The rows are worked diagonally, from the top left-hand corner to the bottom right-hand corner of the area to be covered and all the rows of blocks interlock as shown. Any type of embroidery thread is suitable for broad diagonal cross stitch but care should be taken when matching the weight of the thread to the gauge of the canvas to make sure that the canvas is completely covered by the stitching.

348 Double Dutch stitch ☆
also known as Dutch double cross stitch
Double Dutch stitch is a canvas stitch used on mono canvas. A variation of Dutch stitch *(see pager 137)*, it is used for filling large areas and for backgrounds. It makes a textured surface with strong vertical lines and is worked downward. This stitch uses oblong cross stitches *(see page 133)* worked horizontally over four vertical and two horizontal canvas threads. They are worked in vertical rows, and each alternate cross is tied down with a vertical stitch over three canvas threads. Each row is arranged so that the tied crosses line up next to each other. A second journey of stitching is then begun, using either the same thread, or one of a contrasting color and weight. This journey consists of rows of backstitch *(see page 14)*, worked quite large and covering four horizontal threads, placed between the rows of crosses. Double Dutch stitch gives better coverage of the canvas than Dutch stitch and any type of embroidery thread can be used, provided that it is compatible with the gauge of the canvas.

349 Oblong cross stitch with backstitch and double-tied oblong cross stitch ☆
Oblong cross stitch with backstitch is a simply worked variation of oblong cross stitch *(see page 133)*. It is used on mono canvas and can be worked in two colors. It has the same uses as oblong cross stitch and is worked in exactly the same way, over two vertical and four horizontal threads of the canvas. After the required area has been stitched, a row of backstitch *(see page 14)* is worked over the center of each row of oblong cross stitch. This row can be worked in a contrasting color or a different weight of embroidery thread.

Double-tied oblong cross stitch is similar in appearance to oblong cross stitch with backstitch but the method of working is different and it is worked in one color. Each oblong cross stitch, worked over two vertical and seven horizontal threads, is tied down by two short straight stitches before proceeding to the next cross stitch. This stitch has a more textured appearance than oblong cross stitch or oblong cross stitch with backstitch and has a pronounced ridge running along the center of each row.

350 Broad cross stitch ☆
also known as broad cross
Broad cross stitch is a canvas stitch used for filling large shapes and background areas and is usually worked on mono canvas. Quite a large stitch, it covers a square of six vertical and six horizontal canvas threads, making a raised geometric pattern, which is bold and striking in appearance. It is very straightforward to work and the blocks consist of three vertical straight stitches, which are then crossed by three horizontal stitches of the same length. It is worked in horizontal rows, beginning at the top left-hand corner of the area to be filled. The blocks in one row fit into the spaces at the bottom of the preceding row. Any type of embroidery thread is suitable for broad cross stitch, but care should be taken when matching the weight of the thread to the gauge of the canvas to make sure that the canvas is completely covered by the stitching. A variation of this stitch can be made by working the horizontal stitches first and the vertical stitches last.

351 Canvas herringbone stitch ☆
Canvas herringbone stitch is used on mono canvas for filling large shapes and backgrounds. It makes a dense, plaited texture and is worked in exactly the same way as ordinary herringbone stitch. Each crossed diagonal stitch covers four vertical and four horizontal canvas threads and the rows interlock closely. Any type of thread can be used, but a soft wool thread, such as tapestry or Persian yarn, gives the best coverage of the canvas. Canvas herringbone stitch can be striped in two or more colors to make an attractive chevron pattern.

352 Underlined stitch ☆
Underlined stitch is a canvas stitch used on mono and Penelope canvas to fill a shape or background of any size. A variation of cross stitch *(see page 14)*, it can also be used on an even-weave fabric, provided that a fairly fine thread is used. It is worked in horizontal rows and each cross stitch is underlined by a horizontal straight stitch before the next cross

stitch is formed. Any type of embroidery thread can be used but care should be taken to match the weight of the thread to the gauge of the canvas to make sure that the canvas is covered by the stitching.

353 Half cross stitch ☆
also known as half stitch
Half cross stitch is a line or filling stitch used on even-weave fabrics and Penelope canvas. It is a small, diagonal stitch, always worked in the same direction, which can be used as a filling stitch to fill shapes with a flat area of stitching, or as a line stitch. As its name suggests, half the stitch consists of half an ordinary cross stitch *(see page 14)*. When worked on canvas, half cross stitch looks identical to tent stitch *(see page 121)*. However, the method of working the two stitches is different and they should never be used together, as the different stitches created on the back of the work will result in an uneven, distorted surface. Half cross stitch is very easy to work and the rows should run horizontally from the left to the right of the area. When worked on canvas, this stitch can be trammed *(see Glossary)* to give better coverage. Any type of thread can be used on an even-weave fabric but care should be taken when using half cross stitch on canvas to select a thread that will cover the canvas adequately.

354 Oblong cross stitch ☆
also known as long cross stitch, economic long cross and czar stitch
Oblong cross stitch is a variation of ordinary cross stitch *(see page 14)* and is used on mono and Penelope canvas. It is used for lines and for filling large areas and backgrounds, since it is extremely quick to work. Each row is worked in two journeys and the stitch has a neat, ridged texture. Almost the same as ordinary cross stitch in construction, the stitches of oblong cross stitch are elongated. One set of diagonals is worked from right to left on the first journey and the crosses are completed on the second journey in the opposite direction. This stitch can be worked over four, or six, or more horizontal canvas threads but it is

usually kept at the width shown. Any type of embroidery thread can be used but care should be taken especially when using Penelope canvas, to match the weight of the thread to the gauge of the canvas to ensure that the canvas is completely covered by the stitching.

355 Double cross stitch ☆
also known as double straight cross stitch; see also leviathan stitch
Double cross stitch is a canvas stitch used on mono canvas. It is a very decorative stitch and forms large, raised diamond shapes. The diamonds comprise a row of large, upright cross stitches *(see page 137)* worked over four vertical and horizontal canvas threads, and then over-stitched by a row of smaller ordinary cross stitch *(see page 14)*. Follow the sequence of stitches shown and start stitching from the top left-hand corner of the canvas, working the rows first from left to right, and then from right to left. Any type of embroidery thread can be used but care should be taken to match the weight of the thread to the gauge of the canvas to ensure that the canvas is completely covered.

356 Knotted stitch ☆
also known as Persian cross stitch and Pangolin stitch; see also coral stitch and French knot
Knotted stitch is used on Penelope canvas. It has a closely packed ridged appearance and is quick and easy to work, which makes it suitable for backgrounds and large areas. This stitch can be used with any type of embroidery thread, provided it is compatible with the gauge of the canvas, but a soft wool thread, such as tapestry or Persian yarn, gives better coverage. The stitch consists of a long, slanting stitch over one vertical and three horizontal double threads of canvas, which is tied down by a short, diagonal crossing stitch. The rows of stitching overlap each other by one horizontal double thread, and a pretty, broken striped pattern is created if alternate rows are worked with a contrasting thread.

344/1 Canvas fern stitch ☆

345 Double stitch ☆

347 Broad diagonal cross stitch ☆

344/2 Canvas fern stitch ☆

346/1 Cross stitch plus two ☆

348 Double Dutch stitch ☆

344/3 Canvas fern stitch ☆

346/2 Cross stitch plus two ☆

349 Oblong cross stitch with backstitch ☆

350 *Broad cross stitch* ☆

353 *Half cross stitch* ☆

355 *Double cross stitch* ☆

351 *Canvas herringbone stitch* ☆

354/1 *Oblong cross stitch* ☆

356/1 *Knotted stitch* ☆

352 *Underlined stitch* ☆

354/2 *Oblong cross stitch* ☆

356/2 *Knotted stitch* ☆

357 Leviathan stitch ☆
also known as **double cross stitch, Smyrna cross stitch** *and* **railway stitch**
Leviathan stitch is a canvas stitch which can also be used on even-weave fabrics provided that a fine thread is used. It consists of an upright cross stitch *(see page 137)* worked over a basic cross stitch *(see page 14)* and usually covers four horizontal and four vertical canvas threads. Each stitch forms a neat, raised square unit and these units can be worked in alternate colors to give a chessboard effect. Leviathan stitch worked in tapestry yarn makes an extremly hard-wearing surface, suitable for chair seats and pillow covers.

358 Crossed Gobelin stitch ☆
Crossed Gobelin stitch is a canvas stitch used on mono canvas. A decorative variation of Gobelin filling stitch *(see page 125)*, it has a more textured effect. Each row consists of spaced vertical straight stitches worked over six horizontal canvas threads into alternate holes in the canvas. After each stitch is formed an ordinary cross stitch *(see page 14)* is worked over the center. The rows are worked horizontally in alternate directions. Each row overlaps the preceding row by two horizontal threads to fill in the spaces. As with Gobelin filling stitch, it is important to choose an embroidery thread that will cover the canvas adequately.

359 Rice stitch ☆
also known as **cross corners cross stitch** *and* **William and Mary stitch**
Rice stitch is used on mono or Penelope canvas and has a rather dense texture. It covers the canvas ground well and can be used for small areas and for backgrounds. It can be worked in two colors or two thicknesses of thread. Work the large crosses first and then stitch the corner diagonals with a second thread. If using two thicknesses of thread, use a thick thread for the large crosses and a thinner one for the corner stitches. Rice stitch looks very effective when stitched with a combination of tapestry or Persian yarn with pearl cotton for the corner stitches. Interesting shaded effects can be achieved by working an area of large crosses in one color and varying the colors of the second thread.

360 Reversed cross stitch ☆
Reversed cross stitch is a composite canvas stitch worked on mono canvas, usually in two colors. It is a filling stitch worked in three journeys, which can be shaded by choosing graduating colors for the last journey. It has a dense, closely worked texture and is equally useful for filling any size of shape or for backgrounds. Reversed cross stitch is a combination of ordinary cross stitch *(see page 14)* and upright cross stitch *(see page 137)* worked in two journeys. These stitches are then repeated in reverse sequence on the third journey and worked over the existing crosses. On the third journey, the stitching is usually completed with a contrasting, finer thread, perhaps metallic. The underneath stitches can be worked in any type of embroidery thread, as long as it is compatible with the gauge of canvas chosen.

361 Ridge stitch ☆
Ridge stitch is a canvas stitch used on mono canvas. It makes a distinctive vertically ridged pattern and is used for filling shapes of any size and for background areas. It is most attractive when worked in a fairly heavy wool thread, such as tapestry or Persian yarn, as these threads accentuate the ridged appearance of the stitch. This stitch is worked vertically in rows from the top of the area to be covered, beginning at the left-hand side. It consists of an oblique cross stitch worked over four vertical canvas threads. Each vertical row overlaps the preceding row by one canvas thread so that the rows interlock. Ridge stitch can be striped by using two colors in alternate rows.

362 Horizontal fishbone stitch ☆
Horizontal fishbone stitch is a canvas stitch used on Penelope canvas. It is a variation of fishbone stitch no. 2 *(see page 137)* and forms a strong diagonal pattern. The stitches are worked in diagonal rows from the bottom left to the top right of the canvas and the stitches are all set horizontally. Any type of embroidery thread can be used but care should be taken to match the weight of the thread to the gauge of the canvas to make sure that the canvas is completely covered by the stitching.

363 Upright rice stitch ☆
Upright rice stitch is used on mono and Penelope canvas. It is a simply worked variation of ordinary rice stitch *(see above)* and makes a pattern of diamonds on the surface. It is worked exactly like rice stitch but the foundation stitch is an upright cross stitch *(see page 137)* worked over four vertical and four horizontal threads of the canvas. The corners are then crossed by short vertical and horizontal straight stitches over two canvas threads. Any type of embroidery thread can be used but care should be taken to match the weight of the thread to the gauge of the canvas to make sure that the canvas is completely covered by the stitching. Upright rice stitch can be attractively shaded by varying the colors of the short crossing stitches.

364 *Dutch stitch* ☆
also known as Dutch cross stitch
Dutch stitch is a canvas stitch used on mono canvas. It is used for filling large shapes and for background areas, and makes a raised pattern of crosses. It is worked in two journeys and a contrasting thread can be used for the vertical stitches worked on the second journey. This stitch looks very attractive when tapestry or Persian yarn is used for the first set of stitches and a stranded floss or silk thread is used for the overstitching. The area is first covered by oblong cross stitches *(see page 133)* worked horizontally over four vertical and two horizontal canvas threads. The crosses fit neatly into each other and are arranged as shown. A second journey is then worked to overstitch the crosses with vertical straight stitches over four horizontal canvas threads.

365 *Plaited stitch* ☆
see also herringbone stitch
Plaited stitch is used on Penelope canvas. It makes an attractive, ridged surface and is used for filling shapes and backgrounds. It consists of overlapping vertical rows of top-heavy crosses, and the method of working is very similar to that of canvas fern stitch *(see page 132)*. In that stitch the vertical rows are set side by side but in plaited stitch they overlap; each row overlaps the previous row by one vertical double thread of canvas. A soft wool thread, such as tapestry or Persian yarn, looks best with this stitch and gives good canvas coverage.

366 *Fishbone stitch no. 2* ☆
Unlike fishbone stitch no.1 *(see page 80)*, which is only worked on fabric, fishbone stitch no. 2 is used on Penelope canvas for filling large areas and for backgrounds. It makes an attractive chevron pattern and can be worked in more than one color. It consists of vertical rows of diagonal straight stitches each crossed at the end by a shorter stitch, and is worked alternately up and down over the area. The slant of the diagonal stitches alternates on each row to form the chevrons. Any type of embroidery thread can be used for this stitch but care should be taken to match the weight of the thread to the gauge of the canvas to ensure that the canvas is completely covered by the stitching.

Fishbone stitch makes an attractive pattern when worked in alternate rows with tent stitch *(see page 121)*. When worked like this, the long diagonal stitches of the fishbone rows should all point in the same direction.

367 *Diagonal fishbone stitch* ☆
also known as stepped fishbone stitch
Diagonal fishbone stitch is a canvas stitch used on Penelope canvas. It is a variation of fishbone stitch no. 2 *(see above)* and any type of embroidery thread can be used but care should be taken to match the weight of the thread to the gauge of the canvas to make sure that the canvas is completely covered by the stitching. The stitches are identical to those of fishbone stitch no. 2 but the arrangement of them on the canvas is different and they make a strongly diagonal pattern on the surface. The stitches are worked in diagonal rows with the stitches set horizontally or vertically in alternate rows. The rows run from the bottom left to the top right of the canvas. Diagonal fishbone stitch makes a good background stitch as it is fairly quick and easy to work.

368 *Upright cross stitch* ☆
also known as straight cross stitch
Upright cross stitch is a canvas stitch used on Penelope canvas. The stitch makes a neat, crunchy texture on the surface and it is useful for filling small areas because of the small scale of the stitches. Each stitch is worked over two vertical and two horizontal double threads of the canvas; it is worked diagonally in two journeys, from the bottom right-hand corner to the top left-hand corner of the canvas, and then back again. The vertical stitches are worked first and then crossed by horizontal stitches of the same length. Any type of embroidery thread can be used but care should be taken to match the weight of the thread to the gauge of the canvas to make sure that the canvas is completely covered by the stitching.

369 *Triple rice stitch* ☆☆
and multiple rice stitch
Triple rice stitch is used on mono and Penelope canvas. As the name implies, this stitch is a complex variation of ordinary rice stitch *(see page 136)* and gives a heavier effect. It can be worked in two contrasting colors but looks equally attractive when worked in one. Any type of embroidery thread can be used with this stitch, provided that it is compatible with the gauge of the canvas but a lustrous thread, such as stranded floss, enhances the light and shade effect created by the stitch. Each unit consists of six vertical and six horizontal canvas threads, and each corner is overstitched by three graduated diagonal stitches.

The ordinary cross stitch *(see page 14)* can be made larger, with more diagonal stitches crossing the corners; it is then known as multiple rice stitch. This can be given a pretty striped pattern by working the alternate diagonal stitches in a contrasting color of thread.

357/1 **Leviathan stitch** ☆

358 **Crossed Gobelin stitch** ☆

361 **Ridge stitch** ☆

357/2 **Leviathan stitch** ☆

359 **Rice stitch** ☆

362 **Horizontal fishbone stitch** ☆

357/3 **Leviathan stitch** ☆

360 **Reversed cross stitch** ☆

363 **Upright rice stitch** ☆

364 **Dutch stitch** ☆

366/1 **Fishbone stitch no. 2** ☆

367 **Diagonal fishbone stitch** ☆

365/1 **Plaited stitch** ☆

366/2 **Fishbone stitch no. 2** ☆

368 **Upright cross stitch** ☆

365/2 **Plaited stitch** ☆

366/3 **Fishbone stitch no. 2** ☆

369 **Triple rice stitch and multiple rice stitch** ☆ ☆

370 Chained cross stitch   ☆ ☆

Chained cross stitch is a composite canvas stitch used on mono or Penelope canvas. It is a small stitch worked in rows to make a neat, regular texture and is used for filling shapes or background areas. An extremely hard-wearing stitch, it is very suitable for covering chair seats and footstools, provided that a durable thread has been used. It is straightforward to work and covers a square of four vertical and four horizontal canvas threads. A cross stitch *(see page 14)* is worked across this square, which is then overstitched horizontally with a twisted chain stitch *(see page 21)*. The loop of the twisted chain stitch is anchored by a tiny diagonal stitch and the rows are worked from left to right of the area to be filled. Any type of embroidery thread is suitable for chained cross stitch, but care should be taken to match the weight of the thread to the gauge of the canvas to ensure that the canvas is completely covered by the stitching.

371 Diagonal cross stitch   ☆ ☆

Diagonal cross stitch is a canvas stitch used for filling large shapes and background areas on mono canvas. It is relatively quick to work and covers the canvas well. Worked upward in diagonal rows from the bottom right-hand corner to the top left-hand corner of the area to be filled, it can be stitched in two or more colors to give a pretty, diagonally striped pattern. Each row consists of upright cross stitches *(see page 137)* worked over four vertical and four horizontal canvas threads and separated by diagonal straight stitches. Any type of embroidery thread can be used with diagonal cross stitch, but care should be taken to match the weight of the thread to the gauge of the canvas to ensure that the canvas is completely covered by the stitching. Diagonal cross stitch can also be used to fill shapes on an even-weave fabric.

372 Italian cross stitch   ☆ ☆
also known as **two-sided Italian cross stitch, arrowhead cross stitch** *and* Italian stitch

Italian cross stitch is primarily a canvas stitch used on mono or Penelope canvas. It gives a dense texture and can also be used on even-weave fabrics if the thread is fairly fine. When this stitch is worked on a very loosely woven, even-weave fabric, the stitches can be pulled together tightly to produce an open-work effect. It consists of a cross stitch *(see page 14)* which covers a square of three vertical and three horizontal canvas or fabric threads, and four straight stitches arranged in a square around the cross stitch. Any type of fine embroidery thread can be used on an even-weave fabric but care should be taken, when using Italian cross stitch on canvas, to select a thread that will allow the stitching to cover the canvas completely.

373 Long-armed cross stitch ☆☆
also known as long-legged cross stitch, plaited slav stitch, Portuguese stitch and twist stitch

Long-armed cross stitch is a canvas stitch used primarily on mono and Penelope canvas, although it can also be worked successfully on even-weave fabrics. It can be used both as a border and as a textured filling when it has a pretty, plaited appearance. It is worked in rows from left to right and consists of long diagonal stitches crossed by short diagonal stitches; the long stitches are worked over twice the number of threads as the short stitches. Long-armed cross stitch is straightforward to work and looks equally effective on fabric or canvas. Any type of embroidery thread can be used with this stitch, provided that the weight of the thread is compatible with the fabric or canvas.

374 Woven cross stitch ☆☆
also known as plaited cross stitch

Woven cross stitch is a canvas stitch used on mono and Penelope canvas. This stitch forms square blocks that have a textured, woven appearance. It is used for large areas and backgrounds where a geometric stitch is needed. It can be worked in two contrasting or harmonizing colors and the blocks arranged to make a chessboard pattern; another color can be introduced to frame the blocks with a border of backstitch *(see page 14).* The blocks consist of a large ordinary cross stitch *(see page 14)* worked over four vertical and four horizontal canvas threads and overstitched by four diagonal straight stitches. These diagonal stitches are woven over and under each other as they are worked, and the sequence of stitches should be followed carefully. Any type of embroidery thread can be used with this stitch, but a soft wool thread, such as tapestry or Persian yarn, will accentuate the woven appearance more than a cotton thread.

375 Double cross ☆☆

Double cross is a composite canvas stitch used on mono canvas. It makes a heavy, squared pattern of raised blocks, which can be worked in two colors to make a chessboard pattern. Careful choice of thread and gauge of canvas is important, as this stitch looks its best when worked on quite a small scale; otherwise the pattern can be rather dominant. The blocks cover a square of seven canvas threads and each block is worked in two stages. The square is first crossed by two horizontal and two vertical straight stitches to make an upright cross figure. A second cross, made up of four diagonal straight stitches, is then worked: two run from top right to bottom left and two in the opposite direction. To complete the stitch, a tiny upright cross stitch *(see page 137)* is worked over two vertical and two horizontal canvas threads, where the corners of the blocks meet. Once completed, the blocks can be framed by vertical and horizontal straight stitches.

370/1 *Chained cross stitch* ☆☆

370/4 *Chained cross stitch* ☆☆

371/3 *Diagonal cross stitch* ☆☆

370/2 *Chained cross stitch* ☆☆

371/1 *Diagonal cross stitch* ☆☆

372/1 *Italian cross stitch* ☆☆

370/3 *Chained cross stitch* ☆☆

371/2 *Diagonal cross stitch* ☆☆

372/2 *Italian cross stitch* ☆☆

372/3 Italian cross stitch ☆ ☆

373/2 Long-armed cross stitch ☆ ☆

375/1 Double cross ☆ ☆

372/4 Italian cross stitch ☆ ☆

374/1 Woven cross stitch ☆ ☆

375/2 Double cross ☆ ☆

373/1 Long-armed cross stitch ☆ ☆

374/2 Woven cross stitch ☆ ☆

375/3 Double cross ☆ ☆

376 Plaited Algerian stitch ☆ ☆

Plaited Algerian stitch is used on Penelope canvas and is worked in a similar way to closed herringbone stitch *(see page 60)*, forming neat channels of backstitch on the reverse of the canvas. On the surface, this stitch closely resembles plait stitch *(see below)* but its use of working thread is more economical. Plaited Algerian stitch is most effective when worked on a small-gauge canvas with a smooth thread, such as pearl cotton. It gives a dense, plaited texture and is used for working small areas in one color.

377 Greek stitch ☆ ☆

also known as Greek cross stitch

Greek cross stitch is a canvas stitch used on mono and Penelope canvas. It should always be worked in a fairly thick thread, such as tapestry or Persian yarn. Used for filling large shapes and background areas, it makes a raised, plaited pattern arranged in horizontal bands. It is worked rather like herringbone stitch *(see page 8)* but the crosses are spaced asymmetrically and are usually two double canvas threads tall. It is worked in horizontal rows with the crosses slanting in the opposite direction on every alternate row.

378 Montenegrin stitch ☆ ☆

also known as Montenegrin cross stitch and two-sided Montenegrin cross stitch

Montenegrin stitch is a canvas stitch used on mono or Penelope canvas. Similar in appearance to long-armed cross stitch *(see page 141)* and worked in a similar way, it has additional vertical bars. It is quick to work and can be used for filling large shapes and backgrounds; use a heavy thread so that the canvas is completely covered.

Work Montenegrin stitch upward in horizontal rows, beginning each row at the left-hand side of the area to be filled. First make an irregular cross, in which the longest stitch is twice the length of the shortest stitch, and then make a vertical stitch. When worked in the correct sequence, this stitch is reversible, as the back builds up a pattern of ordinary cross stitches *(see page 14)*, alternating with vertical stitches. Montenegrin stitch can also be worked on an even-weave fabric, provided that a fairly fine thread is used.

379 Plait stitch ☆ ☆

also known as Spanish stitch

Plait stitch is a canvas stitch used on Penelope canvas. It makes a dense, slightly raised and plaited surface, which is rather similar in appearance to plaited Agerian stitch *(see above)* but the method of working is different. This stitch should be worked in a fairly heavy thread, such as tapestry or Persian yarn, to accentuate the raised surface and to cover the double threads of the canvas adequately. It can be used for outlines or for filling large areas and backgrounds, and it is quick and easy to work.

The horizontal rows are worked from left to right over two horizontal double threads of the canvas. A series of irregular cross stitches are made; the needle must always be inserted vertically through the canvas. Every row should begin at the left of the area to be covered and the second and subsequent rows should be worked directly underneath the preceding rows.

380 Rhodes stitch ☆ ☆

Rhodes stitch is a canvas stitch used on mono canvas. The stitch makes a pattern of raised square blocks and is used for large areas and backgrounds. It can be worked over different sizes of square but is usually worked over six canvas threads. Any type of embroidery thread can be used but care should be taken to match the weight of the thread to the gauge of the canvas to make sure that the canvas is completely covered by the stitching.

Each block consists of straight stitches worked across the square, following each other in a counter-clockwise direction, so that they all cross over the same central point. Begin each square by working the first stitch from the bottom left-hand corner to the top right-hand corner and fill every hole around the square. After the block has been covered, work a short vertical stitch in the center over two horizontal threads. This central stitch should be omitted if the stitch is worked over an odd number of threads. When a Rhodes stitch is worked very large, perhaps over ten canvas threads, a neater way of tying it down is to work a straight stitch over each corner, from the mid-point of one side of the square to the mid-point of an adjacent side. The blocks are arranged in horizontal rows, and can be worked in two contrasting colors to give a chessboard effect.

381 Half Rhodes stitch ☆ ☆

Half Rhodes stitch is a canvas stitch used on mono canvas. It makes an attractive textured surface, which is used for filling large shapes and background areas; it is a variation of Rhodes stitch *(see above)*. This stitch is worked in diagonal rows from the top left to the bottom right of the area to be covered, and the stitches on each row interlock with those on the preceding row. Each stitch consists of a half-worked Rhodes stitch, worked over six vertical and six horizontal canvas threads. Form the first stitch in the same way as Rhodes stitch and continue around in a counter-clockwise direction until all the holes at the top and bottom of the square are filled. Any type of embroidery thread can be used, but care should be taken to match the weight of the thread to the gauge of the canvas to make sure the canvas is completely covered by the stitiching.

Half Rhodes stitch can also be worked in horizontal rows with the edges of the stitches touching. A series of diamond shapes of canvas are left showing through and these are filled in with a matching thread, using tent stitch *(see page 121)*.

382 *Plaited Rhodes stitch* ☆ ☆
Plaited Rhodes stitch is a canvas stitch used on mono canvas. It makes an attractive plaited surface and is a variation of half Rhodes stitch *(see page 144)*, which is used for filling shapes of any size and for backgrounds. The stitches are worked in horizontal rows and each row interlocks with the preceding row. The direction of the stitches changes on alternate rows from counter-clockwise to clockwise and the size of each plaited Rhodes stitch is quite small, covering four vertical and four horizontal canvas threads. Any type of embroidery thread can be used with this stitch, provided it is compatible with the gauge of the canvas, but a lustrous thread, such as stranded cotton or silk floss, shows it off to better advantage than a hairy woolen thread.

383 *Captive rice stitch* ☆ ☆
Captive rice stitch is a canvas stitch used on mono or Penelope canvas. A variation of ordinary rice stitch *(see page 136)*, it makes a strongly textured geometric pattern and is used for large areas and backgrounds. Any type of embroidery thread can be used, but care should be taken to match the weight of the thread to the gauge of the canvas to make sure that the canvas is completely covered by the stitching. The stitch consists of a rice stitch surrounded by groups of straight stitches to make a framed block. The second and third straight stitches are worked into the same holes, making a raised bar, and they cover six canvas threads. The blocks are arranged side by side, and a small area is left where the corners of four blocks meet. This can remain unworked, or a tiny ordinary cross stitch *(see page 14)* can be worked to fill it. Captive rice stitch looks very effective when the framing straight stitches are worked in a thread of contrasting color to that of the rice stitch.

384 *Star stitch* ☆ ☆
see also *Algerian eye stitch*
Star stitch is a canvas stitch used on mono canvas. It makes an attractively textured pattern of stars and can be used to fill a shape of any size and for background areas.

Work a grid of large, upright cross stitches *(see page 137)* over six vertical and six horizontal canvas threads to cover the whole shape. They should be worked in horizontal rows and the four adjoining arms of the crosses should share the same holes in the canvas. Next, work a small cross stitch *(see page 14)* over two canvas threads over the upright crosses on every other horizontal row. Then overstitch the upright crosses on the remaining rows with a larger cross stitch worked over four canvas threads. Any type of embroidery thread can be used but care should be taken to match the weight of the thread to the gauge of the canvas to make sure that the canvas is completely covered by the stitching. The cross stitches can be worked in a contrasting color or weight of thread.

385 *Square herringbone stitch* ☆ ☆
also known as *multiplait*
Square herringbone stitch is a canvas stitch used on mono canvas. It makes a large, bold, dramatic pattern, which can be rather dominant, and is used for background areas. The stitch makes a plaited diamond shape, which can be altered in size by increasing or decreasing the number of rows worked. It consists of a central ordinary cross stitch *(see page 14)* enclosed by rows of herringbone stitch *(see page 8)*. The diamond shapes are worked in horizontal rows, so that the rows interlock. The gaps between the edges of the diamond shapes are filled by two straight stitches of commensurate lengths. A soft wool thread, such as tapestry or Persian yarn, is the most suitable for this stitch.

376/1 **Plaited Algerian stitch** ☆ ☆

377/1 **Greek stitch** ☆ ☆

378/2 **Montenegrin stitch** ☆ ☆

376/2 **Plaited Algerian stitch** ☆ ☆

377/2 **Greek stitch** ☆ ☆

378/3 **Montenegrin stitch** ☆ ☆

376/3 **Plaited Algerian stitch** ☆ ☆

378/1 **Montenegrin stitch** ☆ ☆

379/1 **Plait stitch** ☆ ☆

379/2 **Plait stitch** ☆ ☆

381/1 **Half Rhodes stitch** ☆ ☆

383 **Captive rice stitch** ☆ ☆

379/3 **Plait stitch** ☆ ☆

381/2 **Half Rhodes stitch** ☆ ☆

384 **Star stitch** ☆ ☆

380 **Rhodes stitch** ☆ ☆

382 **Plaited Rhodes stitch** ☆ ☆

385 **Square herringbone stitch** ☆ ☆

386 *Velvet stitch* ☆ ☆

also known as rug stitch, tassel stitch, raised stitch, Astrakhan stitch, plush stitch and Berlin plush stitch

Velvet stitch resembles the pile of a carpet and is worked only on Penelope canvas. It became very popular during the Berlin woolwork craze in Europe and America during the middle to late nineteenth century. It was used to give a three-dimensional quality to animals, birds and flowers, against a flat cross stitch background. When working velvet stitch, use one strand of a thick, soft yarn or several strands of a fine yarn. Cut and trim the loops to length after the stitching has been completed. If the stitches are worked very close together on the canvas and a thick yarn is used, the resulting pile will be dense enough to be sculptured with a sharp pair of scissors.

387 *Waffle stitch* ☆ ☆ ☆

also known as Norwich stitch

Waffle stitch is a large canvas stitch used on mono canvas. It makes a pattern of square blocks with superimposed raised diamonds, and is used to fill large shapes and background areas. The blocks can be worked in various sizes, but the squares must contain an odd number of canvas threads. The photograph shows a waffle stitch worked over a square of nine threads: eighteen diagonal straight stitches are worked across the square, following the sequence shown. The second and subsequent straight stitches are worked over each preceding stitch until seventeen have been completed. The eighteenth stitch is taken under the last stitch that it crosses, rather than over it. Any type of embroidery thread can be used with waffle stitch, providing that the weight of the thread is compatible with the gauge of the canvas selected.

388 *Octagonal Rhodes stitch* ☆ ☆ ☆

Octagonal Rhodes stitch is a canvas stitch used on mono canvas. A variation of Rhodes stitch *(see page 144)*, it makes a very raised surface of octagonal blocks, and the spaces in between are filled by individual Rhodes stitches; it is used for filling large areas and for backgrounds. It is worked in the same way as Rhodes stitch, with the stitches following each other in a counter-clockwise direction, so that they all cross over the same central point, but the outline shape followed is an octagon rather than a square. Follow the sequence of stitches carefully and arrange the octagons so that they touch at the vertical and horizontal edges. The remaining squares of canvas should be covered with an ordinary Rhodes stitch in a matching thread. Care should be taken when deciding where to use this stitch, as the pattern can be very dominant and may swamp a smaller, more delicate stitch. Any type of embroidery thread can be used, but care should be taken to match the weight of the thread to the gauge of the canvas to make sure that the canvas is completely covered by the stitching.

389 *Criss-cross stitch* ☆ ☆ ☆

Criss-cross stitch is a large-scale canvas stitch used on mono canvas. A complicated stitch to work, it gives a dense, unusual texture. It is used over large areas or backgrounds, as it covers the canvas well. Any type of embroidery thread can be used, but care should be taken when matching the weight of the thread to the gauge of the canvas selected. As with other complex canvas stitches, a small sample should be worked to test the compatibility of the thread and canvas: if the thread is too fine, the canvas ground will show through; if it is too heavy, the resulting stitch will be too bulky and distorted to give a pleasing appearance.

Criss-cross stitch consists of five slanting stitches radiating from the bottom left-hand corner and crossed by four slanting stitches from the bottom right-hand corner. They are worked alternately, and make a woven surface. Follow the sequence shown carefully, as accuracy is crucial to the formation of the stitch. The completed stitches are arranged in horizontal rows, and are always worked from left to right of the area to be covered.

390 *Plaited double cross* ☆ ☆ ☆

Plaited double cross stitch is a composite canvas stitch and is used on mono canvas. It is a more complex version of double cross stitch *(see page 141)* and has the same raised square pattern but with a woven effect. It is worked in a similar way: first the blocks are made in two stages, and then the small upright crosses are worked. The difference lies in the arrangement of the straight stitches that make the square blocks as they are plaited over and under each other. The sequence of stitches shown should be followed very carefully. As with double cross, choice of thread and gauge of canvas is important, as the pattern can be rather dominant when worked on a large scale.

391 *Double leviathan stitch* ☆ ☆ ☆

Double leviathan stitch is a canvas stitch used on mono or Penelope canvas. It is a more complex variation of leviathan stitch *(see page 136)* and makes a larger, more raised pattern of square blocks. These blocks can be worked in two colors to make a chessboard pattern. A large cross stitch *(see page 14)* worked over four canvas threads is stitched first, followed by further crossing stitches, and, finally, a large upright cross stitch *(see page 137)*. Follow the sequence of stitches carefully. The raised, almost crunchy surface of double leviathan stitch looks best when worked in a fairly thick thread, such as tapestry or Persian yarn.

386/1 *Velvet stitch* ☆ ☆

386/4 *Velvet stitch* ☆ ☆

389/1 *Criss-cross stitch* ☆ ☆ ☆

386/2 *Velvet stitch* ☆ ☆

387 *Waffle stitch* ☆ ☆ ☆

389/2 *Criss-cross stitch* ☆ ☆ ☆

386/3 *Velvet stitch* ☆ ☆

388 *Octagonal Rhodes stitch* ☆ ☆ ☆

390/1 *Plaited double cross* ☆ ☆ ☆

390/2 *Plaited double cross* ☆ ☆ ☆

391/1 *Double leviathan stitch* ☆ ☆ ☆

391/4 *Double leviathan stitch* ☆ ☆ ☆

390/3 *Plaited double cross* ☆ ☆ ☆

391/2 *Double leviathan stitch* ☆ ☆ ☆

391/5 *Double leviathan stitch* ☆ ☆ ☆

390/4 *Plaited double cross* ☆ ☆ ☆

391/3 *Double leviathan stitch* ☆ ☆ ☆

391/6 *Double leviathan stitch* ☆ ☆ ☆

Composite stitches

392 Balcony stitch ☆
Balcony stitch is a canvas stitch that is very quick to work over a large area. It is not suitable for pillows or upholstery, as the stitches are quite long and will snag and catch easily. Mono canvas should be used, and consideration should be given to the gauge of canvas and the weight of thread used in order to cover the canvas ground successfully. If the crossing threads are too long, they will sag and spoil the geometric basketweave appearance of the stitch. Work the five vertical straight stitches first, and then cross them with five horizontal stitches of the same length. Work these groups of stitches diagonally across the area to be covered and fit them together. Balcony stitch can also be used to shade an area if graduated tones of thread are chosen for the horizontal crossing stitches.

393 Chained stitch ☆
Chained stitch is a canvas stitch used on mono canvas. It can also be worked on an even-weave fabric, where the threads can be counted to keep the stitches even. On canvas, it is used for filling shapes and backgrounds since it creates an unusual texture and is quite quick to work. It is similar to cross stitch *(see page 14)* except that the second diagonal is made by a chain loop instead of a straight stitch. Each stitch is worked over an area two canvas threads wide and two threads deep. Care should be taken when matching the weight of the thread to the gauge of the canvas to ensure that the canvas will be completely covered by the stitch.

394 Checker stitch ☆
Checker stitch is a composite canvas stitch used on mono canvas. When worked in one color, the stitch has the look of a woven or brocaded fabric, enhanced by the use of a light-catching flat thread, such as stranded floss or silk. It looks equally attractive worked in two shades or two contrasting colors of tapestry, Persian or crewel yarn, to make a checkered pattern. It is often used for backgrounds when a geometric pattern is needed. Relatively quick to

work, it covers the canvas well. The pattern is arranged in squares, each square covering an area of four vertical and four horizontal canvas threads. Squares of sixteen tent stitches *(see page 121)* alternate with squares composed of seven diagonal straight stitches of graduating lengths. These squares should be worked in diagonal rows from top left to bottom right of the area to be filled.

395 English stitch ☆
English stitch is a modern stitch used on mono canvas. It makes a bold, textured surface and is most effective when worked in tapestry or Persian yarn. It is used for filling large shapes and backgrounds since it covers the canvas well. Work the stitch in rectangular blocks in either horizontal or vertical rows. Each block should cover an area of six vertical and four horizontal canvas threads. First cover the block with five vertical straight stitches. Then overstitch the corners of the block with two diagonal straight stitches of different lengths. The size of the blocks can be altered, if required, but the threads in the block must always be of an even number.

396 Foliage stitch ☆
Foliage stitch is a canvas stitch worked on mono canvas. Since it is relatively quick to work and covers the canvas well, it is used for filling shapes of any size and for backgrounds. It makes a regular geometric pattern of square blocks and each block looks rather like a diagonal leaf. Each block is worked over four canvas threads, and the blocks are repeated in horizontal rows. Each block consists of three vertical and three horizontal straight stitches of graduating lengths, divided by a long diagonal stitch worked over the square from the bottom left-hand corner to the top right-hand corner. Foliage stitch can be worked in any type of embroidery thread, provided that it is compatible with the gauge of the canvas, but it probably looks most attractive when worked with a soft wool thread, such as Persian yarn.

397 Cushion stitch ☆
see also Florentine stitch and tent stitch
Cushion stitch is a composite canvas stitch used on mono canvas. It is worked in two stages with the same thread and has the appearance of a woven or brocaded fabric. It has a neat, geometric pattern and is used for filling background areas. It is relatively quick and simple to work and any type of thread can be used, provided that it is compatible with the gauge of the canvas. However, this stitch will look more striking if it is worked in a lustrous thread, such as stranded floss.

On the first journey, small squares of graduated diagonal stitches are worked over three vertical and three horizontal canvas threads; the stitches should all fall in the same direction. A gap of one canvas thread separates each square and each row of squares. The squares are then framed by a border of tent stitch *(see page 121)* worked in the same thread and with the stitches facing in the same direction. Strictly speaking, the name ''cushion'' refers only to the square blocks, which can be worked without the border of tent stitch.

398 Crossed corners cushion stitch ☆
Crossed corners cushion stitch is a geometric canvas stitch used on mono canvas. It is a very effective stitch for covering backgrounds as it is quick to work and covers the canvas well. The pattern consists of square blocks, which can be worked to any size, arranged in fours so that a square motif is formed. Each block is filled by graduated diagonal straight stitches, running in one direction. Half the square is then overstitched in the opposite direction. Any type of embroidery thread can be used, but care should be taken to match the weight of the thread to the gauge of the canvas to ensure that the canvas is completely covered by the stitching. However, this stitch looks most effective when a lustrous thread, such as stranded floss, is used to enhance the light and shade effect made by the arrangement of the stitches.

399 Beetle stitch and barred beetle stitch ☆

Beetle stitch is a canvas stitch best worked on mono canvas and with a thick thread, such as tapestry or Persian yarn. It forms slightly padded oval shapes, hence its name, and is used for filling backgrounds. It consists of a padding layer of three vertical straight stitches worked in the center three spaces of the oval; and eight horizontal stitches varying in length worked over the padding. If any canvas threads are still visible after the beetle shapes have been worked, the gaps can be filled in with tent stitch (see page 121), or the ovals can be outlined with back-stitch (see page 14), using the same thread.

Barred beetle stitch forms the same oval shapes, but the horizontal straight stitches are worked before the vertical ones. The three vertical stitches are then added, with the base of each stitch sharing the same central hole in the canvas; these three stitches make a V-shaped bar across the beetle shape. As with beetle stitch, gaps between the shapes can be filled with either tent stitch or backstitch.

400 Flower stitch ☆

Flower stitch is a canvas stitch used on mono or Penelope canvas. It has a similar appearance to floral stitch (see below) but the regular pattern created by flower stitch is slightly larger. It can be used to fill any size of shape or background area, and looks most effective when worked in a soft wool thread, such as tapestry or Persian yarn. The pattern is worked in two horizontal rows, which alternate as they fill the area. The first row consists of blocks of two horizontal straight stitches worked over four vertical canvas threads, and alternating with a small cross stitch (see page 14) worked over one thread. The second row consists of blocks of two vertical straight stitches worked over four horizontal canvas threads and alternating with a larger cross stitch worked over two threads and surrounded by four straight stitches, each worked over two threads.

401 Floral stitch ☆

Floral stitch is a composite canvas stitch used on mono or Penelope canvas. It makes an attractive regular pattern, which can be used to fill any size of shape or background area. Any type of thread can be used for this stitch, provided that it is compatible with the gauge of the canvas selected, but a soft wool thread, such as tapestry or Persian yarn, is particularly suitable. The pattern is formed by two horizontal rows of stitching, which are worked alternately to cover the shape. The first row consists of blocks of three horizontal straight stitches worked over three vertical canvas threads, alternating with cross stitch (see page 14) worked over three threads. The second row consists of blocks of three vertical straight stitches worked over three horizontal canvas threads alternating with a smaller cross stitch worked over two threads. The crosses and the blocks of straight stitches alternate.

402 Chessboard stitch ☆

Chessboard stitch is a canvas stitch used on mono canvas. It gives a ridged effect overstitched by crosses, and provides a quick and easy way to fill large areas of canvas. Any type of embroidery thread is suitable for this stitch, provided that it is matched to the gauge of canvas being used. It is worked in alternate squares: one kind of square is worked over the canvas first, then the spaces are filled in by the second kind of square. The first squares consist of four vertical straight stitches worked in a group over four horizontal threads of the canvas. This group of stitches is then overstitched by a large cross stitch (see page 14), extending diagonally across the group; the center of the cross stitch is anchored by a small, horizontal straight stitch. The spaces left uncovered on the canvas after the first set of squares have been completed are filled in by groups of four vertical straight stitches. Although usually worked in monochrome, chessboard stitch can look very effective if two contrasting colors or two shades of the same color are used.

403 French stitch ☆
also known as tied Renaissance stitch

French stitch is a canvas stitch worked on Penelope canvas. It makes a closely worked, slightly textured surface and is ideal for filling large shapes and backgrounds. It looks most attractive when worked with a soft, thick thread, such as tapestry or Persian yarn, and it covers the canvas well. The stitches are arranged in horizontal rows and worked from right to left and then left to right, alternately. Each stitch consists of two vertical straight stitches worked over four double canvas threads, which are worked in the same holes at the ends. The long stitches are tied down at each side over the double threads by two short horizontal stitches. The two long stitches bow slightly when they are anchored. The stitches on the second row interlock with those on the first, and so on. If preferred, French stitch can also be worked in diagonal rows from the top left to the bottom right of the shape but the finished results are identical.

392 **Balcony stitch** ☆

395/1 **English stitch** ☆

397 **Cushion stitch** ☆

393 **Chained stitch** ☆

395/2 **English stitch** ☆

398/1 **Crossed corners cushion stitch** ☆

394 **Checker stitch** ☆

396 **Foliage stitch** ☆

398/2 **Crossed corners cushion stitch** ☆

399 *Beetle stitch and barred beetle stitch* ☆

402 *Chessboard stitch* ☆

403/3 *French stitch* ☆

400 *Flower stitch* ☆

403/1 *French stitch* ☆

403/4 *French stitch* ☆

401 *Floral stitch* ☆

403/2 *French stitch* ☆

403/5 *French stitch* ☆

404 *Wheat sheaf stitch* ☆

Wheat sheaf stitch is a canvas stitch used on mono canvas for filling a shape of any size. It consists of three vertical straight stitches tied down by a tiny horizontal stitch to make a shape like a sheaf of corn. The sheaves can be worked over four or six horizontal canvas threads; if they are to be worked solidly over the canvas, the corners of the sheaves should touch each other. This stitch looks very attractive if the sheaves are spaced two or three canvas threads apart over the entire shape. The unworked canvas can then be covered by tent stitch *(see page 121)* worked in a matching thread. The sheaves can also be worked with a half drop. Any type of embroidery thread can be used to work wheat sheaf stitch, provided that the weight of the thread is compatible with the gauge of the canvas selected.

405 *Rapid stitch* ☆

Rapid stitch is a canvas stitch used on mono canvas. As its name indicates, rapid stitch is extremely quick to work; it is used for filling shapes of any size and backgrounds. Any type of embroidery thread can be used with this stitch, but care should be taken to match the weight of the thread to the gauge of the canvas to make sure that the canvas is completely covered by the stitching. A soft wool thread, such as tapestry or Persian yarn, gives the best coverage, and is preferable to a firm cotton thread. Rapid stitch makes a textured surface. Each stitch covers an area of four vertical and four horizontal canvas threads. An ordinary cross stitch *(see page 14)* is first made across the square and then four slanting stitches are worked across it with one pair at the right and one at the left. If any canvas is still showing, an extra stitch can be made in the center, running from the top to the bottom of the square, and each square can be framed with backstitch *(see page 14)* to give a more closely worked effect. The backstitch can be worked in a matching or contrasting color, or in a lighter weight of thread than the rest of the stitching.

406 *Quodlibet stitch* ☆

Quodlibet stitch is a canvas stitch used on mono canvas. It is suitable for covering large areas and backgrounds and makes a closely worked surface with a pattern of arrowheads. Any type of embroidery thread can be used, although the gauge of the canvas should be taken into consideration. This stitch will benefit from being worked in a fairly flat thread, such as stranded floss or silk. It is quite easy to work and consists of large, lozenge-shaped units which contain two arrowheads, one pointing upward and one downward. First work a central vertical stitch over twelve horizontal canvas threads. Then make the bottom arrowhead, which consists of four slanting stitches radiating from the same hole. Tie down the long stitch with a short, horizontal stitch before making the top arrowhead in exactly the same way. The lozenges are arranged side by side in horizontal rows, each row interlocking with the preceding one. Quodlibet stitch makes an interesting pattern when alternate rows are worked in a contrasting color.

407 *Seven stitch* ☆

Seven stitch is a canvas stitch used on mono and Penelope canvas. It is very quick to work and is useful for filling large areas and backgrounds. The stitch makes a regular pattern of lightly textured blocks, each one consisting of seven stitches. Four vertical straight stitches are worked first, covering four horizontal canvas threads. These are then covered by three horizontal straight stitches. The blocks are worked in horizontal rows, and two colors can be used to make a chessboard pattern. The two threads left uncovered at the corners of the blocks can have an ordinary cross stitch *(see page 14)* worked over them, or, alternatively, a row of small backstitches *(see page 14)* can be worked to frame each block and cover these threads. Any type of embroidery thread can be used, but care should be taken to match the weight of the thread to the gauge of the canvas to ensure that the canvas is completely covered by the stitching.

408 *Pineapple stitch* ☆

Pineapple stitch is a canvas stitch used on mono canvas. It makes a pattern of textured blocks, which are worked with a half drop, and, as its name indicates, it looks very much like the skin of a pineapple. This stitch is very quick and easy to work and is suitable for covering large shapes and background areas. It can be worked in two colors by using a second thread for the superimposed cross and the tying stitch. Any type of embroidery thread can be used, but care should be taken to match the weight of the thread to the gauge of the canvas to ensure that the canvas will be completely covered by the stitching.

Each block is first covered by four vertical straight stitches worked over four horizontal canvas threads. Work an ordinary cross stitch *(see page 14)* over four threads, making sure that the top diagonal stitch crosses from the bottom right-hand corner to the top left-hand corner. Then tie down the cross in the center by working a short, diagonal stitch over the central vertical thread of the canvas.

409 *Tied stitch* ☆

Tied stitch is a canvas stitch used on mono canvas. It makes a neat pattern of barred rectangular blocks arranged with a half drop. It is very quick and easy to work and is ideal for covering large shapes and background areas rapidly. Each stitch consists of two long, vertical straight stitches worked over six horizontal canvas threads and tied down by a short crossing stitch in the center. The stitch is worked diagonally across the area to be filled, working from the top left to the bottom right. Any type of thread can be used, but care should be taken to match the weight of the thread to the gauge of the canvas to ensure that the canvas is completely covered by the stitching.

410 *Scottish stitch* ☆

Scottish stitch is a canvas stitch worked on mono canvas in two colors of thread. It makes a neat pattern of framed squares and is very similar to cushion stitch *(see page 152)*, except that cushion stitch is worked in only one color. Scottish stitch consists of small blocks of five diagonal straight stitches worked over three vertical and three horizontal canvas threads. Each square is framed by a border of tent stitch *(see page 121)* worked in a contrasting color of thread. The diagonal and tent stitches should always fall in the same direction — from bottom left to top right. Any type of embroidery thread can be used, provided that it is compatible with the gauge of the canvas, but a combination of a lustrous, stranded floss with a wool yarn can look extremely effective.

411 *Roman filling* ☆
Roman filling is a canvas stitch used on mono canvas. It makes an attractive diamond pattern and is used for filling large shapes and backgrounds. An adaptation of a fabric stitch called Roman stitch *(see page 44)* for use on canvas, it can be worked with any type of embroidery thread, provided that it is compatible with the gauge of the canvas selected. However, this stitch is shown off to best advantage when pearl cotton or stranded floss is used, and when it is worked on a small scale. Each diamond shape spans seven vertical and eight horizontal threads of canvas, and they are worked in diagonal rows from the top left to the bottom right of the area to be covered. Seven Roman stitches are worked in the center of each diamond shape. Roman filling can be worked in more than one color to give pretty zig-zag stripes across the entire shape.

412 *Crow's foot stitch* ☆☆
Crow's foot stitch is a canvas stitch used on mono canvas. It makes an attractive filling or background stitch and it is fairly quick to work. It is worked in two journeys; the first journey must cover the whole area before the second journey can begin. On the first journey, groups of straight stitches, radiating from a central hole, are worked over three or four horizontal canvas threads, depending on the size of stitch required. A single vertical straight stitch is worked alternately with the

groups on the same journey. The rows are worked horizontally, from left to right and then back again. After the shape has been covered, rows of backstitch *(see page 14)* are worked over four vertical canvas threads to divide the rows with horizontal lines. The backstitch rows are worked in a matching or contrasting color of thread. Any type of embroidery thread can be used, but care should be taken to match the weight of the thread to the gauge of the canvas to ensure complete canvas coverage.

413 *Fir stitch* ☆☆
also known as **leaf stitch**
Fir stitch is a canvas stitch used on mono canvas. It is a bold stitch used for making large shapes and for background areas and makes a lozenge-shaped pattern, which looks rather like a row of fir trees. It can create a shaded background by using threads in graduated shades of one color. Each lozenge is made up of a central vertical straight stitch worked over six horizontal canvas threads, with five slanting stitches worked at each side. The slanting stitches fan out, beginning five spaces below the vertical stitch and, to complete the lozenge, another central stitch is worked over these spaces. Any type of embroidery thread can be used but care should be taken to match the weight of the thread to the gauge of the canvas to make sure that the canvas is completely covered by the stitching.

414 *Large petal stitch* ☆☆
Large petal stitch is a composite canvas stitch used on mono canvas. It makes large square units which have four petal shapes radiating from a central hole to the corners of the area. This stitch has a heavy, textured appearance and careful consideration should be given before using it, as its dominant pattern might swamp a more delicate canvas stitch if the two were used together. Any type of thread can be used, but a smooth, non-hairy thread is preferable. As with other complex canvas stitches, such as perspective stitch *(see page 161)* and sunburst stitch *(see page 165)*, a small sample

should be worked first to check the compatibility of the weight of the thread to the gauge of the canvas.

Although large petal stitch looks rather complicated at first sight, it is fairly simple to work. Each square unit covers ten vertical and ten horizontal canvas threads. The four petals are made by first working five slanting straight stitches of graduated lengths from each corner of the area into a common hole at the center of the square. The thread is brought back through the canvas under one of the petals to a position one canvas thread away from the central hole. It is then wound around in a spiral, passing under the four petals and making five complete rings around the center, as shown. The outer ring is tied down by four tiny straight stitches to complete the unit. A second, contrasting, thread can be used for the circular threading. The units are worked in horizontal rows, and a framework of backstitch *(see page 14)* can be worked to fill any gaps between them.

415 *Fan stitch* ☆☆
also known as **expanded ray stitch** and **fantail stitch;** see also **ray stitch**
Fan stitch is a canvas stitch used on mono canvas. A pattern of fan shapes is made over the canvas, set alternately on the second and subsequent rows. When a patterned background is needed, fan stitch is a very effective stitch to use. The fan shapes cover an area of ten vertical and five horizontal canvas threads and are made up of fifteen straight stitches of varying lengths, radiating from the same hole. A smaller group of five radiating stitches is worked directly underneath, with the central stitch covering three canvas threads. Below this is added a single straight stitch over two horizontal threads. The photograph shows how the two groups of stitches and the single stitch are arranged. Any type of thread can be used but care should be taken to match the weight of the thread to the gauge of the canvas to ensure that the canvas is completely covered by the stitching.

404/1 Wheat sheaf stitch ☆

406 Quodlibet stitch ☆

409 Tied stitch ☆

404/2 Wheat sheaf stitch ☆

407 Seven stitch ☆

410 Scottish stitch ☆

405 Rapid stitch ☆

408 Pineapple stitch ☆

411/1 Roman filling ☆

411/2 *Roman filling* ☆

413/1 *Fir stitch* ☆ ☆

414/1 *Large petal stitch* ☆ ☆

412/1 *Crow's foot stitch* ☆ ☆

413/2 *Fir stitch* ☆ ☆

414/2 *Large petal stitch* ☆ ☆

412/2 *Crow's foot stitch* ☆ ☆

413/3 *Fir stitch* ☆ ☆

415 *Fan stitch* ☆ ☆

416 *Vault stitch* ☆☆
also known as **fan vaulting**
Vault stitch is a canvas stitch used on mono canvas for filling large shapes and background areas. It makes a regularly textured surface, which is enhanced by the use of a soft wool thread, such as tapestry or Persian yarn. The stitch forms a pattern of alternating vertical and horizontal rectangles, each worked individually. A central straight stitch is worked over eight threads and an oblong cross stitch *(see page 133)* of the same height is superimposed. A shorter, wider oblong cross stitch is worked over the previous stitches to complete the rectangle. Small areas of canvas may be visible between each rectangle at this stage, depending on the weight of the thread being used. These can be filled in with a tent stitch *(see page 121)*, or a tiny ordinary cross stitch *(see page 14)* worked in either a matching thread or a contrasting color or weight.

417 *Brighton stitch* ☆☆
Brighton stitch is a composite canvas stitch used on mono canvas. Normally worked in yarn as a geometric background stitch, it looks effective on small-gauge canvas stitched with pearl cotton or stranded floss. The sheen of these threads accentuates the light and shade effect made when blocks of slanting stitches, in alternate directions, are placed side by side.

The stitch consists of blocks of five slanting stitches worked in rows. The direction of the slant changes on every alternate block and each row of blocks is the mirror image of the row above, thus creating a pattern of diamond shapes. After the blocks have been worked over the desired area, an upright cross stitch *(see page 137)* is worked in the space between each block; it can be the same or a contrasting color.

418 *Tile stitch* ☆☆
Tile stitch is a canvas stitch used on mono canvas. It makes a textured surface with a square pattern, and is used for filling shapes and background areas. Work a cross stitch *(see page 14)* over two canvas threads and then surround it with four straight stitches to make a small block. Frame each block with a border of tent stitch *(see page 121)*, as shown; leave one canvas thread unworked around the blocks. Then fill this space with a smaller frame of tent stitch worked in a slightly finer thread. This second frame can be of a contrasting color to the larger frame. Any type of embroidery thread can be used, but care should be taken to match the weight of the thread to the gauge of the canvas to ensure that the canvas is completely covered by the stitching.

419 *Padded satin stitch* ☆☆
Padded satin stitch is a canvas stitch used on mono canvas for filling large shapes and background areas. It makes a pattern of raised diamond shapes which are padded individually after they have been stitched. Each diamond consists of two triangular shapes, each made up of ten satin stitches *(see page 24)* of varying lengths. The same thread is then brought out of the canvas at the top of the left-hand triangle and threaded under the right-hand triangle and back up under the left to the point where the thread emerged. This thread should pass under the satin stitches only and no canvas threads should be picked up. This process is then repeated until the padding reaches the required height and the thread is taken back through the canvas to the place where it originally emerged. A soft wool thread, such as tapestry or Persian yarn, is preferable for working padded satin stitch.

420 *Houndstooth* ☆☆
Houndstooth is used on mono or Penelope canvas and needs a fairly thick thread, such as tapestry or Persian yarn, to cover the canvas well. It makes a neat square surface that is quite textured and can be used for both large and small areas. The squares can be worked over any number of canvas threads, provided that the weight of the threads matches the size of the stitches. The squares are worked over four canvas threads. A diagonal straight stitch is worked from the bottom left-hand corner to the top right-hand corner of the square. Interlocking loops are then worked, one at each of the remaining two corners, encircling the diagonal stitches. The squares are worked in horizontal rows and are set directly underneath each other. This stitch can be worked in two colors to create a chessboard pattern.

421 *Shell stitch* ☆☆
Shell stitch is a canvas stitch used on mono canvas as a decorative border and is also worked solidly to fill shapes. It is worked in horizontal rows from right to left in two journeys, using a contrasting color or weight of thread for the second journey. On the first journey, groups of four vertical straight stitches worked over six horizontal canvas threads are tied together at the center by a short horizontal stitch worked over two threads to form bundles. On the second journey each bundle of stitches is linked together by a second thread, which is laced through the short, tying stitches. The second thread passes through the canvas only at the beginning and end of each row. The rows of bundles are worked underneath each other and can be divided by rows of backstitch *(see page 14)*. An adaptation of this stitch for use on common- and even-weave fabrics is faggot filling stitch *(see page 80)*.

422 *Arrow stitch* ☆☆

Arrow stitch is a canvas stitch usually worked on mono canvas with tapestry or Persian yarn. Three vertical straight stitches are worked over four threads of the canvas and pulled tightly to one side with a small horizontal stitch. Worked side by side, the stitches form textured rows, which are ideal for filling geometric shapes. If small gaps occur at the edge of the filled shape, cover the exposed canvas threads with tent stitch *(see page 121),* using the same yarn. Arrow stitch can be used to create an attractive background pattern: make a half drop between adjoining groups of stitches and pull them alternately to the left and to the right.

423 *Gate stitch* ☆☆

Gate stitch is a modern canvas stitch used on mono canvas. It makes a regular pattern of textured rectangular blocks worked with a half drop. It can be worked in vertical, horizontal or diagonal rows, depending on preference; in each case the finished effect is the same. It is used for filling large shapes and background areas and looks best when a soft, thick thread, such as tapestry or Persian yarn, is used. Each block covers an area of five vertical and six horizontal canvas threads and is worked in three stages before proceeding to the next block. Four vertical straight stitches are worked first over six horizontal threads; an elongated cross stitch *(see page 14)* is then worked over these stitches. Then, a horizontal straight stitch covering five vertical threads is worked over the cross, two threads from the top or bottom.

Both the blocks with the cross stitch near the top and the blocks with the crossing stitch near the bottom are worked directly underneath each other.

424 *Tudor rose stitch* ☆☆

Tudor rose stitch is a canvas stitch used on mono canvas to fill large shapes and background areas. It makes a large, stylized, floral pattern, which looks extremely attractive when worked in more than one color. The stitch is worked in two stages. Alternate horizontal rows of cross stitch *(see page 14)* and rice stitch *(see page 136)* cover the area first. Each of these stitches occupies a square of four canvas threads, and unworked squares of the same size lie between them. These unworked areas are then filled by five straight stitches of graduating lengths. Any type of embroidery thread can be used, but care should be taken to match the weight of the thread to the gauge of the canvas to make sure that the canvas is completely covered by the stitching.

425 *Bouclé stitch* ☆☆

Bouclé stitch is a square canvas stitch used on mono canvas, and has a tight, knobbly texture reminiscent of bouclé fabric. It can be used either to fill small areas or for backgrounds. It is worked over a small square of canvas and consists of two slanting stitches worked side by side in the same holes, each one anchored by a loop. Work the top left-hand portion of the stitch first, taking care to keep the diagonal stitch taut. Then work the bottom right section in the same way. The anchoring loops should be left quite loose and not tensioned in

the way that the diagonal stitches are, in order to create the knobbly texture. Bouclé stitch can be worked over different numbers of threads on the canvas, depending on the size of the shape to be filled, but care should be taken when matching the weight of the yarn to the size of the stitch; the yarn should cover the canvas threads without being too bulky.

426 *Perspective stitch* ☆☆

Perspective stitch is a canvas stitch used on mono canvas. It makes a bold pattern of three-dimensional boxes and is usually worked in two shades of the same color. The pattern of this stitch can be rather dominant and careful consideration must be given when choosing it as it could swamp a more delicate stitch if placed next to it. However, it can make a very attractive background when the colors used are subdued. It is quite simple to work once the sequence of stitches has been mastered, but follow the sequence shown carefully.

One complete pattern is worked in four stages, and each stage consists of vertical groups of three diagonal straight stitches. Each diagonal stitch is worked over two vertical and two horizontal canvas threads. The slant of the stitches alternates from group to group. Each stage should be worked in alternate colors to give the correct sequence, and the stitches made on stages two and four should overlap the stitches made in the previous stages. Perspective stitch looks equally effective worked with stranded floss on a small-gauge canvas or on a larger scale with a heavier thread, such as Persian yarn.

416/1 *Vault stitch* ☆ ☆

417 *Brighton stitch* ☆ ☆

420/1 *Houndstooth* ☆ ☆

416/2 *Vault stitch* ☆ ☆

418 *Tile stitch* ☆ ☆

420/2 *Houndstooth* ☆ ☆

416/3 *Vault stitch* ☆ ☆

419 *Padded satin stitch* ☆ ☆

420/3 *Houndstooth* ☆ ☆

421 Shell stitch ☆ ☆

424 Tudor rose stitch ☆ ☆

426/2 Perspective stitch ☆ ☆

422 Arrow stitch ☆ ☆

425 Bouclé stitch ☆ ☆

426/3 Perspective stitch ☆ ☆

423 Gate stitch ☆ ☆

426/1 Perspective stitch ☆ ☆

426/4 Perspective stitch ☆ ☆

427 Vee stitch   ☆ ☆
Vee stitch is a canvas stitch used on mono canvas for filling large shapes and background areas. It makes a vertically striped pattern which can be worked in two or more colors; a soft wool thread, such as tapestry or Persian yarn, is needed to give adequate coverage of the canvas. The stripes are worked downward, and each stitch overlaps the stitch immediately preceding it. Each vee stitch is quite large, spanning ten vertical and eight horizontal canvas threads, and overlaps the previous stitch by four horizontal threads. A vertical straight stitch covering four threads is worked in the center and four slanting stitches radiate at each side from the base hole of the vertical stitch.

428 Compact filling stitch   ☆ ☆
Compact filling stitch is a canvas stitch used on mono canvas. As its name suggests, it gives a compact textured finish and is ideal for filling small areas or backgrounds. It is quite quick to work once the spacing of the stitches is mastered, and it covers the canvas well. This stitch looks equally attractive when worked in a wool yarn or a cotton embroidery thread.

The stitch consists of two straight stitches, one vertical and one horizontal, worked over three canvas threads and set at a right angle to each other. Two diagonal stitches are then worked at the bottom right of these stitches. The stitch is usually worked in diagonal rows, from the top left-hand corner to the bottom right-hand corner of the area to be covered.

429 Spring stitch   ☆ ☆
also known as coiled stitch
Spring stitch is a modern canvas stitch used on mono canvas. It makes an attractive pattern of springs or coils over the surface and has a strong diagonal feel; it looks most effective when worked with tapestry or Persian yarn on a compatible gauge of canvas. It is used for filling large areas or backgrounds as it has quite a large pattern; the diagonal effect is lost if it is worked over a small area.

Each stitch covers a long rectangle of three vertical and twelve horizontal canvas threads. A large, oblong cross stitch *(see page 133)* is worked over the rectangle, then seven horizontal straight stitches over three vertical threads are worked over the cross. The rectangles are worked in diagonal rows from the top left to the bottom right of the area to be covered; the second and subsequent rectangles on each row are dropped by three threads. The small oblong cross stitch at each end of the springs is worked on a separate journey after all the rectangles are complete.

430 Broad stem stitch   ☆ ☆
also known as canvas stem stitch
Broad stem stitch is a composite canvas stitch used on Penelope canvas; it is not a variation of the stem stitch used on fabric, despite its name. It makes an attractive ridged surface and can be used as a border to fill a shape of any size or a background area. This stitch is worked in two journeys and consists of two vertical rows of diagonal straight stitches arranged to form "V" shapes. The center of the two

rows is then defined by working a row of backstitch *(see page 14)* down it. Backstitch can also be worked to frame each of the rows. Any type of embroidery thread can be used, but pearl cotton or stranded floss enhances the light and shade effect created by the arrangement of the stitches. Broad stem stitch combines well with canvas fern stitch *(see page 132)* when the two are worked in alternate rows and when two different colors are used.

431 Tweed stitch   ☆ ☆
Tweed stitch is a canvas stitch used on mono and Penelope canvas. It makes a tweedy texture on the surface of the fabric, as its name implies, and is very useful for filling a shape or background of any size. It looks most attractive when worked in a soft wool thread, such as tapestry or Persian yarn, and different colors can be used to accentuate its tweedy appearance.

Cover the area with large upright cross stiches *(see page 137)*, each worked over six vertical and six horizontal canvas threads. Super-impose an ordinary cross stitch *(see page 14)* over two threads at the center of each upright cross and work a tiny ordinary cross stitch at the center of the remaining areas of canvas, alternating the top diagonals. Tweed stitch makes a good covering for chair seats and stools, as it is extremely hard-wearing when worked in a durable thread like tapestry yarn.

432 Scallop stitch   ☆ ☆ ☆
Scallop stitch is a canvas stitch used on mono canvas. It makes a large pattern of scallop shapes on the

surface and is used for filling large areas and backgrounds. Care should be taken when considering using this stitch, as the pattern can be rather dominant and may swamp a more delicate canvas stitch if used near it. The scallops are worked over eight vertical and twelve horizontal canvas threads and consist of sixteen slanting straight stitches, radiating from the base of a long, vertical straight stitch worked in the center. The scallops are worked in horizontal rows across the area to be covered, and the second and subsequent rows interlock with each preceding row. A soft wool thread, such as tapestry or Persian yarn, looks very good with this stitch and gives excellent canvas coverage if it is compatible with the gauge of the canvas.

433 *Eastern stitch* ☆ ☆ ☆
also known as Eastern buttonhole stitch

Eastern stitch is a looped canvas stitch used on mono canvas. It has a complex lacy appearance and looks most effective when worked with a lustrous thread, such as stranded floss or silk. It is generally used for filling shapes but can also be used for backgrounds, although it is rather a slow stitch to work. Each stitch covers a square of four canvas threads, and the stitches are worked in horizontal rows from left to right. A foundation of two straight stitches is worked first along the top and left-hand side of the square. The thread is then brought to the surface at the opposite corner, and a looped stitch made over the foundation stitches. The thread enters the canvas through the same hole from which it emerged before making the foundation for the next stitch.

334 *Woven tent stitch* ☆ ☆ ☆
Woven tent stitch is a modern canvas stitch used on mono canvas. It makes a textured surface and can be used for filling shapes or backgrounds of any size. This stitch is a variation of ordinary tent stitch *(see page 11)*, and is based on a square consisting of sixteen tent stitches. The square is worked first, and then two straight stitches are added: one runs along the lower edge of the square and the other is placed along the right-hand side of it. The thread is then interwoven diagonally backward and forward between these two stitches to create a closely woven triangle. During the weaving process do not pick up any of the tent stitches. A soft wool thread, such as tapestry or Persian yarn, works well with this stitch, provided that the gauge of the canvas is compatible.

435 *Sunburst stitch* ☆ ☆ ☆
Sunburst stitch is a modern canvas stitch used on mono canvas. It has a highly textured surface with a large pattern reminiscent of the sun and its rays, and is used for filling large shapes and backgrounds. The stitch is worked in vertical rows, which are then threaded on a second journey with a thicker thread. A soft wool thread, such as tapestry or Persian yarn, is needed to cover the canvas adequately and can be used double in the needle for the threading. Each stitch covers a large, rectangular block of twelve vertical and six horizontal canvas threads. The blocks are worked first over the entire area to be covered, and each consists of two groups of four straight stitches radiating from the same central hole to the left and right of the rectangle. The second, thicker thread is then laced downward through the rows on

the left-hand side, making a circular movement around the central hole of each block. When the lower edge is reached, the thread is taken through the right-hand side of the blocks back up to the top to begin lacing the next row. The thread passes under the stitches and should not pick up any canvas threads.

436 *Curtain stitch* ☆ ☆ ☆
Curtain stitch is a complex canvas stitch used on mono canvas. It makes a very bold pattern in blocks, each block reminiscent of a pair of swagged curtains. Care should be taken in deciding where to use this stitch since the pattern is rather dominant, especially if the stitch is worked in a thick thread on a large-gauge canvas; however, this stitch can look really spectacular. It can be worked in two contrasting threads. Each block fills a square of eight canvas threads, and the blocks are arranged side by side in rows. The blocks are first covered with a series of graduating diagonal straight stitches, the direction of which changes on alternate blocks. This stage should be worked over the whole area first. On the second journey, the "curtains" are made, using the same or a contrasting thread. These consist of eight vertical straight stitches worked loosely across each block, which are then pulled toward the outside of the block in groups of four and tied down by a short horizontal stitch. It is important to maintain the correct tension of the vertical stitches, as they must be loose enough to be tied back. Any type of embroidery thread can be used, provided that it is compatible with the gauge of the canvas.

427/1 Vee stitch ☆ ☆

428/2 Compact filling stitch ☆ ☆

430 Broad stem stitch ☆ ☆

427/2 Vee stitch ☆ ☆

429/1 Spring stitch ☆ ☆

431 Tweed stitch ☆ ☆

428/1 Compact filling stitch ☆ ☆

429/2 Spring stitch ☆ ☆

432 Scallop stitch ☆ ☆ ☆

433/1 Eastern stitch ☆ ☆ ☆

434/1 Woven tent stitch ☆ ☆ ☆

435/1 Sunburst stitch ☆ ☆ ☆

433/2 Eastern stitch ☆ ☆ ☆

434/2 Woven tent stitch ☆ ☆ ☆

435/2 Sunburst stitch ☆ ☆ ☆

433/3 Eastern stitch ☆ ☆ ☆

434/3 Woven tent stitch ☆ ☆ ☆

436 Curtain stitch ☆ ☆ ☆

Other canvas stitches

437 Raised spot stitch ☆
Raised spot stitch is a canvas stitch used on mono and Penelope canvas, which can be used in rows for an outline or border, or worked solidly to fill a shape where a dense, raised texture is needed. It is extremely simple to work and the finished stitch depends greatly on the type of yarn chosen. Each spot stitch is worked over four horizontal canvas threads and consists of straight stitches worked over each other into the same holes at the top and bottom. The stitches should be packed tightly in order to make a really firm raised spot and as many as fifteen or twenty stitches can be worked over each other before the holes become too full to allow the needle to pass through again.

438 Algerian eye stitch ☆
Also known as *star stitch* and *star eyelet stitch*
Algerian eye stitch is used in needlepoint and in open-work embroidery on a loosely woven even-weave fabric. It consists of eight stitches, all worked into the same central point, and forms a star within a square. When used as a canvas stitch, it should be worked on mono canvas with a heavy thread; on an even-weave fabric, the stitches should be pulled quite tight during the stitching to emphasize the holes that form at the center of each eyelet. The eyelets can be spaced alternately to give a chessboard effect or worked as an all-over pattern. Alphabets on early samplers were often worked in Algerian eye stitch.

439 Ray stitch ☆
also known as *fan stitch*
Ray stitch is a canvas stitch used on mono canvas. It makes a regular pattern of square blocks on the surface and can be worked to give three different effects.
   The stitch is normally worked over a square of three canvas threads and is very effective for filling small shapes. The blocks can be made larger by the addition of further stitches and they can be as large as six or eight threads, creating a striking effect for large shapes and backgrounds. When worked over

three threads, each square block consists of seven straight stitches radiating from the same hole at the corner of the square and, if the stitches are pulled tightly, a pattern of holes is also made. The blocks are usually arranged so that the direction of the straight stitches is reversed every alternate block. Different effects can be made by working all the stitches in the same direction, or by working diagonal pairs of blocks into the same central hole, which then becomes quite large. Any type of embroidery thread can be used with ray stitch, provided that it is compatible with the gauge of the canvas, but a lustrous thread, such as stranded floss, enhances the light and shade effect created by the positioning of the stitches.

440 Radiating stitch ☆
Radiating stitch is a canvas stitch used on mono canvas. It is quick and easy to work and ideal for covering large areas and backgrounds. The stitch gives a strong, vertically striped surface, and each stripe consists of a row of triangles. Any type of embroidery thread can be used, provided that it is compatible with the gauge of the canvas. Slight gaps may be visible between the vertical rows, giving a rather untidy appearance to the stitch. This can be remedied by working rows of backstitch *(see page 14)* over the gaps, with each backstitch covering two horizontal canvas threads. The rows of triangles are four vertical canvas threads wide and each triangle consists of five straight stitches radiating from the same central hole. The triangles are worked beneath one another and every alternate triangle faces in the opposite direction.

441 Single knotted stitch ☆
Single knotted stitch is a canvas stitch used on mono canvas. The stitch imitates the knots of a pile carpet and should be worked closely together to cover the canvas completely. It is useful in cases where an area of raised stitching is needed to complement a flat, smoothly stitched surface. Use very thick thread or, alternatively, thread

several strands of a fine thread through the same needle. Interesting color effects can be achieved by mixing contrasting or harmonizing colors of a fine thread. The stitch is simple to work but the loop must be pulled tight after working each stitch. Trim the ends of the threads to the required length after the stitching is completed.

442 Beaded tent stitch ☆ ☆
Beaded tent stitch provides a method of attaching beads to a piece of needlepoint and is mainly used for working small details and highlights. Each bead is secured by a tent stitch *(see page 121)*: bring the thread to the front of the canvas, thread one bead, and go on to work the stitch. The size of the beads should allow them to sit neatly on the surface but, if they are too large to do this, work tent stitch alternately with beaded tent stitch to give more space for the bead. Beaded tent stitch is usually worked in vertical rows.

443 Turkey rug knot ☆ ☆
also known as *Turkey stitch, Ghiordes knot, quilt knot stitch, tufted knot stitch* and *single knotted Smyrna rug stitch*
Turkey rug knot is a pile stitch used on mono canvas. It makes a series of closely worked loops, which are cut and trimmed after the stitching is finished to give a pile which resembles the pile of a carpet. This stitch is used to make very raised areas, sometimes needed to complement a flat, smoothly stitched area of needlepoint. A soft, thick wool thread should be used, or several finer threads can be threaded through the needle at the same time. By using several different-colored threads, this stitch can be made to shade an area gradually by changing some of the colored threads on successive rows. The loops should be worked around a pencil or large knitting needle to keep the size constant. Each loop is secured by a backstitch *(see page 14)*, as shown. Each row is worked above the preceding row: keep the rows as close together as possible.

444 Eye stitch ★★

Eye stitch is primarily a canvas stitch used on mono canvas but it can also be successfully worked on an even-weave fabric, provided that a fine thread is used. A filling stitch, it makes a regular, geometric pattern of square blocks, which can be worked in two or more colors. Each block covers eight vertical and eight horizontal canvas threads and consists of sixteen straight stitches of graduated lengths, radiating from the same central point. Around the outside of each square, the stitches are drawn through alternate holes, leaving two canvas threads unworked. The blocks can be framed by rows of backstitch (see page 14) in the same or a contrasting thread. Any type of embroidery thread can be used, although the thread should not be too thick or the stitches making up the blocks will be difficult to work.

445 Diamond eye stitch ★★

Diamond eye stitch is a canvas stitch used primarily on mono canvas; it can also be successfully worked on an even-weave fabric, provided that a fine thread is used. A variation of eye stitch (see above), it also makes a regular, geometric pattern of blocks but in this case the blocks are diamond-shaped. The blocks can be worked in two colors and, as with eye stitch, any type of embroidery thread can be used, although the thread should not be too thick or the stitches that make up the blocks will be difficult to work. Each block consists of twenty straight stitches of graduated lengths, radiating from the same central point and arranged to make a diamond. Each diamond shape spans ten vertical and ten horizontal canvas threads. After the diamond shapes have been worked, they can be framed by rows of backstitch (see page 14), in the same way as eye stitch can be framed, or by long straight stitches worked from corner to corner around each diamond.

446 Half eye stitch ★★

Half eye stitch is a canvas stitch used on mono canvas with a fairly heavy thread, such as matte embroidery cotton or the heaviest weight of pearl cotton. A variation of eye stitch (see above), it makes a heavy, geometric pattern of rectangular blocks arranged with a half drop. Each block consists of half an eye stitch worked over four vertical and eight horizontal canvas threads. The stitches are packed together very closely, and seventeen straight stitches are worked into the same hole; a small awl may be needed to open up this hole while the stitching is in progress. Each straight stitch should be pulled quite tight, and this stitch is not suitable for use with a soft wool thread as it may snap or shred. For ease of working, the needle should always emerge from the canvas on the outside edge and re-enter by the central hole.

447 Quick stitch ★★

Quick stitch is a canvas stitch used on mono canvas. As its name reveals, this stitch covers the canvas very quickly. It creates a diagonally woven pattern and is an adaptation of a fabric technique, laid-work. It should never be used on an article that is subject to much wear and tear (such as a pillow cover), as the stitches are very long and snag easily, but it works well on a picture as a background. Care should be taken when using quick stitch to choose an embroidery thread which covers the canvas adequately; it is advisable to work a small sample first to test the compatibility of the thread to the canvas. The stitch consists of long threads laid diagonally across the area to be worked and entering the canvas only at the beginning and ends of the rows. It is essential that these threads are laid correctly and follow the intersections of the canvas. The laid threads are then crossed at right angles by groups of three diagonal stitches, arranged as shown. Interesting color changes can be made by graduating the colors used for both the laid threads and the crossing stitches.

448 Surrey stitch ★★

Surrey stitch is a pile stitch used on mono canvas. It forms a series of closely worked loops, which can be cut after the stitching is finished to give a pile which resembles carpet pile. This stitch is used to make very raised areas, which are sometimes needed to complement a flat, smoothly stitched area of needlepoint. Use either a soft, thick wool thread or several finer threads threaded through the needle at once. Work the loops around a pencil or a large knitting needle to keep the size constant. Secure each loop with a short diagonal stitch. Work each row above the preceding row, keeping the rows as close together as possible.

449 Rococo stitch ★★★
also known as queen stitch

Rococo stitch is a canvas stitch used on wide-mesh canvas. Dating from the seventeenth century, it became fashionable again during the nineteenth century and examples of it are found on numerous tiny articles of the period, such as pincushions and purses. It should be worked with a fairly thick thread and it makes a dramatic background stitch. Care should be taken when matching the weight of the thread to the gauge of the canvas to ensure that the canvas is completely covered by the stitching; a small test sample can be worked to check this.

Rococo stitch consists of a group of four vertical stitches worked into the same space with each one crossed by a tiny horizontal stitch. The two outside vertical stitches are anchored to the canvas and curve slightly, giving a globe-shaped appearance to the stitch. The groups are arranged alternately in the spaces of the canvas and make a dense, closely stitched surface punctuated by small holes. They should be worked in diagonal rows, from the top right to the bottom left of the area to be covered.

437 Raised spot stitch ☆

440 Radiating stitch ☆

442 Beaded tent stitch ☆ ☆

438 Algerian eye stitch ☆

441/1 Single knotted stitch ☆

443/1 Turkey rug knot ☆ ☆

439 Ray stitch ☆

441/2 Single knotted stitch ☆

443/2 Turkey rug knot ☆ ☆

444 Eye stitch ☆ ☆

447 Quick stitch ☆ ☆

448/3 Surrey stitch ☆ ☆

445 Diamond eye stitch ☆ ☆

448/1 Surrey stitch ☆ ☆

449/1 Rococo stitch ☆ ☆ ☆

446 Half eye stitch ☆ ☆

448/2 Surrey stitch ☆ ☆

449/2 Rococo stitch ☆ ☆ ☆

Glossary

Accent stitch An embroidery stitch which is chiefly used to provide a splash of color or texture to enliven a monotone or flat area of stitching.

Appliqué or **applied work** A technique in which shapes of different fabrics are placed on the ground fabric to form a design. The edges are secured by tiny stitches which are hardly seen, or by a decorative embroidery stitch.

Assisi work A type of counted thread embroidery originating in Assisi, Northern Italy. The patterns or motifs are outlined before the background is filled in using cross stitch or long-armed cross stitch, leaving the motifs unstitched.

Awl A sharp pointed instrument used for making holes in fabric.

Ayrshire embroidery A type of embroidery stitched in a fine white thread on white muslin and characterized by areas of inset lace stitches. Ayrshire embroidery was worked in Scotland from the late-eighteenth to the mid-nineteenth century and was used for baby garments and collars and cuffs.

Berlin woolwork A technique of working designs in colored yarns on canvas, following a chart on which each square represents one stitch. The yarns and charts were originally produced in Germany but the work spread to the rest of Europe and to the United States and was popular during the nineteenth century.

Blackwork An embroidery technique used on clothing and household linen during the sixteenth century and revived during the twentieth century. It consists of outline and filling stitches worked in black thread on a white fabric to create geometric designs.

Border stitch A wide embroidery stitch which is always used in a straight line and makes a very attractive border. Multiple rows can be worked to make a more complex decorative border.

Canvas The ground material for needlepoint in which vertical and horizontal threads are woven together to produce precisely spaced holes between the threads. Canvas has a regular grid-like structure and is available in several different sizes of grid.

Closed finish The term used when an embroidery stitch is compressed in order to cover the ground fabric completely.

Common-weave fabric A fabric in which the warp and weft threads are woven too irregularly to provide a grid for working stitches by the counted thread method.

Composite stitch A combination of two or more simple embroidery stitches to give a more decorative effect than if they were used singly.

Couching A technique in which a thick thread or group of threads is attached to the ground fabric by means of a finer thread. It is particularly suitable for textured and metallic threads which cannot be stitched directly into the fabric.

Counted thread embroidery An embroidery technique in which the scale and placement of the stitches is determined by counting the warp and weft threads of the ground fabric over which each stitch is worked.

Crane, Walter English illustrator, painter and designer (1845-1915), known primarily for his imaginative illustrations for children's books, who had a great influence on embroidery design.

Crazy patchwork A technique in which irregularly shaped pieces of fabric are sewn at random on a ground fabric. The raw edges where the pieces join are secured by decorative stitching.

Crewel embroidery Embroidery stitched with crewel yarns on a linen background, using a variety of stitches. The designs are often naturalistic.

Crewel yarn A fine two-ply yarn for delicate needlepoint or free embroidery.

Cutwork A technique in which motifs or patterns are outlined with close buttonhole stitching and the ground fabric is cut away in various sections of the design.

Detached stitch An embroidery stitch which is anchored to the ground fabric at the edges only, with the main part of the stitching remaining free.

Drawn fabric work A type of embroidery in which threads are withdrawn from a loosely woven ground fabric and the spaces left are then filled or edged with different stitches.

Edging stitch An embroidery stitch used to finish a raw edge to prevent the fabric from fraying, or to decorate a plain hemmed edge.

Encroaching stitches A term used to describe the overlap of one row of stitching with the preceding row.

Even-weave fabric A fabric with warp and weft threads of identical thicknesses, which provide the same number of threads over a given area, enabling the threads to be counted to keep the stitching even.

Eyelet embroidery A type of cutwork embroidery which evolved from Ayrshire embroidery *circa* 1850, and became very popular as a decoration on children's garments and ladies' underclothes. The formalized designs consist of a series of tiny round and oval holes.

Fabric grain The line of the warp thread in a piece of fabric.

Filling stitch An embroidery stitch which is used to fill a shape on the ground fabric. Filling stitches can be light and delicate with a lacy appearance, or they can completely cover the ground fabric.

Fine crochet cotton A tightly twisted pearlized thread similar to pearl cotton but with a less lustrous finish.

Foundation grid The regular arrangement of threads laid across a shape to provide a framework for an embroidery stitch.

Foundation row A row of stitching which provides the basis for a composite stitch. This term is also used to describe the stitched outline which anchors a detached filling stitch to the ground fabric.

Frame A square or rectangular wooden frame used to keep fabric taut during stitching.

Gauge The number of threads that can be stitched in 1 inch of canvas. Also the number of threads or woven blocks that can be stitched in 1 inch of even-weave fabric.

Grounding stitch A term used in needlepoint to describe a stitch that is suitable for covering large areas of background.

Ground fabric Any fabric on which embroidery is worked.

Half drop A term used in needlepoint to describe an arrangement of stitches. The top of the second and subsequent stitches aligns with the center of the preceding stitch.

Holbein, Hans German painter and engraver (1497-1543) who was Court Painter to Henry VIII from 1536 to 1543. He is noted particularly for his portraits.

Hoop A round frame for stretching the ground fabric while embroidery stitches are worked.

Isolated stitch An embroidery stitch which is worked individually and can be used alone or massed together to fill a shape.

Jacobean embroidery A type of free embroidery worked on linen, popular during the seventeenth and eighteenth centuries.

Journey In embroidery, a term used to describe working a stitch along a line. Many stitches are completed on one journey but others will require two or three.

Laid filling stitch An embroidery stitch consisting of a foundation grid of spaced laid threads which are then anchored to the ground fabric in a decorative manner.

Laid-work An embroidery technique used to fill a shape. Long threads are laid across the shape and anchored to the fabric by a second thread to create a pattern.

Lark's head knot A knot used in macramé to mount the knotting cords onto a support such as a length of cord, a dowel or a ring.

Line stitch Any embroidery stitch which forms a line during the working.

Matte embroidery cotton A tightly twisted five-ply thread with a matte finish, always used as a single thread.

Mono canvas Canvas in which the weave is formed by the intersection of single vertical and horizontal threads.

Morris, William English poet. Pre-Raphaelite painter, designer, craftsman and socialist writer (1834-1896). Among his many achievements he created magnificent wallpaper and fabric designs which remain popular today.

Motif stitch An embroidery stitch which is worked individually, with each stitch making a distinctive shape, such as a star or triangle.

Naturalistic embroidery Embroidery in which natural forms such as plants and animals are depicted in a realistic manner.

Needlepoint A general term for embroidery on canvas. The entire surface of the canvas is covered with stitching and a wide range of stitches is used.

Needlepoint lace Lace made with a needle rather than a bobbin.

Open finish The term used when an embroidery stitch is spaced out to let the fabric ground show though.

Opus Anglicanum The name given to English embroidery, chiefly ecclesiastical, worked during the Middle Ages.

Pearl cotton A twisted two-ply thread with a lustrous sheen. It cannot be divided into separate strands but it is available in three different weights.

Penelope canvas Canvas in which the weave is formed by the intersection of pairs of vertical and horizontal threads.

Persian yarn A loosely twisted three-ply yarn which can be divided into separate strands.

Picot A small loop of twisted thread forming a decorative edging on lace or embroidery.

Powdering A light filling for a shape made by scattering an isolated stitch over an area of ground fabric.

Pulled fabric work An embroidery technique in which stitches are pulled tightly so that the threads of the ground fabric are distorted, creating a pattern of tiny holes in the fabric.

Renaissance embroidery A form of cutwork in which the design is outlined in buttonhole stitch before the ground fabric is cut away. Parts of the design are strengthened by buttonhole bars.

Richelieu embroidery A form of cutwork similar to Renaissance embroidery; the main difference is the addition of picots to the buttonhole bars which join parts of the design.

Royal School of Needlework A school with royal patronage founded in London in 1872.

Sampler A piece of embroidery originally worked by an adult needlewoman as a directory of stitches, patterns, and motifs and used as technical reference. Later, the name was applied to needlework exercises carried out by children for practice in stitching techniques.

Shadow embroidery A type of embroidery worked on a semi-transparent fabric.

Shisha embroidery A traditional embroidery technique using tiny mirrors, which originated in India.

Smock Traditionally, a linen outer garment worn in England by working men in the eighteenth, nineteenth, and early twentieth centuries, decorated with smocking and embroidered motifs which depicted the work done by the owner.

Smocking Evenly spaced gathers in a piece of fabric which are held in place by ornamental stitching.

Stranded floss A loosely twisted, slightly shiny, six-strand cotton thread. For fine embroidery, the threads can be separated and used in twos or threes.

Stranded silk A pure silk thread similar to stranded floss but with a more lustrous finish.

Tapestry needle A long thick needle with a blunt tip and a large eye.

Tapestry yarn A twisted four-ply yarn with hard-wearing properties, mainly used in needlepoint.

Tramming The preparation of double thread canvas, before the decorative stitching is begun, to make the stitched surface hard-wearing. Horizontal straight stitches are worked between the double canvas threads, using colors that match the design. Tramming fills out the stitch that is worked over it and also helps to cover the canvas ground.

Warp The threads in a woven fabric that run lengthwise on the weaving loom.

Waxed thread A thread which has been strengthened by rubbing it against a block of beeswax.

Weft The threads running across the width of a woven fabric that are interwoven with the warp threads.

Whipping A term used in embroidery to describe the method of passing a second thread over and under a simple line stitch to give a raised effect.

Whitework A term referring to all types of embroidery that are traditionally worked in white thread on white fabric. They include cutwork, drawn thread work and pulled fabric work.

Index